COMPUTER NETWORK

COMPUTER NETWORK

(For B.Tech., M.Tech., BCA, MCA, B.Sc. (Comp. Science) and IT Professionals)

By

Bharat Bhushan Agarwal
B.E. (CS & IT) (Honours), M.Tech.
Sr. Lecturer, Deptt. of Computer Engineering
College of Engineering Technology (I.F.T.M.)
Moradabad, Uttar Pradesh

Sumit Prakash Tayal
B.Tech. (Electronics)
Solutions Developer
Engineering and Design Group
Tata Technologies Ltd.,
Pune, Maharashtra

UNIVERSITY SCIENCE PRESS
(An Imprint of Laxmi Publications Pvt. Ltd.)
BANGALORE • CHENNAI • COCHIN • GUWAHATI • HYDERABAD
JALANDHAR • KOLKATA • LUCKNOW • MUMBAI • RANCHI
NEW DELHI

Published by :
UNIVERSITY SCIENCE PRESS
(An Imprint of Laxmi Publications Pvt. Ltd.)
113, Golden House, Daryaganj,
New Delhi-110002
Phone : 011-43 53 25 00
Fax : 011-43 53 25 28
www.laxmipublications.com
info@laxmipublications.com

First Edition : 2009

OFFICES

✆ **Bangalore**	080-26 61 15 61	✆ **Chennai**	044-24 34 47 26
✆ **Cochin**	0484-237 70 04, 405 13 03	✆ **Guwahati**	0361-254 36 69, 251 38 81
✆ **Hyderabad**	040-24 65 23 33	✆ **Jalandhar**	0181-222 12 72
✆ **Kolkata**	033-22 27 43 84	✆ **Lucknow**	0522-220 95 78
✆ **Mumbai**	022-24 91 54 15, 24 92 78 69	✆ **Ranchi**	0651-221 47 64

UCN-9250-140-COMPUTER NETWORK **C—15885/08/05**

Typeset at : Kalyani Computer Services, New Delhi. Printed at : Repro Knowledgecast Limited, Thane

Dedicated

to

Our Parents

CONTENTS

PREFACE

Today, students waiting to understand the concepts & mechanisms underlying telecommunications & networking coming from a variety of academic & professional backgrounds.

This book attempts to provide a unified overview of the broad field of data and computer communications. The organizations of the book reflects an attempt to break this massive subject into comprehensible parts and to build, piece by piece, a survey of the state of the art. The book emphasizes the basic principles and topics of the fundamental importance concerning the technology and architecture of this field, and provides a detailed discussion of leading edge topics.

The book is primarily intended to serve as a textbook in accordance with the syllabus of computer networks offered by various universities in India.

The text is designed to make it particularly easy for students of B.Tech., M.Tech., MCA, BCA, to understand data communications and networking.

The book highlights the basic principles, and contrasts their application in the specific areas of technology. It contains a number of examples, various diagrams and exercises, which enhance its suitability for classroom instructions.

We hope that the book will fulfill the need of readers and would welcome any suggestions regarding the improvement of the book.

—Authors

ACKNOWLEDGEMENT

First and foremost, we must extend our deepest gratitude to the Almighty God for showering love and grace on us to make us write this book.

We feel privileged and fortunate enough to retain the affection of the following distinguished personalities, Shri Rajeev Saran Kothiwal, Chairman, IFTM Moradabad, Dr. R. M. Dubey, the Managing Director IFTM Moradabad & Mr. Prakash M. Telang, Executive Director (Commercial Vehicles), Tata Motors Limited, Pune who have been the driving force behind this effort.

We are extremely indebted to Prof. Anupam Srivastava, Director, C.E.T, IFTM, Moradabad for inspiring and motivating us, without whose valuable suggestions it would have been difficult to complete the book.

We express our special gratitude, very heartly, to Prof. B.N. Kaul Dean Administration CET, IFTM Moradabad, time-to-time suggestions & guidance.

Special thanks are also to Mr. G.S. Singh, Practice Head, Tata Technologies Ltd. Pune, Mr. Ramraj Pandey, Consultant, Chrysler, U.S.A., Mr. Rahul Shandilya, Project Manager, Mr. P.W. Dandekar, Tata Technologies Ltd. Pune, and Mr. R. Pandian, Project Manager who have guided, encouraged and advised us during the process of writing the book.

We would also like to thank to Prof. S.K. Srivastava, Advisor, CET., I.F.T.M, Moradabad & Mr. M.I.H Ansari (Head, Dept. of Computer Applications, I.F.T.M. Moradabad) for their moral support & encouragement for the completion of this book.

We wish to put on record our sincere thanks, honor, and gratitude to our close family members Shri K.B. Agarwal, Shri Akhilesh Kothiwal and Shri Sandeep Agarwal (brother), consecutive four times elected as MLA of Moradabad (U.P.) for their soft words, continuous encouragement & necessary help whenever required.

We would also like to offer their warm thanks to Prof. (Dr.) A.K. Nayak, Director, School of Computer Sciences Indian Institute of Business Management Patna, Dr. A.K. Raghav, Director of Alfalah School of Engg. & Tech. Dauj (Faridabad) for their valuable contributions.

Sincere thanks are also due to Prof. Dinesh Chandra & Shri Suneet Shukla, HOD. Department of Computer Science, CET, IFTM Moradabad & Dr. Vivek Kumar, HOD. Department of Info. Tech., Galgotia, Gr. Noida, Dr. Parmanand Astya, HOD. Department of Computer Science, Galgotia, Gr. Noida, Mr. S. S. Bedi, Head of Deptt. CS & IT Engg. & Tech., Rohilkhand, Bareilly, Dr. O.P. Singhal, Head—CS Dept. IDEAL, Ghaziabad, Mr. L.S. Maurya, HOD. Department of Information Technology, SRMS, Bareilly & Dr. R.K. Gupta (Tauji) Principle of MBBS, TMIMT, Moradabad, Mr. Vikas Mittal, Head of Deptt. CS & IT, M.I.T., Moradabad, Mr. Yogesh Sharma, Head of CS-Deptt., S.D. College of Engg. & Tech., for their encouragement & critical suggestions.

Along with our colleagues—(Dr. B.K. Singh (Chief Proctor), Dr. Nikhil Rastogi, Mr. lntezar Mahdi, Dr. Vikas Gupta, Mr. Rahul Mishra—CET, IFTM MBD) who have helped & motivated us for writing this book.

We would like to acknowledge our special thanks to our well-wishers (Dr. Manish Saxena, Dr. Animesh Agarwal, and Shri Kshitij Shinghal, MIT, MBD) for valuable suggestions. We would like to thank Mr. Akhtar Hussain, (MJP, Rohilkhand, Bareilly) & Manoj Kr. Chubey (GLA, MATHURA) for their cooperation in this project.

Also, we would like to express our heartiest thanks to Ms. Shivangi Dhall & Mr. Dhiraj Dhall for their deep involvement in this project.

So, special acknowledgement to the postgraduate colleagues Raj Kumar Goel, Vikram Bali, Prateek Srivastava, Anita Sahoo, Kanchan Singh, Pavitra Rani Gautam, Sarika Khandelwal, Rashmi Singh, Hitendra Agarwal, Vikas Lamba, Anupama Sharma, Dharmendra Kumar Tripathi, Kulwant Singh Patel, Lavkush Sharma, Mahendra Prasad Sharma, Varsha, Pritee Gupta, Narendra Kumar, Niraj Kumar Singh, Nitin Goyal, Prachi Vats, Promod Kumar Yadav, Narvada Chaudhary, Rinki, Sachin Ahuja, Sanjay Kumar Nayak, Uma Shankar Sharma, Ankit Vishnoi, Mohit Agarwal.

We are indebted to all the seniors, colleagues and juniors of Tata Technologies Ltd. and CS & IT Dept. of CET, IFTM Moradabad during the whole process of writing the book.

We through our indebtedness to our parents, Shri Ravi Prakash Agarwal and Smt. Bindu Agarwal for their perpetual love and concern, which cannot be summed up in words.

Sincere thanks are also due to our sister Smt. Anupam Agarwal & brother-in-law Shri Shakshi Goel for their words of cheer & encouragement & special thanks to little Shubhangi & Gauri for bearing with us at odd hours.

Finally, we thank every one, who contributed significantly in accomplishing this job.

—Authors

Chapter 1

NETWORK CONCEPTS

1.1 INTRODUCTION

1.1.1 Computer Networks

A computer network refers to the collection of several computing machines, peripheral devices and storage unit. The computer systems may communicate over a computer network and share their resources. These networks enable the computer to communicate with a remote computer which may be located at a distance of a few meters to several thousands kilometers. The users of a computer system on the network are able to share the software resources such as programs, database and program utilities. The computer network has become a basic necessity and has triggered the development of several applications. The conventional concept of installing a high performance and large computer system has now been replaced with computer networks where several low cost and low performance computer systems collectively exhibit high performance at lower cost. The computer network connects several peripheral devices, databases and computer systems as shown in Fig. 1.1.

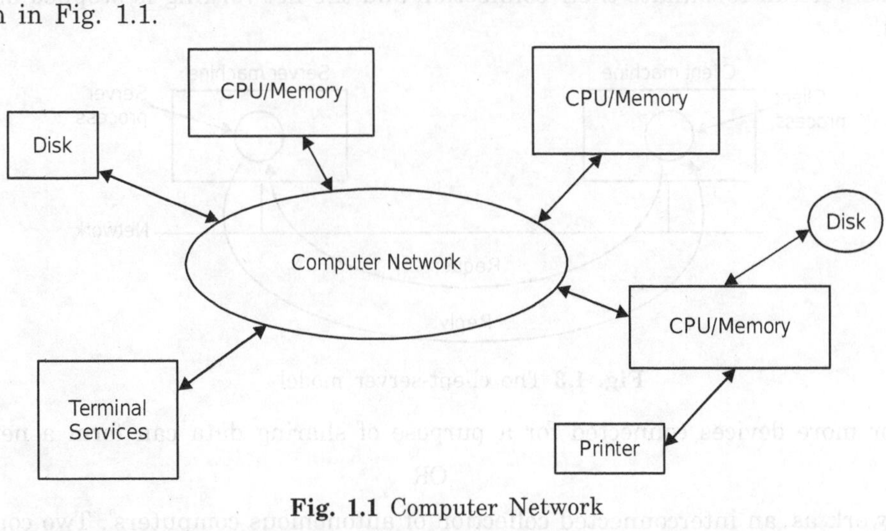

Fig. 1.1 Computer Network

1.1.2 Networking

A group of computers and other devices connected together is called a network. The interconnected computers can share resources, which called networking. It is linking of two or more different entities together to form a group or network to perform some specific task. The networking enhances the capacity of computer to share, exchange, preserve and protect information. When the computers are connected over a network it is possible to exchange the information easily and faster. A group of computer connected together is a network.

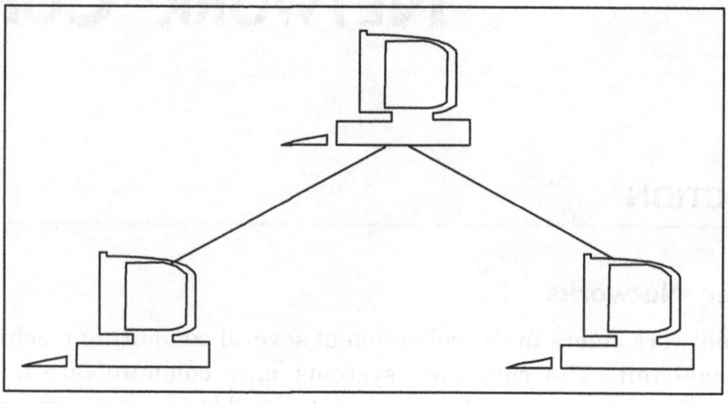

Fig. 1.2 Networking

The client server relationship exists in networking in which client requests that some action to be performed and server performs the action returning the results to the client. The client first has to establish the connection to server and then the data can be transmitted. The server may deny or accept the connection. If the connection is accepted then the client and server communicate through sockets as similar to the operations being performed on the input/output file. When the connection is not required the client server can terminate their connection and the networking is stopped as shown in Fig. 1.3.

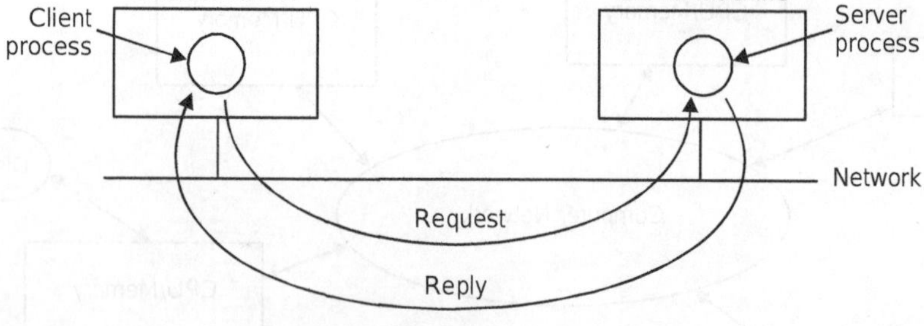

Fig. 1.3 The client-server model

Two or more devices connected for a purpose of sharing data can form a network.

OR

A network as 'an interconnected collection of autonomous computers'. Two computers are said to be interconnected if they are capable of exchanging information. Central to this definition is the fact that the computers are autonomous. This means that no computer on the network can start, stop or control another.

OR

A group of computers and other devices connected together is called a network.

1.1.3 Internetworking

The interconnected computers can shape resources which called **networking.**

internet: An interconnection of network is called internet.

Internet: It is the name of a specific worldwide network.

1.1.4 The Advantages (Benefits) of Networking

1. Connectivity and Communication

Networks connect computers and the users of those computers. Individuals within a building or work group can be connected into local area networks (LANs); LANs in distant locations can be interconnected into larger wide area networks (WANs). Once connected, it is possible for network users to communicate with each other using technologies such as electronic mail. This makes the transmission of business (or non-business) information easier more efficient and less expensive than it would be without the network.

2. Data Sharing

One of the most important uses of networking is to allow the sharing of data. Before networking was common, an accounting employee who wanted to prepare a report for her manager would have to produce it on his PC, put it on a floppy disk, and then walk it over to the manager, who would transfer the data to her PC's hard disk.

3. Hardware Sharing

Networks facilitate the sharing of hardware devices. For example, instead of giving each of 10 employees in a department an expensive color printer (or resorting to the "sneaker net" again), one printer can be placed on the network for everyone to share.

4. Internet Access

The Internet is itself an enormous network, so whenever you access the Internet you are using a network. The significance of the Internet on modern society is hard to exaggerate especially for those of us in technical fields.

5. Data Security and Management

In a business environment, a network allows the administrators too much better manage the company's critical data. Instead of having this data spread over dozens or even hundreds of small computers in a haphazard fashion as their users create it; data can be centralized on shared servers. This makes it easy for everyone to find the data, makes it possible for the administrators to ensure that the data is regularly backed up, and also allows for the implementation of security measures to control who can read or change various pieces of critical information.

6. Entertainment

Networks facilitate many types of games and entertainment. The Internet itself offers many sources of entertainment, of course. In addition, many multi-player games exist that operate over a local area network. Many home networks are set up for this reason, and gaming across wide area networks (including the Internet) has also become quite popular.

1.1.5 The Disadvantages (Costs) of Networking

1. Network Hardware, Software and Setup Costs

Computers don't just magically network themselves, of course. Setting up a network requires an investment in hardware and software, as well as funds for planning, designing and implementing the network. For a home with a small network of two or three PCs, this is relatively inexpensive, possibly amounting to less than a hundred dollars with today's low prices for network hardware, and operating systems already designed for networks. For a large company, cost can easily run into tens of thousands of dollars - or more.

2. Growing Concerns Over Security

As Internet use increased in the 1990s, more "bad guys" started using the network also. The more machines a company had directly connected to the Internet, the greater their potential exposure to security risks.

3. Undesirable Sharing

With the good comes the bad; while networking allows the easy sharing of useful information, it also allows the sharing of undesirable data. One significant "sharing problem" in this regard has to do with viruses, which are easily spread over networks and the Internet. Mitigating these effects costs more time, money and administrative effort.

4. Illegal or Undesirable Behavior

Similar to the point above, networking facilitates useful connectivity and communication, but also brings difficulties with it. Typical problems include abuse of company resources distractions that reduce productivity, downloading of illegal or illicit materials, and even software piracy . In larger organizations, these issues must be managed through explicit policies and monitoring, which again, further increases management costs.

1.2 GOALS OF COMPUTER NETWORK

The most important goals are security, reliability, performance and cost of network.

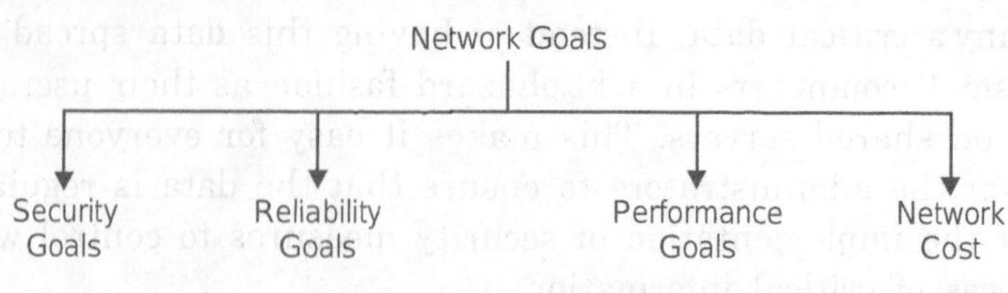

Goals of Computer networks are discussed as follows:

1. **Security Goals:** Network security issues comprise of prevention from virus attacks and protecting data from unauthorized access.

(*a*) *Viruses:* As a network is accessible from many points, it can be susceptible to computer viruses. A virus is an illicitly introduced code to damage the functionality of a system. A good network is protected from viruses by software and hardware designed specifically for that purpose.

(*b*) *Unauthorized access:* Protection from unauthorized access of sensitive data is mandatory for any network to be useful. Protection can be accomplished at a number of levels. At the lowest level are user login codes and passwords. At high level are encryption techniques.

2. **Reliability Goals:** Network reliability is measured by failure frequency average down time of network and the networks robustness in a catastrophe.

(*a*) *Failure Frequency:* Network failure is always a possibility. A network that fails rarely is good for a user but a network that fails oftenly is of little value to a user.

(*b*) *Average Down Time:* How long does it take to restore service is known as downtime for the network. A network with less average down time is more useful than one that does not.

(*c*) *Catastrophe:* Network must be protected from catastrophe events such that earthquake or theft. One protection against these is a reliable system to backup network software.

3. **Performance Goals:** The network performance can be measured by its transit time and response time. Transit time is the amount of time required for a message to travel from one device to another device in network. Response time is the time elapsed between an inquiry and a response. Network performance depends on a number of factors including, network transmission medium, network hardware, network software and traffic load.

(*a*) *Network Transmission Medium:* A network medium may be wired (optical fiber, copper cables, etc.) or wireless (microwave, satellite etc.). The medium defines the data rate (speed at which data can travel through a connection). As the uses of network are increasing, faster and faster transmission media is required for networks; such as fiber optic cabling. Amount of data that a media can handle defines its capacity and in turn how powerful media it is. A medium that can carry 200 megabits per second is 20 times more powerful than a medium that can carry data at only 10 megabits per second.

(*b*) *Hardware:* The types of hardware included in a network affect both the speed and capacity of transmission. A higher speed system with greater storage capacity provides better performance.

(*c*) *Software:* Moving a message from node to node through a network requires processing for transformation of raw data into transmittable signals, to route these signal to the proper destination, to ensure error free delivery and to recast the signals into a form the receiver can use. The software that provides these services affects both the speed and the reliability of a network link. Well-designed software can speed the process and make transmission more effective and efficient.

(*d*) *Traffic Load:* The design of a network is based on an assessment of the average number of users that will be communicating at any moment of time. Having a large number of concurrent users can slow response time in a network not designed to coordinate heavy traffic loads. In peak load periods however the 'actual number of users' may exceed the 'average number of users' and thereby detoriate the performance. How a network responds to peak load is a measure of is performance.

4. **Network cost:** While designing cost of a network is an important factor. The network cost can be calculated on the basis of fixed cost and runtime cost.

(*a*) *Fixed cost:* The cost of medium and devices (like switch, router, hub etc.) which are required to make a network functional plays an important role while designing the network. For better network design in minimum cost the network design engineer must understand the function's to be performed by the network and accordingly performance parameters of medium and device (capacity and quality of medium, processing speed, capacity etc., of device) should be chosen.

(*b*) *Runtime cost:* To maintain a Network functionally strong, very good maintenance is required and as much complexity we increase in design chances of failure increases accordingly which in turn leads to more down time and maintenance cost of network. So increasing the runtime cost of network. So while designing not only fixed cost but run-time costs must be taken into account for minimization of total cost.

1.3 APPLICATIONS OF COMPUTER NETWORK

Some of the applications of computer network are as follows:

1. **Sharing:** The potential advantage of network is to provide an easy and flexible means of sharing. There are three distinct types of sharing.

(*a*) *Peripherals:* These are often expensive. It is impractical for each computer on the network to have both its laser printer (for quality printing) and dot-matrix printer (for all general printouts). A main frame may have one of each connected to it allowing all users controlled access in a cost effective manner.

(*b*) Users of a multi-user system can share and exchange information in a number of ways. Examples are sending electronic mail or having controlled access to the same files or database.

(*c*) In a traditional time-sharing system, all control is performed centrally; if the processor fails then the entire system fails. In a network system, this need not be the case. The failure of one node should not have a 'domain' effect on the rest. This is called distributed control and is a very lively area of research at present.

2. **Access to remote database:** Another major area of network use is access to remote database. It is easy for the average person sitting at his PC to make reservation for aeroplanes, trains, and hotels and so on anywhere in the world with instant confirmation.
3. **Communication facilities:** A third category of potential widespread network use is as a communication medium. It is possible for everyone, not just people in the computer business, to send and receive electronic mail. This mail is also able to contain digitized voice, still pictures and even moving television and video images.
4. **Tele conferencing:** Teleconferencing allows conferences to occur though participants are not in the same place. Applications include simple text conferencing (users communicate through their keyboards and computer monitors). Voice conferencing (users at a number of place communicate simultaneously over the phone) and video conferencing. (User can see as well as talk to each other).

To meet above applications effectively and efficiently a network must meet a number of goals. Using computer network as a sophisticated communication system may reduce the amount or traveling done, thus saving energy. The information revolution is expected to change society as much as the Industrial Revolution did.

1.4 DISTRIBUTED PROCESSING

Networks use distributed processing, in which a task is divided among multiple computers. Instead of a single large machine being responsible for all aspects of a process, each separate computer (usually a personal computer or workstation) handles a subset.

The distributed processing can more precisely be defined as: " the ability of network nodes to execute shared network applications or parts of network applications, independently of other nodes of the network." Thus each node has its own central processing unit with its own memory and communication hardware.

Advantages of Distributed Processing

Advantages of distributed processing include the following:

- *Encapsulation:* A system designer can limit the kinds of interactions that a given user can have with the entire system. For example, a bank can allow users access to their own accounts through an automated teller machine (ATM) without allowing them access to the bank's entire database.
- *Distributed database:* No one system needs to provide storage capacity for the entire database. For example, the World Wide Web gives users access to information that may be actually stored and manipulated anywhere on the Internet.
- *Faster problem solving:* Multiple computers working on parts of a problem concurrently often can solve the problem faster than a single machine working alone. For example, networks of PCs have broken encryption codes that were

presumed to be unbreakable because of the amount of time it would take a single computer to crack them.

- *Security through redundancy:* Multiple computers running the same program at the same time can provide security through redundancy. For example, in the space shuttle, three computers run the same program so that if one has a hardware error, the other two can override it.
- *Collaborative processing:* Both multiple computers and multiple users may interact on a task. For example, in multi-user network games the actions of each player are visible to and affect all the others.

Disadvantages of Distributed Processing

Distributed networks have disadvantages, too, and these must be considered before a system is decentralized. They include:

- *Technical problems of connecting dissimilar machines:* Technical problem can sometimes be overwhelming for a distributed system. Additional layers of operating system software are needed to translate and coordinate the flow of data between machines. Sometimes a link between mainframes and microcomputers can be difficult to establish.
- *Need for sophisticated communication systems:* Distributed processing requires the development of a data communication system. These systems can be costly to develop and use. In addition, their maintenance can be a costly affair.
- *Data integrity and security problems:* Because data maintained by distributed systems can be accessed at many locations in the network, controlling the integrity of a database can be difficult.
- *Lack of professional support:* Finally, distributed computers are often place in locations where little or no data processing support is available. Consequently, they will be run by non-professionals. Another aspect is that the communication systems also require highly trained personnel for their maintenance.

Salient Features of a Distributed Processing

The salient features of a distributed processing system are:

- The node or computers can be different sizes, makes and computing powers. They are physically located at separate location and communicate through communication network.
- Each node has its own specific operating system. However, all the nodes are integrated into a communication system by a networking operating system.
- Each node, if required, can work independently *i.e.*, the computers are not permanently linked to the network.

1.5 TOPOLOGIES

Topology defines the physical or logical arrangement of links in a network.

OR

Network topology defines how various computers or nodes are connected to one another.

OR

Network topology refers to the connection of different computers and deals with problem of how best various computers can be interconnected.

OR

Topology is the geometric arrangement of the computers in a network.

OR

Network topology defines the manner in which the nodes are geometrically arranged and connected to one another.

- The meaning of physical topology indicates the way in which a network is physically laid out.
- Two or more devices connect to a link; two or more links form a topology.
- The topology of a network is the geometric representation of the relationship of all the links connecting the devices (or nodes).

OR

In the computer network each computer is known as nodes and how these nodes are connected with each other's is called the network topology.

OR

In the context of a communication network, the term topology refers to the way in which the end points, or stations, attached to the network are interconnected.

1.5.1 Classification of Network Topology

The five basic topologies are as shown in Fig. 1.4

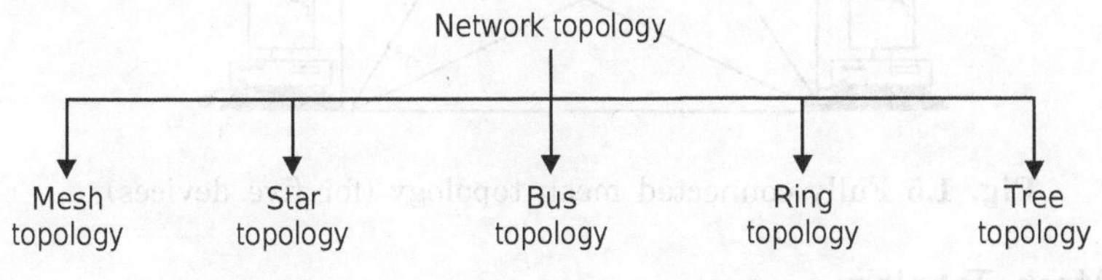

Fig. 1.4 Classification of network topology

- Two relationships on the basis are possible as follows:
  1. Peer to Peer
  2. Primary-secondary

- Peer to peer is the relationship where the devices share the link equally. The examples are ring and mesh topologies.
- In primary-secondary relationship, one-device controls and the other devices have to transmit through it. For example star and tree topology.

1. Mesh Topology

- It is also called as complete topology.
- In mesh topology, every device has a dedicated point to point link to other device where point to point means that only one terminal/wire directly connects only the two devices (see Fig. 1.5).
- The term dedicated means the link carries traffic only between the two devices it connects.
- A mesh network has $(n\ (n-1))/2$ physical channels to link n devices.
- The accommodate that many links; every devices on the network work must have (n-1) input output ports.
- Mesh topology is employed for long-distance transmission of data between nodes.
- Mesh topology is of two types:
  - ❑ True mesh topology
  - ❑ Hybrid mesh topology

Examples

Examples of mesh topology are WFW, WIN'95.

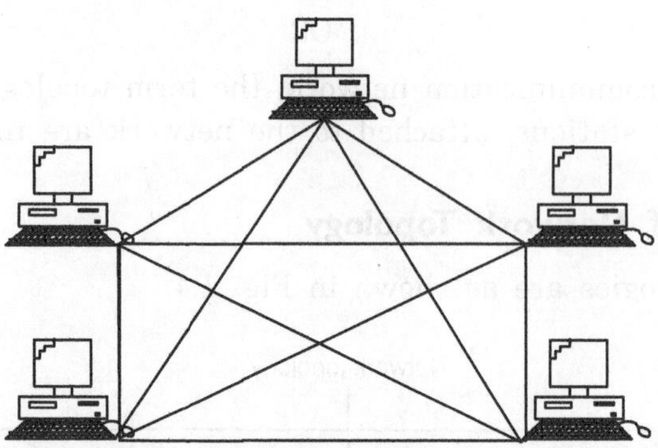

Fig. 1.5 Fully connected mesh topology (for five devices)

Advantage of Mesh Topology

(*i*) *No traffic problem:* The use of dedicated links assures that each connection can carry its own data load, thus eliminating the traffic problems that can occur when links are shared by more than one devices. That mean's no bottleneck problem.

(*ii*) *Better security:* As every message travels on a dedicated line, only the intended recipient can receives it.

(iii) *A mesh topology is robust to link failures*: If one link fails the data can be transmitted through alternate path.

(iv) Fault identification and fault isolation is easy due to 'point to point link'. Traffic can be routed through other paths to avoid links with suspected problems.

Disadvantages of Mesh Topology

1. Amount of cabling and number of input output ports required.
2. Every device must be connected to every other device.
3. The installation and reconnection are difficult.
4. The sheer bulk of the wiring can be greater than the available space.
5. The hardware required to connect each link (input output ports and cable) can be expensive.

Example 1.1 Assume six devices are arranged in a

(*a*) Fully connected mesh topology, how many cables are needed? How many ports are needed for each device?

(*b*) Ring topology how many cable links are required?

Solution:

(*a*) Number of links for a fully connected mesh of N nodes

$$= (n\ (n - 1))/2$$

Here, N = 6, Therefore

Number of links = (6 (6 – 1))/2 = 15

Number of ports per device = N – 1 = 6 – 1 = 5

(*b*) To connect *n* devices in a ring topology, we need n cable links. A six-device ring requires six cable links.

Example 1.2 The Lucky Ducky Corporation has a fully connected mesh network consisting of eight devices. Calculate the total number of cable links needed and the number of ports for each device.

Solution:

The formula for the number of links for a fully connected mesh is $n(n - 1)/2$, where n is the number of devices.

$$\text{Number of links} = n\ (n - 1)/2 = 8\ (8 - 1)/2 = 28$$

$$\text{Number of ports per device} = n - 1 = 8 - 1 = 7$$

2. Star Topology

In a star topology, each device has a dedicated point-to-point link only to a central controller, usually called a hub. The devices are not directly linked to each other. Unlike a mesh topology, a star topology does not allow direct traffic between devices. The controller acts as an exchange: If one device wants to send data to another, it sends the data to the controller, which then relays the data to the other connected device (see Figure 1.6).

The star is probably the most commonly used topology today. It uses twisted pair (10baseT or 100baseT) cabling and requires that all devices are connected to a hub.

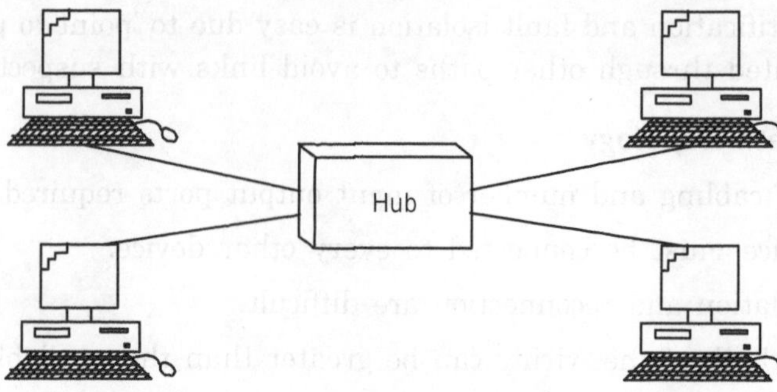

Fig. 1.6 Star Topology

Example

ARCNET is an example of star topology

Advantages of the Star Topology

1. *Ease of service*. The star topology has a number of concentration points (where connections are joined). These provide easy access for service or reconfiguration of the network.
2. *One device per connection*. Connection points in any network are inherently prone to failure. In the star topology, failure of a single connection typically involves disconnecting one node from an otherwise fully functional network.
3. *Centralized control problem diagnosis*. The fact that the central node is connected directly to every other node in the network means that faults are easily detected and isolated. It is a simple matter to disconnect failing nodes from the system.
4. *Simple access protocols*. Any given connection in a star network involves only the central node. In this situation, contention for who has control of the medium for the transmission purposes is easily solved. Thus in a star network, access protocols are very simple.
5. Each device needs only one link and one I/O port makes star topology less expensive, easy to install and easy to configure.
6. Robust topology.
7. If any link fails, it does not affect entire network.
8. Easy fault identification and fault isolation.
9. It is easy to modify and add new needs to a star network without disturbing to the rest of the network.
10. Star topology is useful when a centralized control is required.

Disadvantages of the Star Topology

1. *Long cable length*. Because each node is directly connected to the center, the star topology necessitates a large quantity of cable. Whilst the cost of cable is often

small, congestion in cable ducts and maintenance and installation problems can increase cost considerably.

2. *Default to expand.* The addition of a new node to a star network involves a connection all the way to the central node.
3. *Central node dependency.* If the central node in a star network fails, the entire network is rendered inoperable. This introduces heavy reliability and redundancy constraints on this node.

   The star topology has found extensive application in areas where intelligence in the network is concentrated at the central node.
4. If the central hub fails, the whole network fails to operate.
5. Each device requires its own cable segment.
6. In hierarchical network, installation and configuration is difficult. This is like if you were to burn down the phone company's central office, then anyone connected to it wouldn't be able to make any phone calls.
7. If one link fails there is no alternate to connect it with rest of network.

3. Ring Topology

It is also called as circular topology. In a ring topology, each device has a dedicated point-to-point line configuration only with the two devices on either side of it. A signal is passed along the ring in one direction, from device to device, until it reaches its destination. Each device in the ring incorporates a repeater. When a device receives a signal intended for another device, its repeater regenerates the bits and passes them along (see Fig. 1.7).

The ring topology looks are same as the star; except that it uses special hubs and Ethernet adapters. The ring topology is used with Token Ring networks.

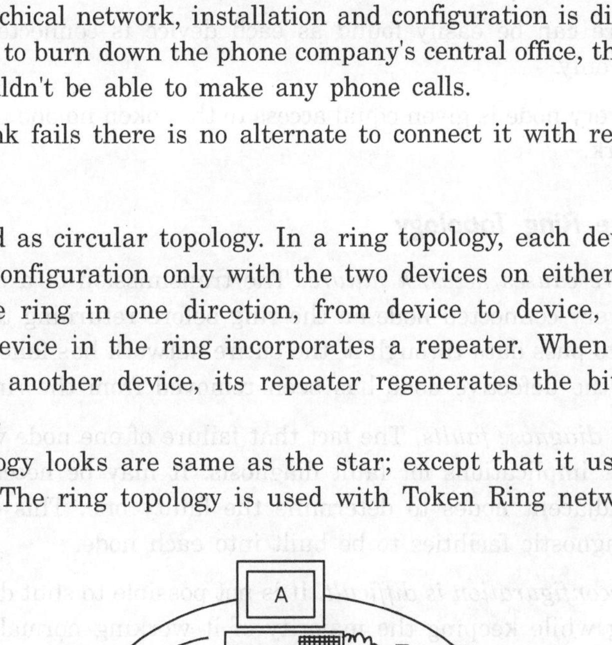

Fig. 1.7 Ring Topology

Example

Example of ring topology is Token Ring.

Advantages of the Ring Topology

1. *Short cable length.* The amount of cabling involves in a ring topology is comparable to that of a bus and is small relative to that of a star. This means that less connection will be needed, which will in turn increase network reliability.
2. *No wiring closet space required.* Since there is only one cable connecting each node to its immediate neighbors, it is not necessary to allocate space in the building for wiring closets.
3. *Suitable for optical fibers.* Using optical fibers offers the possibility of very high speed transmission. Because traffic on a ring travels in one direction, it is easy to use optical fibers as a medium of transmission.
4. A ring is relatively easy to install and reconfigure.
5. Link failure can be easily found as each device is connected to its immediate neighbors only.
6. Because every node is given equal access to the token no one node can monopolize the network.

Disadvantages of the Ring Topology

1. *Node failure causes network failure.* The transmission of a data on a ring goes through every connected node on the ring before returning to the sender. If one node fails to pass data through it, the entire network has failed and no traffic can flow until the defective node has been removed from the ring.
2. *Difficult to diagnose faults.* The fact that failure of one node will affect all others has serious implications for fault diagnosis. It may be necessary to examine a series of adjacent nodes to determine the faulty one. This operation may also require diagnostic facilities to be built into each node.
3. *Network reconfiguration is difficult.* It is not possible to shut down a small section of the ring while keeping the majority of it working normally.
4. Maximum ring length and number of devices is limited.
5. Failure of one node on the ring can affect the entire network.
6. Adding or removing nodes disrupts the network.

Characteristics of Ring LANs

- The basic ring topology is shown in Fig. 1.8, which shows that a number of repeaters are used and that the transmission in unidirectional.
- The data is transferred in a sequential manner bit by bit around the ring. Note that each repeater will regenerate and retransmit each bit.

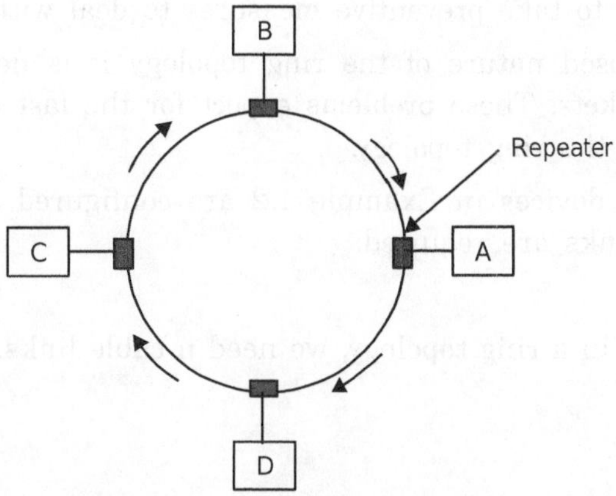

Fig. 1.8 Basic Ring Topology

Functions of a Ring

- A ring can operate as a communication network if it performs the following three functions:
  1. Data insertion
  2. Data reception
  3. Data removal
- The above-mentioned functions are actually provided by the repeaters.
- Each repeater also acts as the device attachment point. Hence the function of data insertion is accomplished by the repeaters.
- Data is transmitted in the form of packets.
- Each packet consists of a destination address field. As this packet by a repeater, the destination address field is copied by the repeater.
- If the destination address field corresponds to the address of a device then that repeater copies the remaining contents of packet as well.
- Data insertion and reception can be done easily by the repeaters but data removal is more difficult on a ring.
- As the ring is a closed loop, a packet will circulate on it identify if it is not removed.
- A packet can be removed by the addressed repeater or each packet can be removed by the transmitting repeater itself after the packet has made one trip around the ring. The second approach is more desirable.

Problems faced in the Ring Topology

- If any link brakes or if any repeater face then the entire network will be disabled.
- To install a new repeater for supporting a new device, it is necessary to have the identification of two near by, topologically adjacent repeaters.

- It is necessary to take preventive measures to deal with the time jitter.
- Due to the closed nature of the ring topology it is necessary to remove the circulating packets. These problems expect for the last one can be rectified by refinements of the ring topology.

Example 1.3 If the devices in Example 1.2 are configured as a ring instead of a mesh, how many cable links are required.

Solution:

To connect n devices in a ring topology, we need n cable links. An eight - device ring needs eight cable links.

4. Bus Topology

- It is also called as linear topology.
- All other topologies (mesh, star, ring) described point-to-point configuration.
- A bus topology is multipoint. One long cable acts as a backbone to link all other devices in the network.
- The speed of the bus topology is slow because only one computer can send a message at a time. A computer must wait until the bus is free before it can transmit.
- The bus topology requires a proper termination at both the ends of the cable.
- Since the bus is a passive topology, the electrical signal from a transmitting computer is free to travel the entire length of the cable.
- Nodes are connected to the bus cable by droplines and taps (see Fig. 1.9).

Dropline: A drop line is a connection between the devices and the main cable.

Tap: A tap is a connection that punctures with the metallic core.

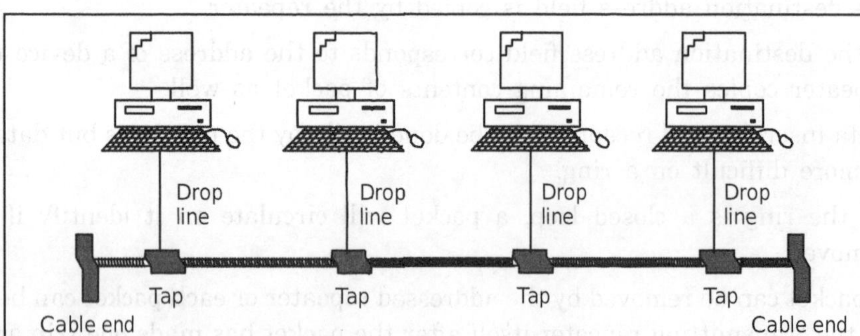

Fig. 1.9 Bus Topology

Example

Example of bus topology is ETHERNET.

Advantages of the Linear Topology

1. *Short cable length and simple wiring layout*. Because there is a signal common data path connecting all nodes, the linear topology allows a very short cable length to be used. This decreases the installation cost, and also leads to a simple, easy to maintain wiring layout.
2. *Resilient Architecture*. The LINEAR architecture has an inherent simplicity that makes it very reliable from a hardware point of view. There is a single cable through which all the data propagates and to which all nodes are connected.
3. *Easy to extend*. Additional nodes can be connected to an existing bus network at any point along its length. More extensive additions can be achieved by adding extra segments connected by a type of signal amplifier none as repeater.

Disadvantages of the Linear Topology

1. *Fault diagnosis is difficult*. Although simplicity of the bus topology means that there is very little to go wrong, fault detection is not a simple matter. Control of the network is not centralized in any particular node. This means that detection of a fault may have to be performed from many points in the network.
2. *Fault isolation is difficult*. In the star topology, a defective node can easily be isolated from the network by removing its connection at the center. If a node is faulty on the bus, it must be rectified at the point where the node is connected to the network.
3. *Repeater configuration*. When BUS type network has its backbone extended using repeaters, reconfiguration may be necessary.
4. *Nodes must be intelligent*. Each node on the network is directly connected to the central bus. This means that some way of deciding who can use the network at any given time must be performed in each node.

Characteristics of the Bus Topology

Following are some of the important characteristics of the bus topology:

1. This is a multipoint configuration. There are more than two devices connected to the medium and they are capable of transmitting on the medium. Hence the medium access control is essential for the bus topology.
2. The signal strength of the transmitted signal should be adequately high so as to meet the minimum signal strength requirements of the receiver.
3. Adequate signal to noise ratio should be maintained.
4. The signal should not be too strong. This is necessary to avoid the overloading of transmitter and hence the possibility of signal distortion.
5. This is called as signal balancing, which is not an easy task at all. Especially the signal balancing becomes increasingly difficult with increase in the number of stations.
6. The solution to this problem is to divide the transmission medium into small segments and within each segment a pair wise balancing is done using amplifiers or repeaters between the segments.

5. Tree Topology

- It is also called as hierarchical topology.
- A tree topology is a variation of a star. As in a star, nodes in a tree are linked to a central hub that controls the traffic to the network.

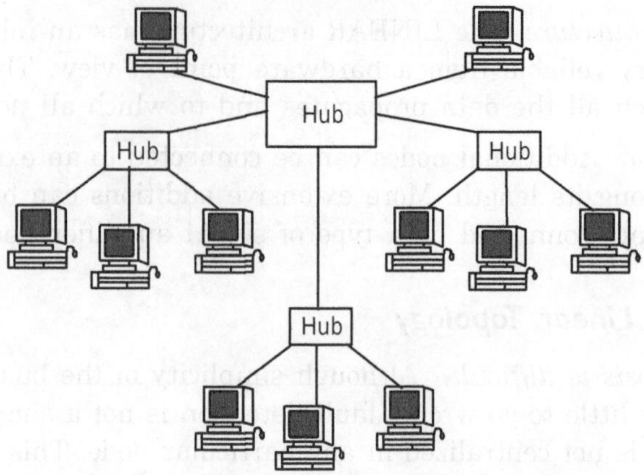

Fig. 1.10 Tree Topology

- However not every computers plugs into the central hub, majority of them are connected to a secondary hub which in turn is connected to the central hub as shown in Fig. 1.10.
- The central hub in the tree is an active hub, which contains repeater. The repeater amplifies the signal and increase the distance a signal can travel.
- The secondary hubs may be active or passive. A passive hub provides a simple physical connection between the attached devices.
- Tree Topology is somewhat similar to bus topology. We can say that tree topology is another form of bus topology. But unlike bus topology, the nodes in a tree extend similar to the branches of a tree with the trunk or we can say bus is a special case of tree in which there is only one trunk.

Advantages of Tree Topology

1. It allows more devices to be attached to a single hub and can therefore increase the distance of a signal can travel between devices.
2. It allows the network to isolate and priorities communications from different computers.

Disadvantages of Tree Topology

1. If the central hub fails the system breaks down.
2. The cabling cost is more.

Note: The advantages and disadvantages of a tree topology are generally the same as those of a star.

Difference between Bus and Tree

Besides this, the difference between bus and tree is that the bus topology uses baseband transmission techniques and the tree topology uses the broadband techniques. In tree topology usually a coaxial cable is used to implement it. The data transmitted by a node traverses through the trunk on head end before reaching the destination.

1.6 CATEGORIES OF NETWORK

A computer network means a group of 'networked' computers i.e., computers that are linked by means of a communication system. A network can mean a small group of linked computers to a chain of a few hundred computers of different types (e.g., PCs, minis, mainframes etc.) spread around the world. Thus, networks vary in size, complexity and geographical spread. Mostly, computers are classified on the basis of geographical spread and on this basis; there can be three types of networks (see Fig. 1.11).

- Local Area Networks (LANs)
- Wide Area Networks (WANs)
- Metropolitan Area Networks (MANs)

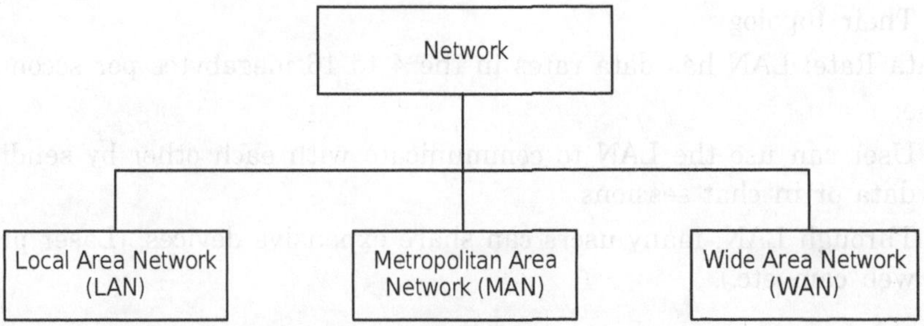

Fig. 1.11 Categories of Networks

I. Local Area Network (LAN)

- A LAN is a data communication system within a building or campus or between near by buildings (see Fig. 1.12).
- The most common LAN topologies are Bus, Ring, and Star.
- LAN is that network which covers the distance from 1m. To 1km.
- LAN is the cheap way of interconnecting the systems.
- LAN is capable of transmitting data at very fast rates. Much faster than data can be transmitted over a telephone line.
- LANs are easy to design and troubleshoot. The personal computers and workstations in the offices are interconnected via LAN.
- The exchange of information and sharing of resources becomes easy because of LAN.
- In LAN all the machines are connected to a single cable. Different types of topologies such as Bus, Ring, Star, Tree etc. are used for LANs.

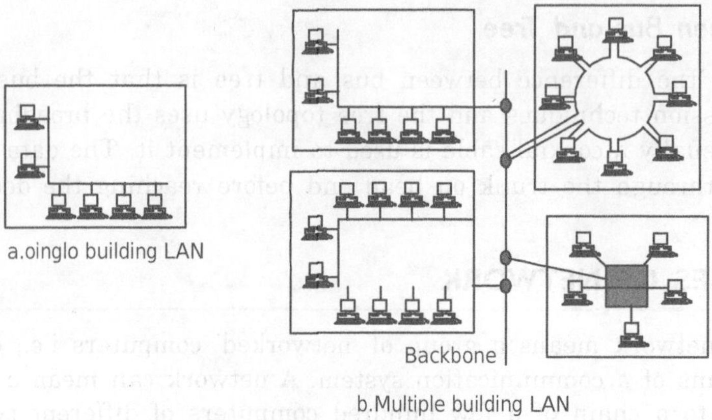

Fig. 1.12 Local Area Network (LAN)

- LAN uses a layered architecture and they are capable of operating at hundreds of Mbits/sec.
- LANs are distinguished from other kinds of networks by three characteristics:
  1. Their size
  2. Their transmission technology, and
  3. Their topology
- Data Rate: LAN has data rates in the 4 to 16 megabytes per second.
- Use:
  1. User can use the LAN to communicate with each other by sending e-mails, data or in chat sessions
  2. Through LAN, many users can share expensive devices. (Laser printer, data, web cam etc.).

Advantages of LAN

1. It allows large number of users to access the data from single memory.
2. The files are stored on single memory.
3. The processing can be done by number of users simultaneously.

Characteristics of LAN

1. Low cost is an important characteristic of LAN.
2. Resource sharing is the greatest advantage of LAN.
3. In LAN, every device can communicate with any other device.
4. The independent devices are interconnected with high degree in LAN.

Key Purpose

Key purpose of a LAN is to serve its users in resources sharing. The main reason for designing a LAN is to share resources such as disks, printers, programs and data. It also enables the exchange of information.

System of LAN

There are 3 types of systems used in LAN.

1. Client-server

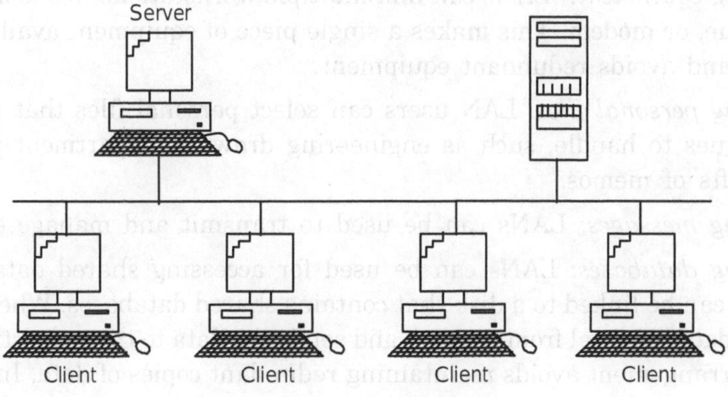

Fig. 1.13 Client-server

This LAN does not provide network resources. In this case, the client computer accesses the main computer through the server.

2. Peer based LAN

This LAN provides interconnection between the computers and various devices. All computers can be interconnected to each other by networking.

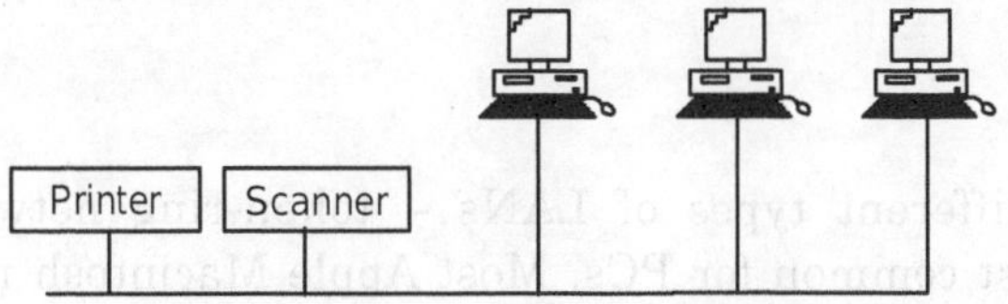

Fig. 1.14 Peer Based LAN

3. Server Based LAN

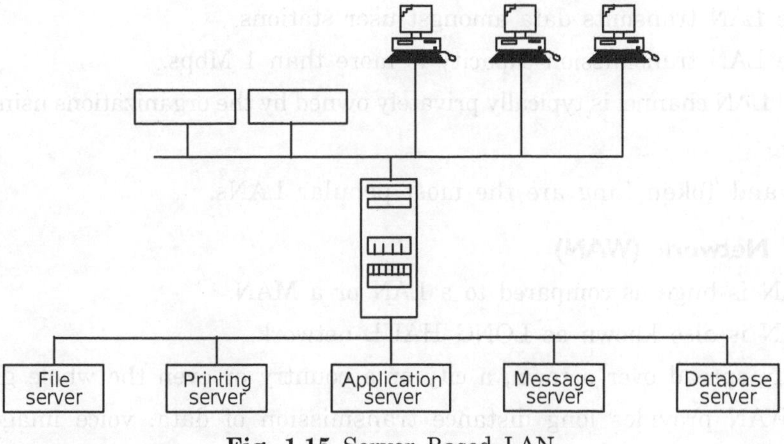

Fig. 1.15 Server Based LAN

This is hybrid network, in which Peer connection are made by joining the connections.

Applications of LANs

1. *Sharing equipment:* LANs can link multiple workstations to one laser printer, fax machine, or modem. This makes a single piece of equipment available to multiple users and avoids redundant equipment.
2. *Sharing personal files:* LAN users can select personal files that they want their colleagues to handle, such as engineering drawing, department plans, contracts or drafts of memos.
3. *Sending messages:* LANs can be used to transmit and manage electronic mail.
4. *Sharing databases:* LANs can be used for accessing shared databases. The file server can be linked to a disk that contains shared databases. When a workstation needs data retrieval from the disk and sends the data to the requesting workstation. This arrangement avoids maintaining redundant copies of data. In addition to not wasting storage, and having the databases in one place avoids problems with inconsistent data.
5. *Administering software:* Instead of storing separate copies of spreadsheet or word processing software at each workstation, the LAN can deliver a temporary copy to a workstation that needs the software. This ensures everyone the use of latest version of the software. Upgrading to a new software version involves only one replacement instead of finding and replacing each copy. This approach also reduces the number of copies of the software that must be purchased.

Types of LANs

There are many different types of LANs – token-ring networks, Ethernets, and ARCNETs being the most common for PCs. Most Apple Macintosh networks are based on Apple's AppleTalk network system, which is built into Macintosh computers.

Attributes of LAN

- The LAN transmits data amongst user stations.
- The LAN transmission capacity is more than 1 Mbps.
- The LAN channel is typically privately owned by the organizations using the facility.

Example

Ethernet and Token Ring are the most popular LANs.

2. Wide Area Network (WAN)

- WAN is huge as compared to a LAN or a MAN.
- WAN is also known as LONG HAUL network.
- WAN spread over a town, a city or a country or even the whole globe.
- A WAN provides long distance transmission of data, voice image and video information over large areas.

- The data is communicated in the form of small pieces and sent over the network.
- It is cheaper and more efficient to use phone network for the links.

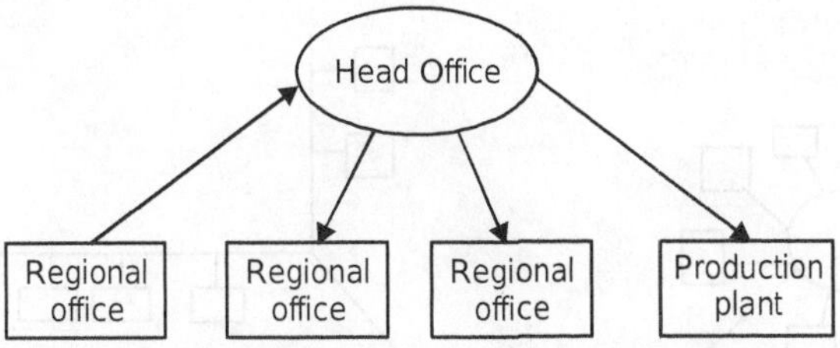

Fig. 1.16 Wide Area Network (WAN)

Uses of WAN

1. A WAN uses telephone links, mobile phones, satellite transmission and under sea cables.
2. The WAN used direct distance dialing, leased links and satellite.
3. The remote computers are connected to each other by use of these lines.
4. A WAN uses various communication facilities to connect the user not located in the single building.

Example

Example of WAN is an airline reservation system.

Types of WAN

WANs can be classified into two types. They are:

1. Discontinuous connection WANs and.
2. Continuous connection WANs.

3. Metropolitan Area Network (MAN)

- MAN is a network that is designed to cover an entire city.
- A MAN can support both data and voice.
- A MAN does not contain switching elements (connectivity).
- Its range from 5 to 50 km. high data rate from LAN.
- It may be a single network such as Television network or it may be a means of connecting a number of LANs into a larger network, so that resources may be shared LAN-to-LAN as well as device-to-device.
- MAN is designed with two unidirectional buses. Each bus is independent of the other in the transfer of traffic. The topology can be designed as an open bus or a closed configuration.
- MANs are based on fiber optic transmission technology and provide high-speed interconnection between sites. It can support both data and device.
- MANs as a special category is that a standard has been adopted for them and this standard is now being implemented. It is called IEEE 802.6.

Example 1

A company can use a MAN to connect the LANs in all the offices throughout the city.

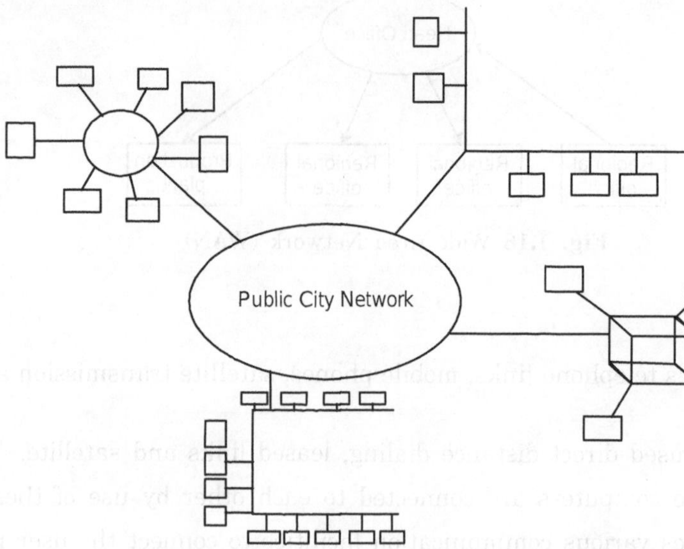

Fig. 1.17 Metropolitan Area Network (MAN)

Example 2

Cable TV networks that are spread over a city can be turned as metropolitan area networks.

- **Uses:** It uses high-speed data transfer medium, like fiber optics.
- **Purpose:** The purpose of a MAN is also the sharing of hardware and software resources among its users.
- **Transfer Rate:** MAN provides the transfer rates from 34 to 150 Mbps.

Table 1.1 Comparisons between LAN, WAN & MAN

Parameter	*LAN*	*WAN*	*MAN*
Area covered	Covers small area. i.e. within the building	Covers large geographical area	Covers larger than LAN & smaller than WAN
Error rates	Lowest	Highest	Moderate
Transmission speed	High speed	Low speed	Moderate speed
Equipment cost	Uses inexpensive equipment	Uses most expensive equipment	Uses moderately expensive equipment

Table 1.2 Comparison between LAN and WAN

Sr. No.	*LAN*	*WAN*
1.	It covers small Area	WAN covers large geographical area
2.	LAN operates on the principle of broadcasting	WAN operates on the principle of point to point
3.	Used for time critical application	Not used for time critical application
4.	Transmission speed is high	Transmission speed is low
5.	Easy to design & maintain	Design & maintain is not easy
6.	LAN is broadcasting in nature	WAN is point to point in nature
7.	Transmission medium is co-axial or UTP cable	Transmission or communication medium is PSTN or satellite link
8.	LAN does not suffer from propagation delay	WAN suffer from propagation delay
9.	LAN can operate on very high data rates	WAN operates on low data rates
10.	In a LAN each station can transmit and receives over the communication medium	In WAN each station cannot transmit.
11.	The LAN is owned by a person, college, factory etc. It is a privately owned network.	WAN can be private or it can be public leased type network.
12.	LAN is designed to operate over a small physical area such as office, factory or group of buildings.	WAN is used for the network that spans over a large distance such as system spanning states countries etc.

1.7 LINE CONFIGURATION

Line configuration refers to the way two or more communication devices attach to a link. A link is the physical communication pathway that transfers data from one device

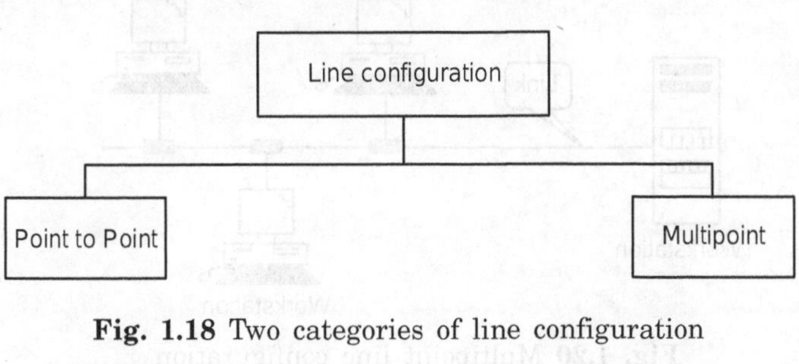

Fig. 1.18 Two categories of line configuration

to another. For the purposes of visualization, it is simplest to imagine any link as a line drawn between two points. For communication to occur, two devices must be connected in some way to the same link at the same time. There are two possible line configurations: point-to-point and multipoint (see Fig. 1.18).

Line configuration defines the attachment of communication devices to a link.

1. Point-to-point Line Configuration

A point-to-point line configuration provides a dedicated link between two devices. The entire capacity of the channel is reserved for transmission between those two devices. The most point to point line configuration use an actual length of wire or cable to connect two ends, but other options, such as microwave or satellite links are also possible (see Figure 1.19). When you change television channels by infrared remote control, you are establishing a point-to-point line configuration between the remote control and the television's control system.

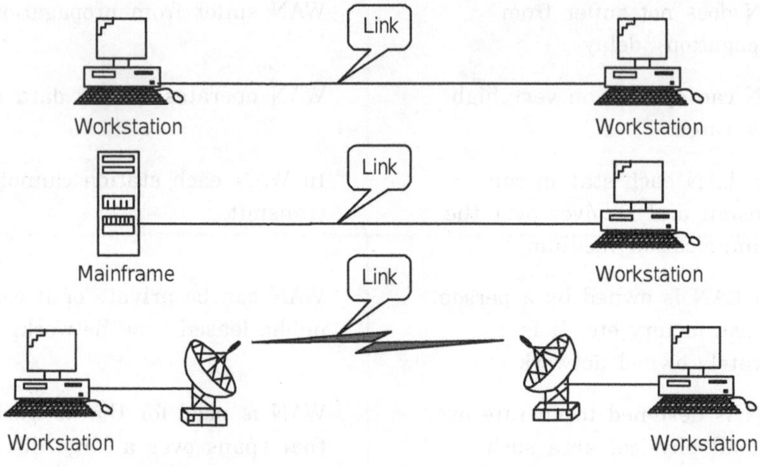

Fig. 1.19 Point-to-point line configuration

2. Multipoint Line Configuration

A multipoint (also called multidrop) line configuration is one in which more than two specific devices share a single link (see Fig. 1.20).

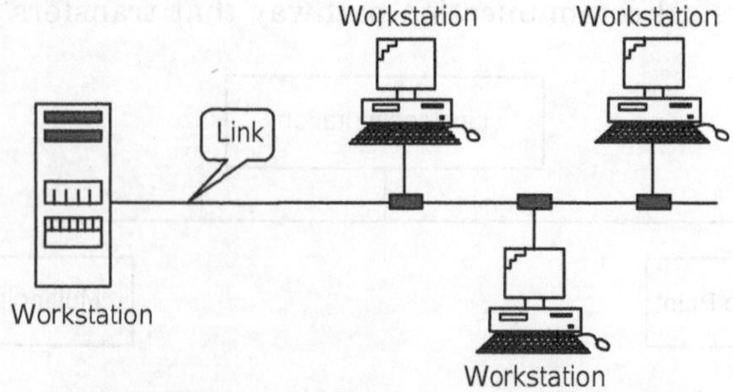

Fig. 1.20 Multipoint line configuration

In a multipoint environment, the capacity of the channel is shared, either spatially or temporally. If several devices can use the link simultaneously, it is a spatially shared line configuration. If users must take turns, it is a time-shared line configuration.

1.8 BROADCAST NETWORKS

- Broadcast systems generally also allow the possibility of addressing a packet to all destinations by using a special code in the address field. When a packet with this code is transmitted, it is received and processed by every machine on the network. This mode of operation is called broadcasting.
- Broadcast networks have a single communication channel that is shared or used by all the machines on the network. Short messages called packets sent by any machine are received by all the others.
- Some broadcast systems also support transmission to a subset of the machines known as multicasting.
- Upon receiving a packet, a machine checks the address field. If the packet is addressed to it then the packet is processed, otherwise the packet is ignored.

1.9 INTRODUCTION TO SMDS

Switched multimegabit data services (SMDS) are a service for handling high-speed communications for metropolitan area networks. It was developed to support organizations that need to exchange data between LANs located in different parts of a city or large campus. The goal was to produce a high-speed data service and get it out into the world with a minimum of fuss. SMDS is the first broadband (i.e., high-speed) switched service offered to the public.

Example

To see a situation in which SMDS would be useful, consider a company with four offices on four different cities, each with its own LAN. The company would like to connect all the LANs, so that packets can go from one LAN to another. One solution would be to lease six high-speed lines and fully connect the LAN as shown in Fig. 1.21 (*a*). Such a solution is certainly possible, but expensive.

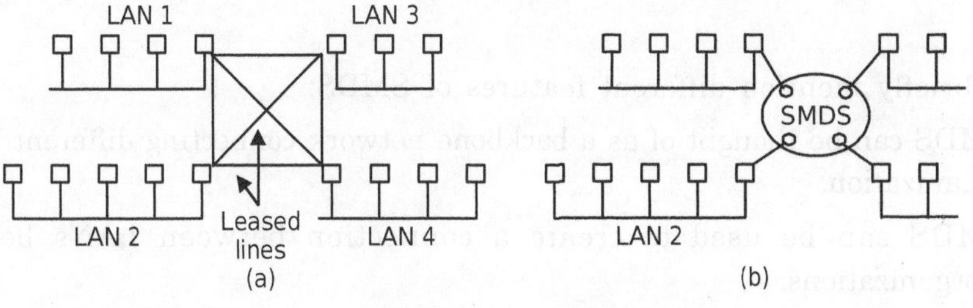

Fig. 1.21 (*a*) Four LANs interconnected with leased lines
(*b*) Interconnection using SMDS

An alternative solution is to use SMDS, as shown in Fig. 1.21 (*b*). The SMDS network acts like a high-speed LAN backbone, allowing packets from any LAN to flow to any other LAN. Between the LANs in the customer's offices, and the SMDS network, in the telephone company's offices, is a (short) access line leased from the telephone company. Usually, this line is a MAN and uses DQDB, other options may also be available.

1.9.1 SMDS Packet Format

The basic SMDS service is a simple connectionless packet delivery service. The packet format is shown in Fig. 1.22. It has three fields: the destination (where the packet is to go to), the source (who sent it), and a variable length for up to 9188 bytes of user data. The machine on the sending LAN that is connected to the access line puts the packet on the access line, and SMDS makes a best effort attempt to deliver it to the correct destination. No guarantee is given.

Bytes	8	8	≤9188
	Destination address	Source address	User data

Fig. 1.22 The SMDS packet format

The source and destination addresses consist of a 4-bit code followed by a telephone number of up to 15 decimal digits. Each digit is coded in a separate 4-bit field. The telephone numbers contain country code, area code, and subscriber number so the service could eventually be offered internationally. It was thought that having decimal telephone numbers as network addresses would make the new offering seem familiar to nervous users.

When a packet arrives at the SMDS network, the first router checks to make sure that the source address corresponds to the incoming line, to prevent billing fraud. If the address is incorrect, the packet is simply discarded. If it is correct, the packet is sent along toward its destination.

A useful SMDS feature is broadcasting. The customer can specify a list of SMDS telephone numbers, and be assigned a special number for the whole list. Any packet sent to that number is delivered to all members on that list. The National Association of Securities Dealers uses this feature of MCI's SMDS service to broadcast new stock prices to all of its 5000 members.

Features

We will briefly mention different features of SMDS:

- SMDS can be thought of as a backbone network connecting different LANs same organization.
- SMDS can be used to create a connection between LANs belonging to diorganizations.
- Although used mostly as a MAN, SMDS can also be used as a WAN.
- SMDS is a switched-packet network; the same network is available to all us.

- Subscribers pay only when they actually use the network.
- Since the user payload can be up to 9188 bytes, SMDS can receive and encapsulate frames from all LANs.
- The data rate ranges from 1.544 Mbps to 155 Mbps.
- Each user is assigned as average data rate.
- The instantaneous data rate can vary as long as the average is below the data rate assigned to a specific customer. This means that the transmission of data can be bursty.
- Since the addressing system is a telephone number, there is no need for a new addressing system to be assigned to each user.
- Multicasting is available; a user can send data that can be received by several users.

1.10 X.25 NETWORKS

- X.25 is a standard used by many older public networks specially outside the U.S.
- This was developed in 1970s by CCITT for providing as interface between public packet-switched network and their customers.
- The packet switching networks use X.25 protocol. The X.25 recommendations were first prepared in 1976 and then revised in 1978, 1980 and 1984.
- This protocol is based on the protocols used in early packet switching networks such as ARPANET, DATAPAC, and TRANSPAC etc.
- A protocol X.21 that is a physical layer protocol is used to specify the physical electrical and procedural interface between the host and network.
- The problem with this standard is that it needs digital signal rather than analog signals on telephone lines.
- So not many networks support this standard. Instead RS 232 standard is defined.
- The data link layer standard has a number of variations. It is designed for error detection and corrections.
- The network layer protocol performs the addressing, flow control, delivery confirmation etc.
- It allows the user to establish virtual circuits and send packets on them. These packets are delivered to the destination reliably and in order.
- X.25 is a connection-oriented service. It supports switched virtual circuits as well as the permanent circuits.
- A switched virtual circuit is established between a computer and network when the computer sends a packet to the network requesting to make a call to other computer.

- Packets can then be sent over this connection from sender to receiver.
- X.25 provides the flow control, to avoid a fast sender overriding a slow or busy receiver.
- A permanent virtual circuit is analogous to a leased line. It is set up in advance with a mutual agreement between the users.
- Since it is always present, no call set up is required for its use.
- In order to allow the computers which do not use the X.25 to communicate with the X.25 network a packet assembler disassembler (PAD) is used.
- PAD is required to be installed along with each computer, which does not use X.25.
- X.25 defines the interface for exchange of packets between a DTE and switch data sub network node.

Figure 1.23 gives a conceptual overview of X.25. Although X.25 is an end-to-end protocol, the actual movement of packets through the network is invisible to the user. The user sees the network as a cloud through which each packet passes on its way to the receiving DTE.

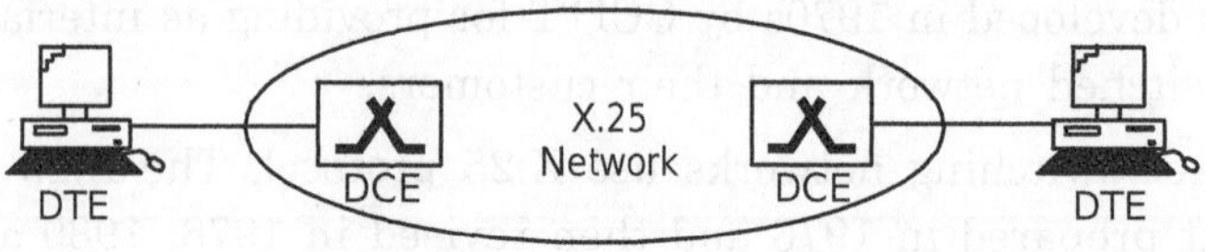

Fig. 1.23 X.25

Three Layers of X.25

The X.25 interface is defined at three levels. The three levels are:

1. Physical layer (level 1)
2. Data link layer (level 2)
3. Packet layer (level 3).

   - These three layers correspond to the three lower most layers of the ISO-OSI reference model. The physical layer takes care of the interface between a computer terminal and the link, which attaches it to the packet switching node.
   - The X.25 defines the interface for exchange of packets between the user's machine (DTE) and the packet switching node to which this DTE is attached which is called as DCE.
   - The three layers of X.25 interface are as shown in Fig. 1.24 (*a*).
   - At the physical level X.21 physical interface is being used which is defined for circuit switched data network. At the data link level, X.25 specifies the link access procedure-B (LAP-B) protocol, which is a subset of HDLC protocol.
   - At the network level (3rd level), X.25 defines a protocol for an access to packet data subnetwork.

- This protocol defines the format, content and procedures for exchange of control and data transfer packets. The packet layer provides an external virtual circuit service.
- Fig. 1.24 (*b*) shows the relationship between the levels of X-25. User data is passed down to X.25 level 3.

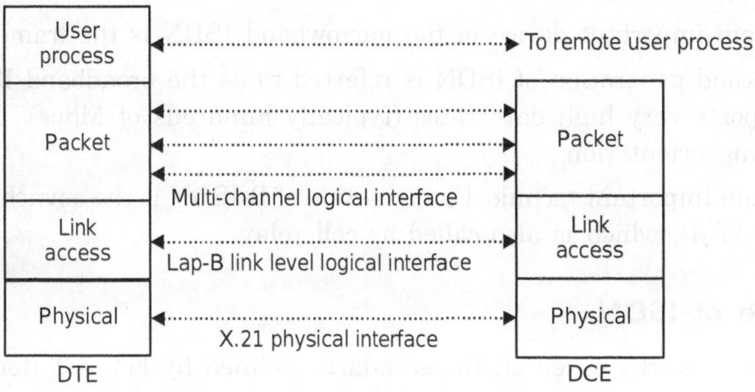

Fig. 1.24 (*a*) Different layers of X.25 and interface DTE and DCE

- This data then appends the control information as a header to form a packet. This control information is then used in the operation of the protocol.
- The entire X.25 packet formed at the packet level is then passed down to the second layer i.e. the data link layer.
- The control information is appended at the front and back of the packet forming a LAP-B frame. The control information in LAP-B frame is needed for the operation of the LAP-B protocol.
- This frame is then passed to the physical layer for transmission.

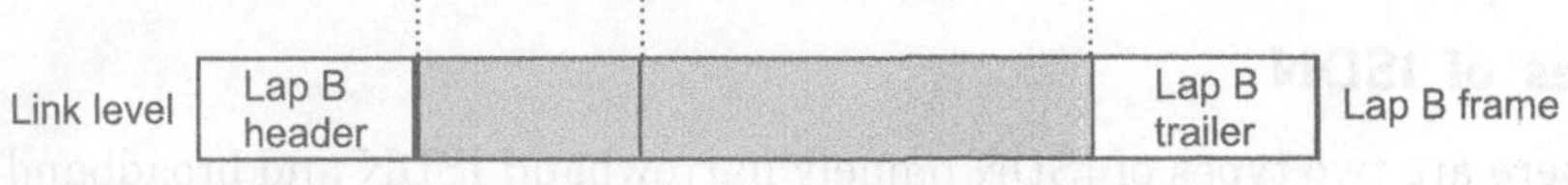

Fig. 1.24 (*b*) Relationship between the levels of X.25

1.11 ISDN

- The long form of ISDN is integrated services digital network. It is a wide area network becoming widely available.

- Due to rapid advances in computer and communication technologies these two fields have virtually merged into each other.
- ISDN is the product of such a merger of these technologies.
- The first generation of ISDN is called as a narrowband ISDN and it is based on the user of 64 kbps channel as the basic unit of switching and has a circuit switching orientation.
- The main important device in the narrowband ISDN is the frame relay.
- The second generation of ISDN is referred to as the broadband ISDN (B-ISDN). It supports very high data rates (typically hundreds of Mbps). It has a packet switching orientation.
- The main important technical contribution of B-ISDN is the asynchronous transfer mode (ATM), which is also called as cell relay.

1.11.1 Principle of ISDN

- The ISDN works based on the standards defined by ITU - T (formerly CCITT).
- The principle of ISDN according to ITU - T is as stated below.
- The ISDN is supported by a wide range of voice and non-voice applications of the same network. It provides a range of services using a limited set of connections and multipurpose user-network interface arrangements.
- ISDN supports a variety of applications that include both switched and non-switched connections. The switched connections include both circuit switched and packet switched connections.
- As far as possible, new services introduced into an ISDN should be arranged to be compatible with the 64 kbps switched digital connections.
- An ISDN will contain the intelligence for providing service features, maintenance and network management functions.
- A layered protocol structure should be used for the specification of access to an ISDN.
- This is same as the OSI reference model. The standards which have already been developed for OSI applications such as X.25 can be used for ISDN.
- ISDNs may be implemented in a variety of configurations.

1.11.2 Types of ISDN

- There are two types of ISDN namely narrowband ISDN and broadband ISDN. The narrowband ISDN has a smaller bandwidth and it can support the data rates of upto 64 kbits/s only.
- Due to low bit rates the quality of service provided by the narrowband ISDN is poor. That means the quality of video signals in the narrowband ISDN is very poor.
- The quality of service is improved by using the broadband ISDN. The broadband ISDN can support higher data rates due to the use of optical fiber cables.

- The bandwidth of an optical fiber cable is very high. So the broadband ISDN can allow transmission of very high quality video images through it.

1.11.3 Services of ISDN

The purpose of the ISDN is to provide fully integrated digital services to users. These services fall into categories: better services, teleservices and supplementary services (see Figure 1.25).

1. Bearer Services

Bearer services provide the means to transfer information (voice, data and video) between users without the network manipulating the content of that information. The network does not need to process the information and therefore does not change the content. Bearer services belong to the first three layers of the OSI model and are well defined in the ISDN standard. They can be provided using circuit-switched, packet-switched, frame-switched, or cell-switched networks.

2. Teleservices

In teleservicing, the network may change or process the contents of the data. These services correspond to layers 4-7 of the OSI model. Teleservices relay on the facilities of the bearer services and are designed to accommodate complex user needs without the user having to be aware of the details of the process. Teleservices include telephony, teletex, telefax, videotex, telex and teleconferencing. Although the ISDN defines these services by name, they have not yet become standards.

3. Supplementary Services

Supplementary services are those services that provide additional functionality to the bearer services and teleservices. Examples of these services are reverse charging, call waiting, and message handling, all familiar from today's telephone company services.

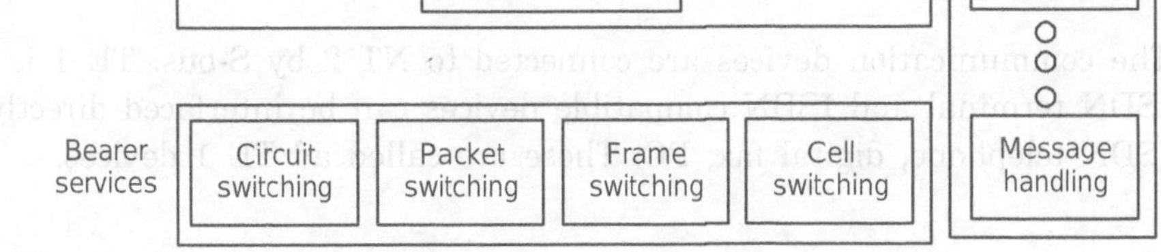

Fig. 1.25 ISDN services

1.11.4 ISDN Interface

Even though ISDN uses existing telephone network, it requires special interfaces for connecting equipments. The interface can be used for voice, data, video, fax, and digital data transmission. Fig. 1.26 shows ISDN interfaces. These are the parts of communication system for ISDN network.

Non-ISDN terminal

- PBX
- Telephone (Analog)

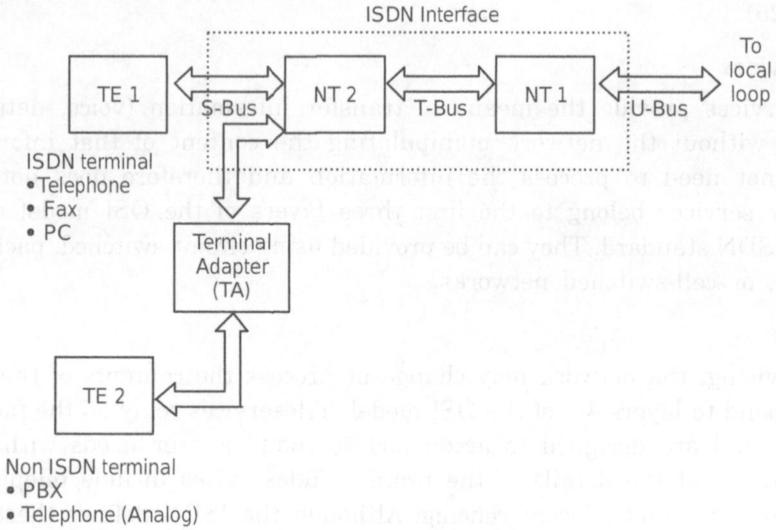

Fig. 1.26 ISDN interface

NT I

- NT 1 provides the physical and electrical terminations of twisted pair wiring (U–Bus). NT 1 provides multilevel encoding, decoding, multiplexing and timing.

NT 2

- NT 2 provides interface to user equipments such as connection to LAN, PBX, telephone and other devices. These are ISDN or non-ISDN equipment. NT 2 also provides 2 wire-to-4 wire conversions for basic rate access to common carrier.
- NT 2 and NT 1 are interconnected by T-bus and together called as ISDN interface.

TE I

- The communication devices are connected to NT 2 by S-bus. TE 1 is called as ISDN terminal and ISDN compatible devices can be interfaced directly such as ISDN telephone, digital fax, PC. These are called ad TE 1 devices.

TE 2

- TE 2 is called as non-ISDN terminal i.e. equipments that are not compatible to ISDN are interfaced. To interface such devices a Terminal Adapter (TA) is needed. Different TAs are available, depending on the type of equipment suitable TA is selected. Examples of non-ISDN equipment are PBX, analog telephone (pulse operated).

- Two basic ISDN connections are:
  1. Basic Rate Interface (BRI)
  2. Primary Rate Interface (PRI)

BRI

The basic rate interface BRI specifies a digital pipe consisting of two B channels and one 16 Kbps D channel (see Fig. 1.27).

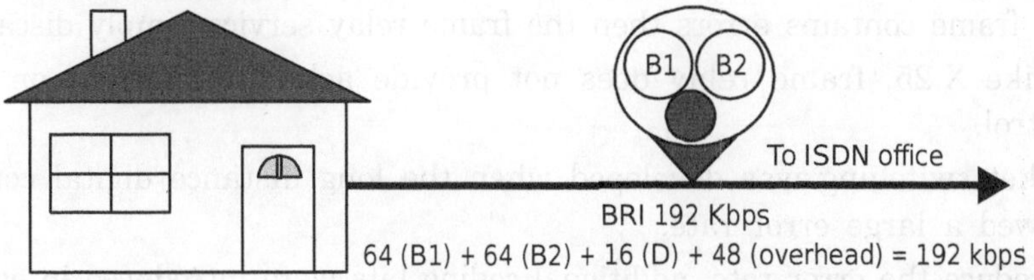

Fig. 1.27 BRI

Two B channels of 64 Kbps each, plus one D channel of 16 Kbps, equal 144 Kbps. In addition, the BRI service itself requires 48 Kbps of operating overhead. BRI therefore requires a digital pipe of 192 Kbps. Conceptually, the BRI service is like a large pipe that contains three smaller pipes, two for the B channels and one for the D channel. The remainder of the space inside the large pipe carries the overhead bits required for its operation. In figure 1.27 the shaded portion of the circle surrounds the B and D channels shows the overhead.

PRI

The usual primary rate interface (PRI) specifies a digital pipe with 23 B channels and one 64 Kbps D channel (see Fig. 1.28).

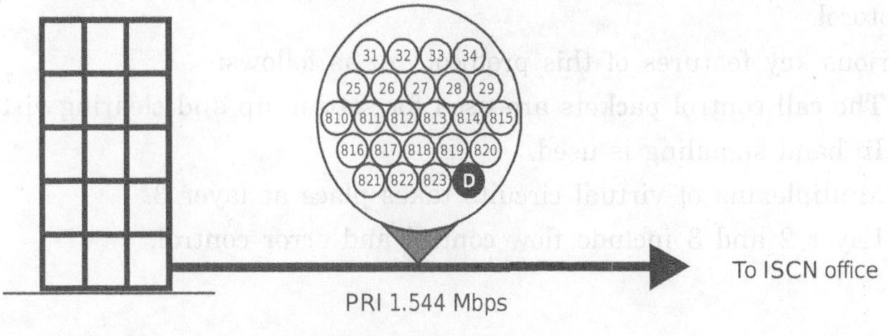

Fig. 1.28 PRI

Twenty-three B channels of 64 Kbps each, plus one D channel of 64 Kbps equals 1.536 Mbps. In addition, the PRI service itself uses 8 Kbps of overhead. PRI therefore requires a digital pipe of 1.544 Mbps. Conceptually; the PRI service is like a large pipe containing 24 smaller pipes, 23 for the B channels and 1 for the D channel. The rest of the pipe carries the overhead bits required for its operation. In Fig. 1.28, the shaded portion of the circle surrounding the B and D channels shows the overhead.

1.12 FRAME RELAY

- Frame relay is a connection-oriented service. It can be imagined to be equivalent to a virtual leased line.
- On a virtual line data bursts can be sent ad full speed.
- Frame relay provides a service to determine the start and end of each frame. It also detects the transmission errors. But the frame relay does not have error control or flow control.
- If a frame contains errors then the frame relay service simply discards it.
- Unlike X.25, frame relay does not provide acknowledgement or normal flow control.
- Packet switching was developed when the long distance digital communication showed a large error rate.
- To reduce the error rate, additional coding bits were introduced in each packet in order to introduce redundancy to detect and recover errors.
- But in the modern high-speed telecommunication systems, this overhead is unnecessary and infact counter productive.
- Frame relay was developed for taking the advantage of the high data rates and how error rates in the modern communication system.
- The original packet switching networks were designed with a data rate at the user end of about 64 Kbps.
- But the frame relay networks are designed to operate efficiently at the user's data rate upto 2 Mbps.
- This is possible practically because most of the overhead (additional bits) is striped off.
- Frame relay also is meant for more efficient transmission scheme than the X.25 protocol.
- Various key features of this protocol are as follows:
  1. The call control packets are used for setting up and clearing virtual circuits.
  2. In band signaling is used.
  3. Multiplexing of virtual circuits takes place at layer 3.
  4. Layer 2 and 3 include flow control and error control.

Advantages

Frame Relay has several advantages over comparable wide area networks such as X.25 and T-lines.

1. Frame Relay operates at a higher speed (1.544 Mbps and recently 44.376 Mbps). This means that it can be easily be used instead of a mesh of T-1 or T-3 lines.
2. Streamlined communication process.
3. The number of functions of a protocol at the user-network interface is reduced.
4. Lower delay.

5. Higher throughput.
6. Frame relay can be used at access speeds upto 2 Mbps.
7. Frame Relay allows bursty data. Users do not have to adhere to a fixed data rate as in the case of X.25 or T-lines.
8. Frame Relay allows a frame size of 9000 bytes, which can accommodate all local area network frames.
9. Frame Relay is less expensive than other traditional WANs.

Disadvantages

Frame Relay is not perfect. Despite its low cost, there are some disadvantages:

1. Although some Frame Relay networks operate at 44.376 Mbps, this is still not high enough for protocols with even higher data rates (such as B-ISDN).
2. Frame Relay allows variable-length frames. This way creates varying delays for different users. A Frame Relay switch handles a large frame from one user and a small frame from another user the same way. They are stored in the same queue if they are going out the same-interface. The delay of a small frame following a large frame may be different than the delay of a small frame following another small frame; users of small frames are punished.
3. Because of the varying delays, which are not under user control, Frame Relay is not suitable for sending delay sensitive data such as real-time voice or video. For example, Frame Relay is not suitable for teleconferencing.

1.13 COMPARISON BETWEEN X.25 AND FRAME RELAY

The difference between the X.25 and frame relay are given in the tabular form as follows:

Table 1.3 Comparison between X.25 and Frame Relay

Feature	*X.25*	*Frame relay*
1. Connection establishment	At the network layer	None
2. Hop-by-Hop flow control and error control	At the data link layer	None
3. End-to-End flow control and error control	At the network layer	None
4. Data rate	Fixed	Bursty
5. Multiplexing	At the network layer	At the data link layer
6. Congestion control	Note necessary	Necessary
7. Support	Both switched virtual circuits and permanent ones	Only virtual leased line.
8. Acknowledge signal	Provide	Does not Provide
9. Speed	Upto 64 kbps	1.5 Mbps
10. Reliability	More reliable than frame relay	Less reliable than X.25

1.14 ATM

- The long form of ATM is asynchronous transfer mode. It is a streamlined packet transfer interface. ATM also is a connection-oriented network.
- ATM uses packets of fixed size for the communication of data. These packets are called as ATM cells.
- ATM is used for efficient data transfer over high-speed data networks.
- ATM provides real time and non real time services.
- The services provided are
  1. Synchronous TDM streams such as T-1.
  2. Services using the constant bit rates.
  3. Compressed voice and video.
  4. Traffic with specific quality requirement using the non real time variable bit rate.
  5. IP based services using available bit rate (ABR) and unspecified bit rate (UBR) services.
- The ATM needs an adaption layer for supporting the information transfer protocols that are not based on ATM.

Cell relay

- ATM is also known as cell relay.
- It has advantages of better reliability and fidelity, which allows faster packet switching than X.25.

Applications

- ATM was developed as a part of work on ISDN.
- But now it is used in non-ISDN systems where the data rates are very high.

1.14.1 ATM Protocol Architecture (ATM Reference Model)

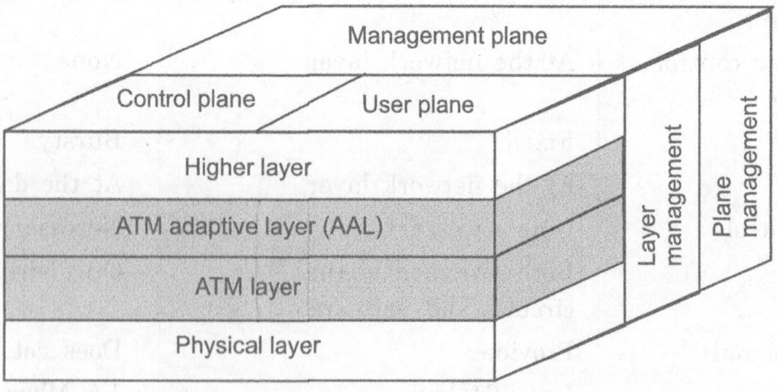

Fig. 1.29 ATM protocol architecture

- ATM is a streamlined protocol. It has minimal error and flow control capabilities. Hence the number of overhead bits required with each cell is reduced which enables ATM to operate at high data rates.
- Also, due to the ATM cells of fixed size, the processing required at each node is simplified. This also supports the use of ATM at high data rates.
- Fig. 1.29 shows the ATM protocol architecture for an interface between user and network.
- The standards issued for ATM by ITU-T are based on this protocol architecture.

Physical layer

- The physical layer of the protocol involves the specification of a transmission medium and signal-encoding scheme.
- The data rates specified at this layer are between 25.6 Mbps and 622.08 Mbps, but data rates higher and lower than these are possible.

Layers related to ATM functions

The two shaded layers in Fig. 1.29 correspond to the ATM functions. The two layers are:

1. ATM layer
2. ATM adaption layer (AAL)

1. *ATM layer:* This layer is common to all the services that provide the packet transfer capabilities. This layer defines the transmission of data in fixed size cells and it also defines the use of logical connections.
2. *ATM adaption layer (AAL):* This layer is a service dependent layer. It is used for supporting the information transfer protocol not based on ATM. The AAL maps the higher layer information onto the ATM cell and cell is transported over the ATM network.

Various planes in the ATM protocol model

The ATM protocol architecture of Fig. 1.29 consists of three separate planes.

1. User plane
2. Control plane
3. Management plane

1. *User plane:* It is used for transferring user information along with associated controls such as flow control, error control etc.
2. *Control plane:* It is supposed to perform the call control and connection control functions.
3. *Management plane:* It includes the plane management. The management plane performs management functions related to a system. They include,

   (*i*) Provision of coordination between all planes

   (*ii*) Layer management

(*iii*) Management functions relating to resources and parameters residing in its protocol entities.

1.14.2 ATM Virtual Circuits

- ATM networks are connection oriented. Hence before sending data first it is necessary to send a packet to set up a connection.
- The setup packet passes through the subnet. All the routers on its path make entry in their table about this new connection.
- Connections are called as virtual circuits. Most ATM networks also support the permanent virtual circuits. They are permanent connections between two distant hosts. They are similar to leased telephone lines.
- A virtual circuit is shown in Fig. 1.30
- Once a connection is established, both the sides can start transmitting data.

The basic data unit in an ATM network is called a cell. A cell is only 53 bytes long with 5 bytes allocated to header and 48 bytes carrying payload (user data may be less than 48 bytes). We will study in detail the fields of a cell, but for the moment it suffices to say that most of the header is occupied by the VPI and VCI that define the virtual connection through which a cell should travel from an end point to a switch or from a switch to another switch. Figure 1.31 shows the cell structure.

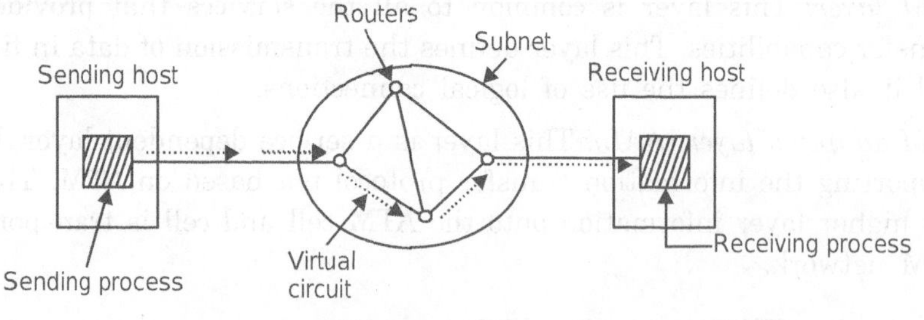

Fig. 1.30 A virtual circuit

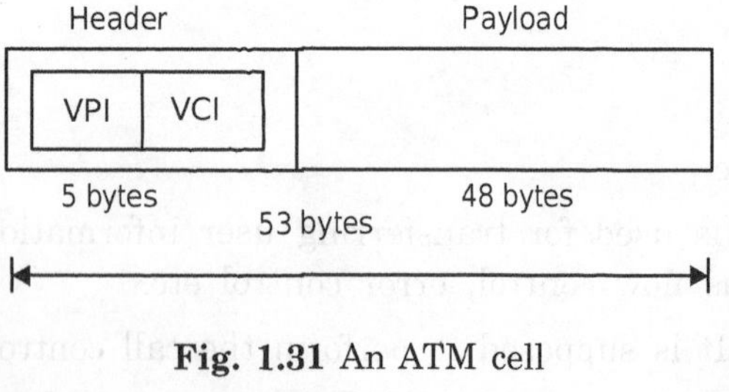

Fig. 1.31 An ATM cell

- Cell routing is done in hardware at a high speed. All the cells follow the same root to destination. So their order (sequence) does not change in transmit. Cell delivery is not guaranteed.
- Common speeds of ATM networks are 155 Mbps and 622 Mbps.

1.14.3 Service Classes

The ATM Forum defines four service classes: CBR, VBR, ABR and UBR, VBR is divided into two subclasses VBR-RT and VBR-NRT (see Fig. 1.32).

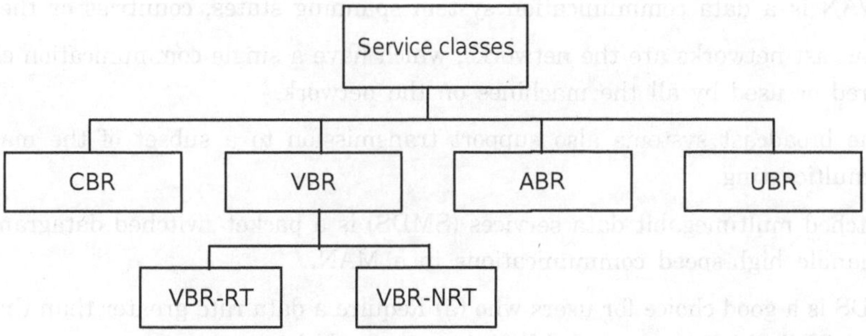

Fig. 1.32 Service classes

1. CBR. The constant bit rate (CBR) class is designed for customers that need real-time audio or video services. The service is similar to that provided by a dedicated line such as a T-line.
2. VBR. The variable bit rate (VBR) class is divided into two subclasses: real time (VBR-RT) and non-real time (VBR-NRT). VBR-RT is designed for those users that need real-time services (such as voice and video transmission) and use compression techniques to create a variable bit rate. VBR-NRT is designed for those users that do not need real-time services but those compression techniques to create a variable bit rate.
3. ABR. The available bit rate (ABR) class delivers cells at a minimum rate. If more network capacity is available, this minimum rate can be exceeded. ABR is particularly suitable for applications that are bursty in nature.
4. UBR. The unspecified bit rate (UBR) class is a best-effort delivery service that does not guarantee anything.

SUMMARY

- Networks allow shared access to information devices.
- Networks use distributed processing in which a task is divided among multiple computers.
- Networks are judged by their performance, reliability and security.
- A line configuration defines the relationship of communication devices to a communications pathway.
- In a point-to-point line configuration, two and only two devices are connected by a dedicated link.
- In a multipoint line configuration, three or more devices share a link.
- Topology refers to the physical or logical arrangement of a network.
- In topology technique devices may be arranged in a mesh, star, tree, bus, ring topology.
- A network can be categorized as a local area network (LAN), a metropolitan area network (MAN) or a wide area network (WAN).

- A LAN is a data communication system within a building, plant or campus or between nearby buildings.
- A MAN is a data communication system covering an area the size of a town or a city.
- A WAN is a data communication system spanning states, countries or the whole world.
- Broadcast networks are the networks, which have a single communication channel that is shared or used by all the machines on the network.
- Some broadcast systems also support transmission to a subset of the machines known as multicasting.
- Switched multimegabit data services (SMDS) is a packet-switched datagram service used to handle high-speed communications in a MAN.
- SMDS is a good choice for users who (a) Require a data rate greater than that of switched/56 or DDS. (b) Do not need full time use of a link.
- Access to SMDS is coordinated through SMDS interface protocol (SIP)
- SMDS uses DQDB for media access.
- X.25 is a popular packet-switching wide area network.
- The X.25 protocol defines the procedures for data transmission between a DTE and a DCE for terminal operation in the packet mode on public data networks.
- The X.25 protocol specifies three layers: the physical layer, the frame layer and the packet layer.
- An ISDN provides digital services to users over integrated digital networks.
- Digital services fall into one of three classes:

(*a*) Bearer Services-no network manipulation of the information contents.

(*b*) Teleservices–network may change or process information contents.

(*c*) Supplementary services-cannot stand-alone; must be used with bearer or teleservices.

- A digital pipe is a high-speed path composed of time-multiplexed channels. There are three types of channels.

(*a*) Bearer (B)–basic user channel.

(*b*) Data (D)–for control of B channels, low-rate data transfer & other application.

(*c*) Hybrid (H)–high data rate applications.

- A BRI is a digital pipe composed of two B channel and one D channel.
- A PRI is a digital pipe composed of 23B channel and one D channel.
- Asynchronous Transfer Mode (ATM) is a cell relay protocol that, in combination with B-ISDN will allow high-speed interconnection of the world's networks.
- The ATM data packet is a cell composed of 53 bytes (5 bytes of header and 48 bytes of payload).
- ATM eliminates the varying delay times associated with different sized packets.
- ATM can handle real time transmission.
- ATM uses asynchronous time-division multiplexing and is based on permanent virtual circuits.

- ATM standard defines three layers:
  (*a*) Application adaptation layer (AAL)
  (*b*) ATM layer
  (*c*) Physical layer
- Frame Relay is a cost-effective technology that connects LANS.
- Frame Relay can handle bursty data.
- Frame Relay eliminates the extensive error checking necessary in X.25 protocol.
- Frame Relay operates in the physical & data link layer of OSI model.

EXERCISE

1. What do you mean by the term computer networks? Give the list of goals of computer networks.
2. What is meant by the terms networking and internetworking?
3. Write a short note on applications of computer network.
4. Explain the term distributed processing? Also state its advantage & disadvantages.
5. Explain in detail the various classification of topology.
6. What do you mean by the term topology? Explain any two types of topologies.
7. What is the difference between bus and tree topology?
8. Explain in detail the various categories of network.
9. What is the difference between the various categories of network?
10. What do you mean by the term broadcast networks?
11. What is the difference between point-to-point and multipoint line configurations?
12. Explain each of the words in "Integrated Services Digital Network".
13. Contrast the three categories of services provided by ISDN.
14. Who are the subscribers to a BRI & to a PRI?
15. What is an NT1, NT2, TE1, TE2, TA & a reference point with reference to ISDN?
16. What are the X.25 layers? How does each relate to the OSI model?
17. Name the X.25 frame types and their primary functions.
18. How are flow and error control handled by X.25? Are all the layers involved?
19. How is flow control handled in frame Relay?
20. Name some advantages of Frame Relay over X.25?
21. How does a frame get retransmitted in Frame Relay?
22. Write short notes on:
    (*a*) Frame Relay
    (*b*) ISDN
    (*c*) ATM

23. What do you mean by the term ATM? Explain it in detail?
24. Write a short note on SMDS. How is LAN connected to SMDS?
25. What are the different features of SMDS? How is DQDB related to SMDS?
26. Explain the different categories of networks in detail? Also given their advantages and disadvantages.
27. What is ISDN? Explain the different services provided by ISDN.
28. Explain the concept of computer networks. Also explain the terms networking and internetworking.
29. What are the different applications of computer networks? Also name the different goals of computer networks.
30. What do you mean by the term distributed processing in reference to computer networks? Also state its advantages.
31. What do you mean by the term network topology? Explain bus topology in detail.
32. What is the difference between point-to-point and multipoint line configuration with the help of suitable diagrams?
33. Mention some of the features of SMDS. Draw the SMDS packet format and explain the purpose of its fields.
34. Give any four differences between X.25 and Frame Relay.
35. Explain the ATM protocol architecture in detail.

Chapter 2

NETWORK ARCHITECTURE

2.1 CONCEPT OF PROTOCOL SERVICES

"A set of layers and protocols is called as network architecture."

Protocols

In computer networks, communication occurs between entities in different systems. An entity is anything capable of sending or receiving information. Examples include application programs, file transfer packages, browsers, database management systems, and electronic mail software. A system is a physical object that contains one or more entities. Examples include computers and terminals.

A protocol is a set of rules that govern data communication. A protocol defines what is communicated, how it is communicated, and when it is communicated. The key elements of a protocol are syntax, semantics, and timing.

Syntax

Syntax refers to the structure or format of the data, meaning the order in which they are presented. For example, a simple protocol might expect the first eight bits of data to be the address of the sender, the second eight bits to be the address of the receiver, and the rest of the stream to be the message itself.

Semantics

Semantics refers to the meaning of each section of bits. How is a particular pattern to be interpreted, and what action is to be taken based on that interpretation? For example, does an address identify the route to be taken or the final destination of the message?

Timing

Timing refers to two characteristics: when data should be sent and how fast they can be sent. For example; if a sender produces data at 100 Mbps but the receiver can process data at only 1 Mbps, the transmission will overload the receiver and data will be largely lost.

2.1.1 Protocol Hierarchies

- Most of all networks are organized as a series of layers, each one built upon the one below it. Because of layer, it reduces the design complexity.
- In layer protocols, a layer is a service provider and may consist of several service functions. Function is a sub system of a layer.
- Each subsystem may also be made up of entities. An entity is a specialized module of a layer or subsystem.
- Name of the layer, total number of layer, function and content of each layer differ from network to network.
- Protocols are the rules that govern network communication.
- Fig. 2.1 shows the five-layer network.

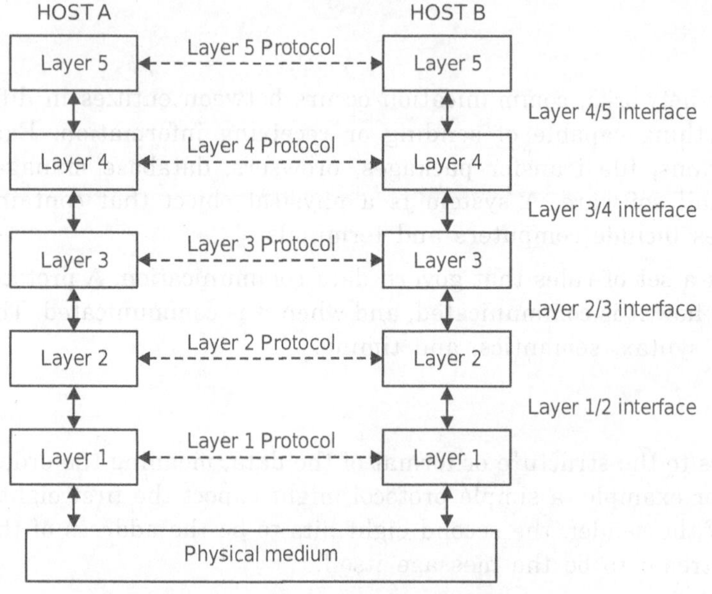

Fig. 2.1 Layers, protocols and interfaces

- Layer n on one node carries on a conversation with layer n on other node.
- The entities comprising the corresponding layers on different machine are called *peers.*
- The actual data flow is from upper layer to its below layer and then from physical medium to destination layer.
- Between each pair of adjacent layers is called *interface.* The interface defines which primitive operations and services the lower layer offers to the upper one.
- A set of layers and protocols is called *network architecture.*

2.1.2 Design Issues for the Layers

Some of the key design issues that occur in computer networking are present in several layers. Below, we will briefly mention some of the more important ones.

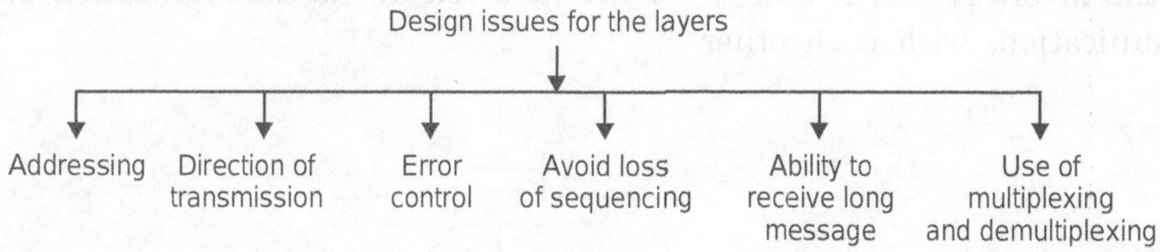

1. Addressing

Every layer needs a mechanism for identifying senders and receivers. Since a network normally has many computers, some of which have multiple processes, a means is needed for a process on one machine to specify with whom it wants to talk. As a consequence of having multiple destinations, some form of addressing is needed in order to specify a specific destination.

2. Direction of Transmission

Another set of design decisions concerns the rules for data transfer. In some systems, data only travel in one direction *(simplex communication).* In others they can travel in either direction, but not simultaneously *(half-duplex communication).* In still others they travel in both directions at once *(full-duplex communication).*

3. Error Control

Another important issue is the error control because physical communication circuits are not perfect. Error detection and correction both are essential. Many error detecting and correcting codes are known out of which those agreed by sender and receiver should be used. The receiver should be able to tell the sender by some means, that it has received a correct message or a wrong message.

4. Avoid loss of sequencing

All the communication channels cannot preserve the order in which messages are sent on it. So there is a possibility of loss of sequencing. To avoid this, all the pieces should be numbered so that they can be put pack together at the receiver in the appropriate sequence.

5. Ability of receiving long messages

At several levels, another problem should be solved, which is inability of all processes to accept arbitrarily long messages. So a mechanism needs to be developed to disassemble, transmit and then reassemble messages.

6. To use multiplexing and demultiplexing

Multiplexing and demultiplexing is to be used to share the same channel by many sources simultaneously. It can be used for any layer. Multiplexing is needed in the physical layer.

2.1.3 Interfaces and Services

The process provides a common technique for the layer to communicate with each other. The standard terminology used for layered networks to request services is provided. In Fig. 2.2 the layers N + 1, N and N – 1 are involved in the communication process for layer communication, with each other.

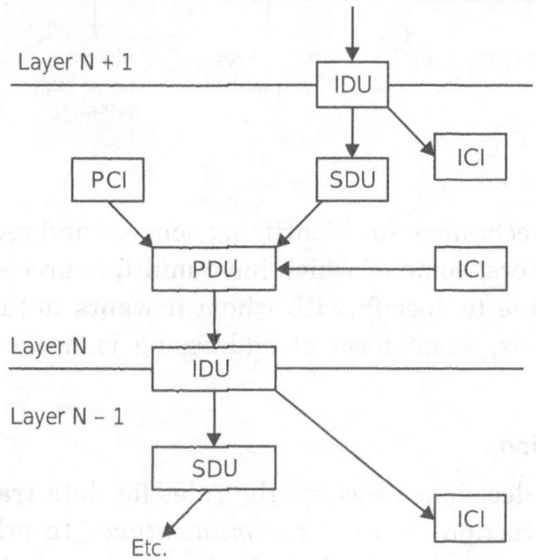

Fig. 2.2 Communication between layers

Following components are involved and their function is as follows:

1. Service data unit (SDU)
2. Protocol control information (PCI)
3. Protocol data unit (PDU)
4. Interface control information (ICI)
5. Interface data unit (IDU)

Table 2.1 Functions of components used for communication between layers

Sr. No.	*Name*	*Function*
1.	SDU	Transfer user data by layer N + 1 to layer N and N – 1
2.	PCI	To perform service function, it is used to exchange information by peer entities at different sites on the network.
3.	PDU	Combination of the SDU and PCI
4.	ICI	It passes temporary parameter between N and N – 1 to invoke service function.
5.	IDU	The total unit of information transferred across the layer boundaries.

When the IDU from layer N + 1 passes to layer N, it becomes the SDU to that layer. PCI is added to SDU at layer N. ICI performs its function and is discarded. Another ICI is added to PDU at layer N and it becomes IDU to layer N – 1. Thus a full protocol unit is passed through each layer.

Each layer adds header to data. This header is used by the peer layer entity at another node of the network to invoke function. This process repeats itself through each layer.

As each unit traverses through the layer, it has a header added to it i.e. user data and header (SDU and PCI). This full protocol data unit is passed onto the communication path, where it arrives at the receiving site.

In short, each layer added its header to user's data and passes to its next layer. This layer process on that data and adds its own header and provides to next layer for processing. Through transmission channel data passes to receiving site. Figure 2.3 shows the communication between two sites in a network.

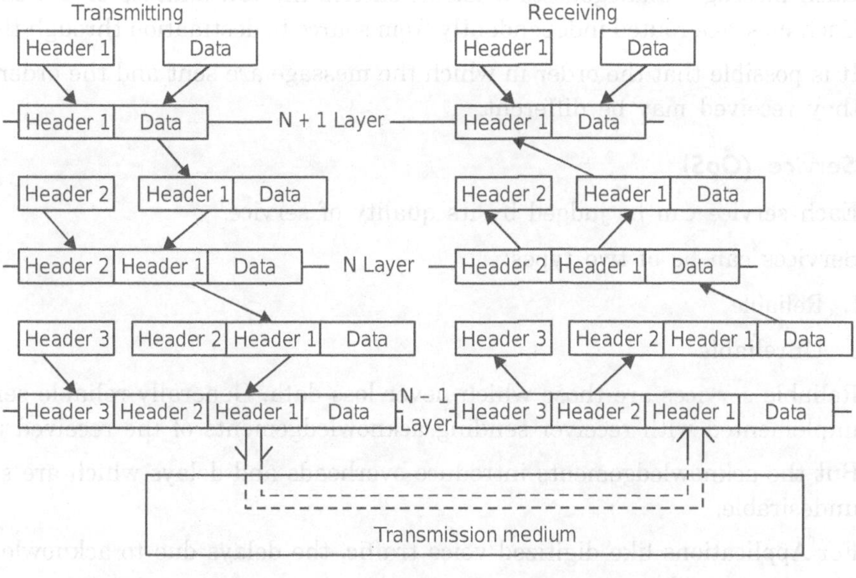

Fig. 2.3 Communication between two sites in a network

2.1.4 Connection Oriented and Connectionless Services

Layers can offer two types of services to the layers above them:

1. Connection oriented service
2. Connectionless service

Connection oriented service

- The connection oriented service is similar to the one provided in the telephone system.
- The service users of the connection-oriented service undergo the following sequence operation.

1. Establish a connection
2. Use the connection
3. Release the connection

- The connection acts like a tube. The sender pushes bits from one end of the tube and the receiver takes them out from the other end.
- The order is generally preserved. That means the order in which the bits are sent is same order in which they are received.
- Sometimes after establishing a connection, the sender and receiver can discuss and neglect about parameters to be used such as maximum message size, quality of service and some issues.

Connectionless Service

- The connectionless service is similar to the postal service.
- Each message (analogous to a letter) carries the full address of the destination. Each message routed independently from source to destination through the system.
- It is possible that the order in which the message are sent and the order in which they received may be different.

Quality of Service (QoS)

- Each service can be judged by its quality of service.
- Services can be of two types:
  1. Reliable
  2. Unreliable
- Reliable services are those which never loss data. Generally reliable services are implemented with receiver sending acknowledgements of the received messages.
- But the acknowledgements introduce overheads and delays which are sometimes undesirable.
- For Applications like digitized voice traffic, the delays due to acknowledgements are unacceptable.
- Applications such as electronic mail do not require any connections. The cost associated, complexity and overheads of reliable services is not required here.
- Such applications require high reliability of message arrival but no guarantee i.e. unreliable services will be ok.
- The unacknowledged services are unreliable connectionless services. Such services are called as *datagram* service, which is similar to telegram service.
- However note that *acknowledged datagram service* could also be provided.
- One more type of service is the *request-reply service.* In this type, the sender transmits a single datagram, which contains a request, and a reply obtained from the receiver contains the reply.
- Table 2.2 lists various types of services and their examples.

Table 2.2 Six different types of services

Sr. No.	*Service*	*Type*	*Example*
1.	Reliable message stream	Connection oriented	Sequence of pages
2.	Reliable byte stream	Connection oriented	Remote login.
3.	Unreliable connection	Connection oriented	Digitized voice
4.	Unreliable datagram	Connectionless	Electronic mail
5.	Acknowledged datagram	Connectionless	Registered e-mail
6.	Request-Reply	Connectionless	Database query

- The unreliable service is used only if the reliable service is not available or is too expensive. Fig. 2.4 shows the connection oriented and connectionless service operation.

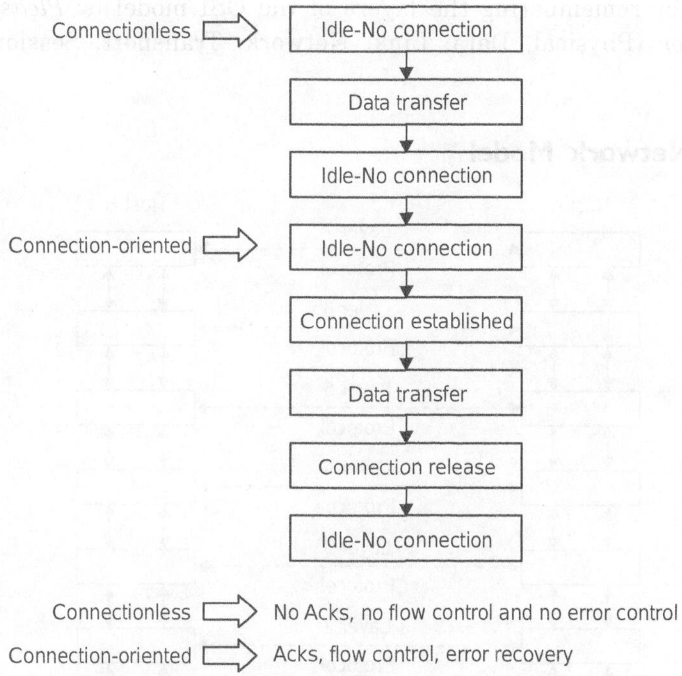

Fig. 2.4 Connectionless and connection oriented service

2.1.5 The Relationship of Services to Protocols

Services and protocols are distinct concepts, although they are frequently confused. This distinction is so important, however, that we emphasize it again here. A service is a set of primitives (operations) that a layer provides to the layer above it. The service defines what operations the layer is prepared to perform on behalf of its users, but it says nothing at all about how these operations are implemented. A service relates to an interface between two layers, with the lower layer being the service provider and the upper layer being the service user.

A *protocol*, in contrast, is a set of rules governing the format and meaning of the frames, packets, or messages that are exchanged by the peer entities within a layer. Entities use protocols in order to implement their service definitions. They are free to change their protocols at will, provided they do not change the service visible to their users. In this way, the service and the protocol are completely decoupled.

2.2 OSI MODEL

The *Open Systems Interconnection* (OSI) model was intended to be a blueprint for a set of worldwide communication standards, which would enable all computers everywhere to get interconnected easily. This model is also called ISO OSI standard for networks as it is designed by ISO (International Standards Organization). The OSI model itself is a useful tool for discussing how a LAN works.

A mnemonic for remembering the layers of the OSI model is: *Please Do Not Touch Steve's Pet Alligator* (Physical, Data, Link, Network, Transport, Session, Presentation, and Application).

2.2.1 General Network Model

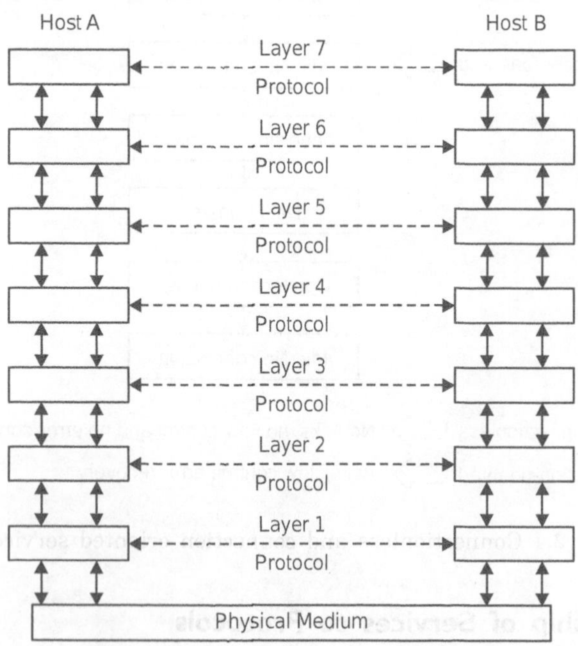

Fig. 2.5 The general network model

The OSI reference model has seven layers. These were derived on the basis of following principles:

1. A layer should be created where a different level of abstraction is needed.
2. Each layer should perform a well defined function.
3. The layer boundaries should be chosen to minimize the information flow across the interface.
4. The number of layers should be large enough to distinct functions need not to be thrown together in same layer out of necessity and small enough that the architecture does not become very large.

The OSI reference model has seven layers each performing a well - defined function. The function of layer should be chosen accordingly to develop a protocol. The purpose of classification of layers in OSI model is to define specific protocol, function, independent design and testing of components for a particular class of a problem.

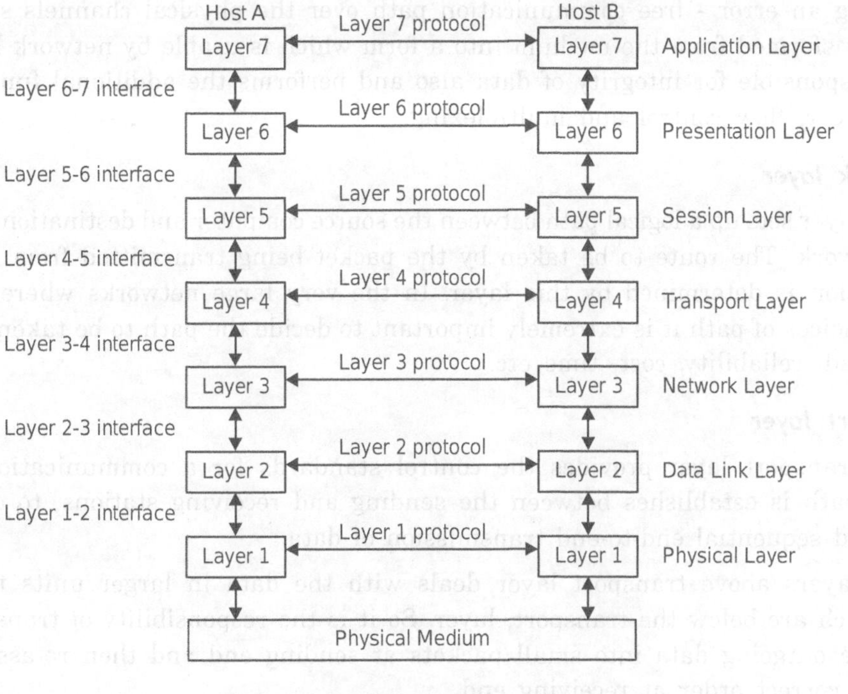

Fig. 2.6 OSI reference model

OSI model itself is not a network architecture. It does not specify the exact services and protocols to be used in each layer. It just tells what each layer should do. It provides a basis for coordinating the development of a standard that would facilitate a flexible interconnection of systems. The seven layers of OSI model are:

1. Physical layer
2. Data link layer
3. Network layer
4. Transport layer
5. Session layer

6. Presentation layer
7. Application layer.

1. Physical layer

Physical layer covers the physical interfaces between the devices so that the digital signal transmits from the transmitting node to other nodes. The mechanical, electrical, procedural and functional characteristics of transmission are dealt with at this layer. The specification of physical layer concerns with the signal layers, cable lengths, how to set up the physical links, maintain and disconnect them.

2. Data link layer

The data link layer is responsible for managing the access to the physical layer and establishing an error - free communication path over the physical channels so that the data is transformed from the medium into a form which is usable by network layer. This layer is responsible for integrity of data also and performs the additional functions like error recovery, flow control and multiplexing.

3. Network layer

This layer sets up a logical path between the source computer and destination computers of the network. The route to be taken by the packet being transmitted from the source to destination is determined by this layer. In the very large networks where there are multiple choices of path it is extremely important to decide the path to be taken according to the speed, reliability, cost, time etc.

4. Transport layer

The transport layer provides the control standards for a communication session, after the path is establishes between the sending and receiving stations, to ensure the reliable and sequential end-to-end transmission of data.

The layers above transport layer deals with the data in larger units then those layers, which are below the transport, layer. So it is the responsibility of transport layer to split the outgoing data into small packets at sending end and then re-assemble the packets in correct order at receiving end.

5. Session layer

The session layer provides the services related to the establishment, maintenance and termination of dialogue or session between two end - users. It regulates the direction of data flow; this layer is infact, responsible for complete transmission and restart if some error occurs.

6. Presentation layer

The sixth layer of the OSI model provides the application layer, the services which deals with conversion of encoded transmitted data into presentable form, so that it might may be displayed on a video unit or printed on a printer. So the presentation layer is responsible for data encoding, data encryption and compression.

7. Application layer

This layer is the topmost layer of OSI model and is user-oriented layer i.e. it is custom-made according to the user's requirement.

The application layer provides the services that directly supports the end - user. These services include file transfer, electronic - mail, directory services, network management, data base management, messaging protocol, virtual terminals, remote file access, etc. It also develops a transparent environment so that users don't knows about the physical distribution of the network resources being used by them.

Here is an easy way to memorize the order of the 7 layer model and it is as follows: *All People Seem To Need Data Processing.* The first letter of each word corresponds to the first letter of one of the layers.

Layer	*Description*	*Device*	*Protocol*
Application	Provides network access for applications, flow control and error recovery	Gateway	SMTP, ETP, SNMP, Telnet, Appletalk, DNS, TFTP, MIME, LOGIN, NFS, BOOTP
Presentation	Performs protocol conversion, encryption and data compression	Gateway and redirectors	AFP, TDI, SMB, NCP
Session	Allows two applications to communicate over a network by opening a session and synchronizing the involved computers	Gateway	NetBios, RPC
Transport	Repackages messages into smaller formats, provides error free delivery and error handling functions	Gateway	NetBEUI, TCP, SPX, and NW Link, ARP, RARP, NETBios
Network	Handles addressing, translates logical addresses and names to physical addresses, routing and traffic management.	Router and Brouter	IP, IPX, NW Link, NetBEUI, DECENT, ICMP, IGMP
Data Link	Packages raw bits into frames and includes a cyclical redundancy check (CRC)	Switch, bridge and brouter, NIC	LLC
Physical	Transmits data over physical medium	Multiplexer and repeater, hub, Amplifier, Oscilloscope	IEEE802, IEEE802.2, ISO2110, ISDN

2.2.2 Merits of OSI Reference Model

It distinguishes very clearly between the services, interfaces and protocols.

- The protocols in OSI model are better hidden. So they can be easily replaced by new protocol the technology changes.
- OSI model is truly a general model.
- This model supports connection oriented as well as connectionless services.

2.2.3 Demerits of OSI Model

- Sessions and presentation layers are not of much use.
- This model was devised before the protocols were invented. So in real life there is a problem fitting protocol into a model.

2.3 TCP/IP REFERENCE MODEL

- TCP/IP stands for Transmission Control Protocol/Internet Protocol.
- The TCP/IP reference model is a set of protocols that allow communication across multiple diverse networks.
- TCP/IP is normally considered to be a four layer system. Layers of TCP/IP are Application layer, Transport layer, Internet layer, Host to network layer.
- Host to network layer is also called physical and data link layer.
- The application layer in TCP/IP can be equated with the combination of session. Presentation, application layer of the OSI reference model.
- Fig. 2.7 shows TCP/IP reference model.

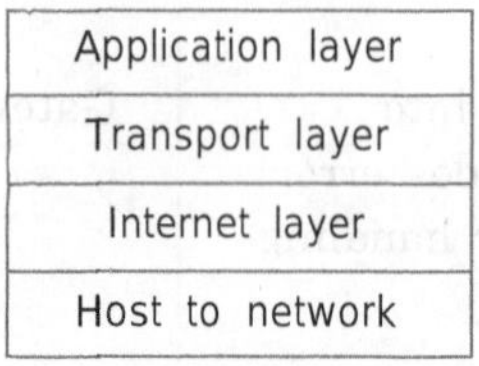

Fig. 2.7 TCP/IP reference model

- TCP/IP defines two protocol at transport layer: TCP and UDP
- *User Datagram Protocol (UDP)* is connectionless protocol.
- UDP is used for application that requires quick but necessarily reliable delivery.
- Internet layer also called *network layer*. Internet layer handles communication from one machine to the other. Routing of packet takes place in internet layer.
- TCP/IP does not define any specific protocol in host to network layer. This layer is responsible for accepting and transmitting IP datagrams. This layer normally includes the device driver in the operating system.
- Detail function of each layer is given below.

1. Application layer

TCP/IP model does not have session or presentation layers, because they are of title importance in most applications.

Application layer includes all process and services that use the transport layer to deliver data. The most widely known application protocols are: TELNET, File Transfer Protocol (FTP), Simple Mail Transfer Protocol (SMTP) and Simple Network Management Protocol (SNMP). TELNET is the Network Terminal Protocol, which provides remote login over the network. FTP is used for interactive file transfer. SMTP delivers the electronic mail.

2. Transport layer

Application programs send data to the transport layer protocols TCP and UDP. An application is designed to choose either TCP or UDP based on the services it needs.

The transport layer provides peer entities on the source and destination hosts to carry on a conversation. Both ends protocol is defined in this layer. TCP is reliable connection oriented protocol that allows a byte stream originating on one computer to be delivered without error or any other computer in the internet. It converts the incoming byte stream into discrete message and passes each one onto the internet layer. At the destination side, the receiving TCP reassembles the received data or messages into the output format. TCP also handles flow control. It synchronizes between fast sender and slow receiver. UDP is a connectionless protocol. Sometimes this type of protocol is used for prompt delivery. The relation of the protocols is shown in the Fig. 2.8

3. Internet layer

The Internet network layer protocol (IP, ARP, ICMP) handle machine to machine communications.

These protocols provide for transmission and reception of transport requests and handle network level control. The TCP/IP internet layer moves data from one host to another; even if the hosts are on different networks. The primary protocol used to move data is the Internet Protocol (IP), which provides the following services:

(*a*) *Addressing:* Determining the route to deliver data to the destination host.

(*b*) *Fragmentation:* Breaking the messages into pieces if an intervening network cannot handle a large message.

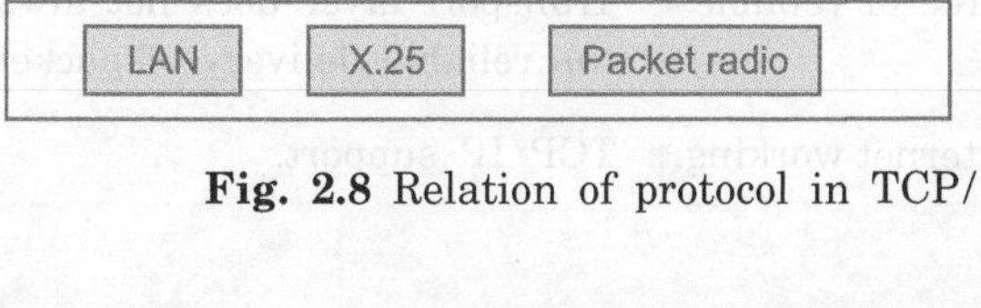

Fig. 2.8 Relation of protocol in TCP/IP model

It provides a connectionless method of delivering data from one host to another. It does not guarantee delivery and does not provide sequencing of datagrams. It attaches a header to datagram that includes source address and the destination address both of which are unique internet addresses.

4. Host-to-network layer

This is the lowest layer in TCP/IP reference model. This layer is also called network interface layer.

This layer is same as *physical and data link layer of OSI model. Host to network layer cannot define any protocol.* It is responsible for accepting and transmitting IP datagrams. This layer may consist of a device driver in the operating system and the corresponding network interface card in the machine.

2.3.1 Comparison of OSI and TCP/IP Models

Refer to Fig. 2.9 for the comparison of the two reference models.

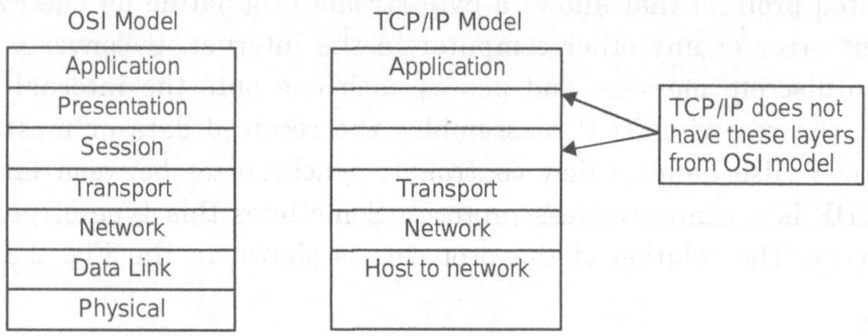

Fig. 2.9 Relationship between OSI and TCP/IP models

2.4 DIFFERENCE BETWEEN OSI AND TCP/IP MODEL

Table 2.3 Comparison of two reference models

Sr. No.	*OSI*	*TCP*
1.	7 layers	4 layers
2.	Model was first defined before implementation takes place.	Model defined after, protocol were implemented.
3.	OSI model based on three concept i.e. service, interface and protocol.	TCP/IP model did not originally clearly distinguish between service, interface and protocol.
4.	OSI model gives guarantee of reliable delivery of packet.	Transport layer does not always guarantee the reliable delivery of packet.
5.	OSI does not support internet working.	TCP/IP support.

6.	Strict layering.	Loosely layered.
7.	Support connectionless and connection-oriented communication in the network layer.	Support only connection-oriented communication in the transport layer.
8.	Horizontal layer.	Vertical approach
9.	Separate session layer.	No session layer, characteristics are provided by transport layer
10.	Separate presentation layer.	No presentation layer, characteristics are provided by application layer.

SUMMARY

- Protocol is a set of rules that govern data communication.
- The three key elements of protocols are: syntax, semantics and timings.
- A layer is a service provider and may consist of several service functions.
- An entity is a specialized module of a layer or subsystem.
- The entities comprising the corresponding layers on different machine are called peers.
- Network architecture is a set of layers & protocols.
- Interface defines which primitive operations and services the lower layer offers to the upper one.
- The various design issues for the layers are addressing, direction of transmission, error control; avoid loss of sequencing, ability to receive long messages, use of multiplexing and de-multiplexing.
- Direction of transmission of data can be done in three ways: simplex systems, half duplex systems and full duplex systems.
- To share the same channel by many sources simultaneously the concept of multiplexing and de-multiplexing is done.
- The various components which are used for the purpose of communication between layers are: Service data unit (SDU), Protocol control information (PCI), Protocol Data Unit (PDU), Interface control information (ICI), Interface Data Unit (IDU)
- SDU transfers the user data by layer N + 1 to layer N and N – 1
- PCI component is used to perform service function i.e. it is used to exchange the information by peer entities at different sites on the network.
- PDU is the combination of both SDU and PCI.
- ICI passes the temporary parameter between N an N – 1 to invoke service function.
- IDU is the total unit of information transferred across the layer boundaries.
- Any layer can provide two types of services to the above layer, these two services are: connection oriented service and connectionless service.
- A service is a set of primitives/operations that a layer provides to the layer above it.

- OSI reference model consists of several different layers each of which has a well-defined function.
- The phrase by which the name of seven layers of OSI reference model can be memorized are Please Do Not Touch Steve's Pet Alligator or All People Seem To Need Data Processing.
- OSI model is not a network architecture because it just tells what each layer should do.
- TCP/IP reference model is a set of protocols that allow communication across multiple diverse networks.
- TCP/IP consists of four layers: Application layer, transport layer, Internet layer and Host to network layer.
- At transport layer TCP/IP defines two protocols TCP (Transmission Control Protocol) and UDP (User Datagram Protocol).
- The OSI model was first defined before implementation takes place while in TCP/IP reference model, model defined after the protocols were implemented.

EXERCISE

1. What do you mean by the term protocol? Also explain its key elements?
2. Explain the concept of protocol services in detail.
3. Explain the concept of layers, protocol and interfaces with the help of a suitable diagram.
4. What are the various design issues for the layers?
5. Give the names of the various design issues for the layers?
6. Explain how the communication between layers is done.
7. Name the various components, which are involved during the communication of layers and also explain their functions.
8. Explain with the help of the schematic diagram how the communication between two sites in a network takes place.
9. Explain the differences between the connection oriented and connectionless services?
10. What do you mean by the term "Quality of Services" (QoS)?
11. Give the names of different services & their types with the help of an example?
12. What is the relationship of services to protocols?
13. Explain in detail the OSI model with all its seven layers.
14. Explain in detail the TCP/IP reference model?
15. What is the difference between the OSI reference model and the TCP/IP reference model?

Chapter 3

DATA COMMUNICATION CONCEPT

3.1 COMPONENTS OF DATA COMMUNICATION

Data communication is the exchange of data (in the form of 0s and 1s) between two devices via some form of transmission medium (such as a wire cable). Data communication is considered local if the communicating devices are in the same building or a similarly restricted geographical area, and is considered remote if the devices are farther apart.

For data communication to occur the communicating devices must be part of a communication system made up of a combination of hardware and software.

3.1.1 Characteristics of Data Communication

Data communication system depends on three fundamental characteristics:

1. *Delivery.* The system must deliver data to the correct destination. Data must be received by the intended device or user and only by that device or user.
2. *Accuracy.* The system must deliver data accurately. Data that have been altered in transmission and left in corrected are unusable.
3. *Timeliness.* The system must deliver data in a timely manner. Data delivered late are useless. In the case of video, audio, and voice data, timely delivery means delivering data as they are produced, in the same order that they are produced, and without significant delay. This kind of delivery is called real-time transmission.

3.1.2 Components of Data Communication

A data communication system is made up of five components (see Fig. 3.1).

1. *Message.* The *message* is the information (data) to be communicated. It can consist of text, numbers, pictures, sound or video-or any combination of these.
2. *Sender.* The *sender* is the device that sends the data message. It can be a computer, workstation, telephone handset, video camera, and so on.

3. *Receiver.* The *receiver* is the device that receives the message. It can be a computer, workstation, telephone handset, television, and so on.

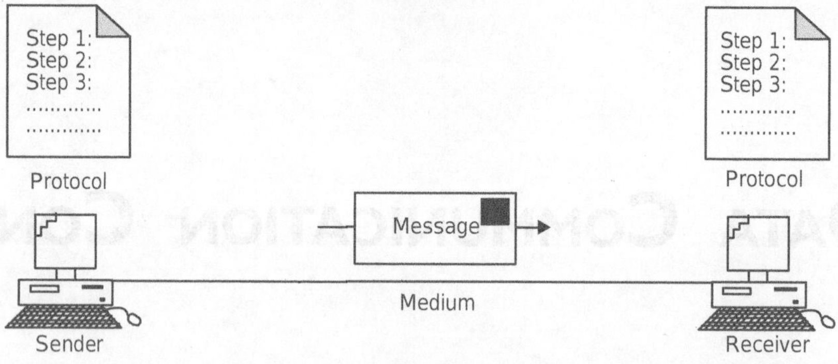

Fig. 3.1 Data communication system components

4. *Medium.* The transmission medium is the physical path by which a message travels from sender to receiver. It can consist of twisted pair wire, coaxial cable, fiber-optic cable, laser, or radio waves (terrestrial or satellite microwave).
5. *Protocol.* A protocol is a set of rules that govern data communication. It represents an arrangement between the communicating devices. Without a protocol, two devices may be connected but not communicating, just as a person speaking French cannot be understood by a person who speaks only Japanese.

3.1.3 Block Diagram

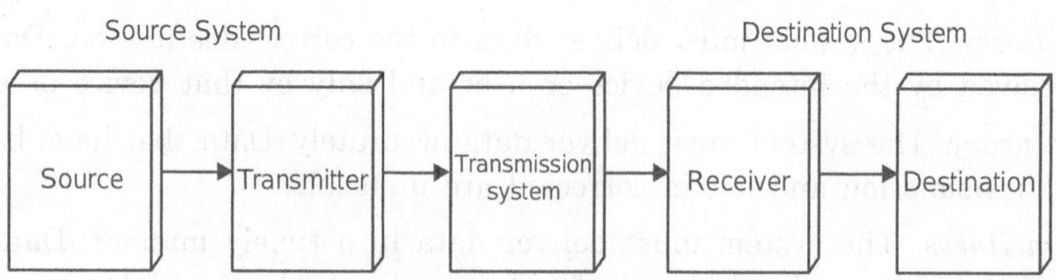

Fig. 3.2 General block diagram

The key elements of the model are as follows:

- *Source.* This device generates the data to be transmitted; examples are telephones and personal computers.
- *Transmitter.* Usually, the data generated by a source system are not transmitted directly in the form in which they were generated. Rather, a transmitter transforms and encodes the information in such a way as to produce electromagnetic signals that can be transmitted across some sort of transmission system. For example, a modem takes a digital bit stream from an attached device such as a personal computer and transforms that bit stream into an analog signal that can be handled by the telephone network.

- *Transmission system.* This can be a single transmission line or a complex network connecting source and destination.
- *Receiver.* The receiver accepts the signal form the transmission system and converts it into a form that can be handled by the destination device. For example, a modern will accept an analog signal coming from a network or transmission line and convert it into a digital bit stream.
- *Destination.* Takes the incoming data from the receiver.

Example

The fundamental purpose of a communications system is the exchange of data between two parties. Figure 3.3 presents one particular example, which is communication between a workstation and a server over a public telephone network.

Another example is the exchange of voice signals between two telephones over the same network.

Fig. 3.3 Simplified communications model

3.2 SYSTEM TRANSMISSION MODES

The term transmission mode is used to define the direction of signal flow between two linked devices. There are three types of transmission modes: simplex, half-duplex, full-duplex (see Fig. 3.4).

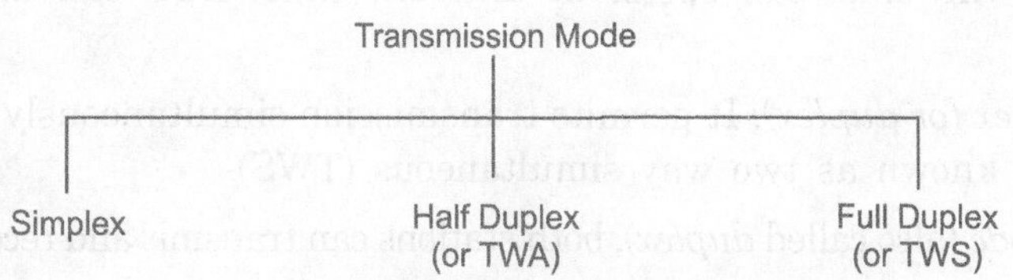

Fig. 3.4 Types of transmission mode

1. *Simplex.* Transmission in one direction only (see Fig. 3.5). One end will always transmit and other end will always receive. Examples are traditional keyboards and printers for simplex devices; as the keyboard can only introduce input, the printer can only accept output. Television and commercial ratio are also example of simplex communication.

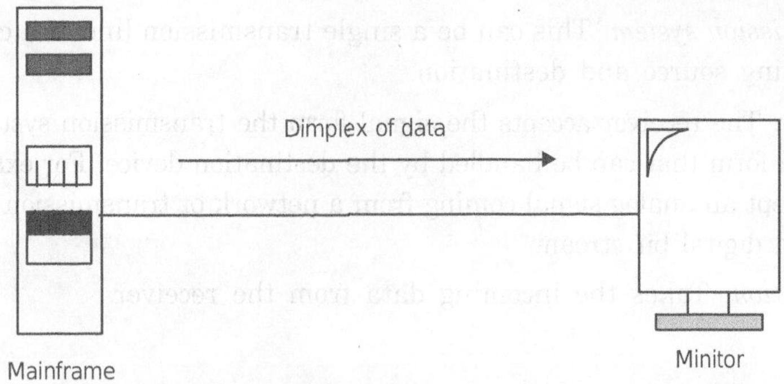

Fig. 3.5 Simplex

2. *Half duplex:* It permits transmission in both direction but at a time in only one direction. So it is also known as 'two way alternate (TWA)'.

   In other words, in *half-duplex mode,* each station can both transmit and receive, but not at the same time. When one device is sending, the other can only receive, vice versa (see Fig. 3.6).

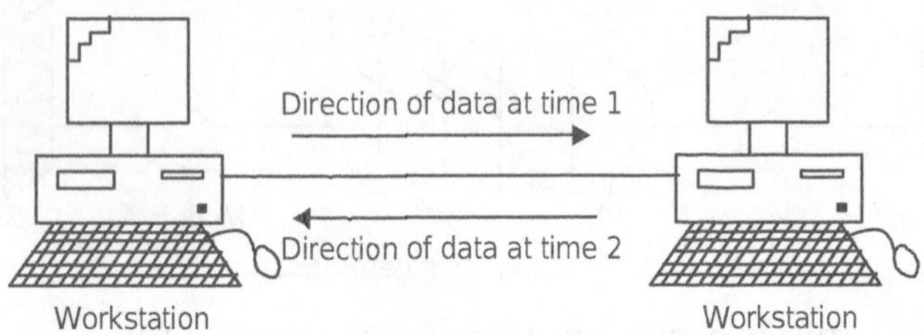

Fig. 3.6 Half duplex

   Half duplex mode can be understood as narrow bridges over which only one side traffic is permitted at a time that means when one end traffic is moving, other end traffic will wait and vice-versa.

   Communication or walkie-talkie is also example of half-duplex mode of communication as only one end can speak and other has to listen only at a time but both the ends can speak at different time. DTS can use full capacity of channel.

3. *Full-duplex (or duplex):* It permits transmission simultaneously in both directions. It is also known as two way simultaneous (TWS).

In *full-duplex mode* (also called *duplex*), both stations can transmit and receive simultaneously (see Fig. 3.7).

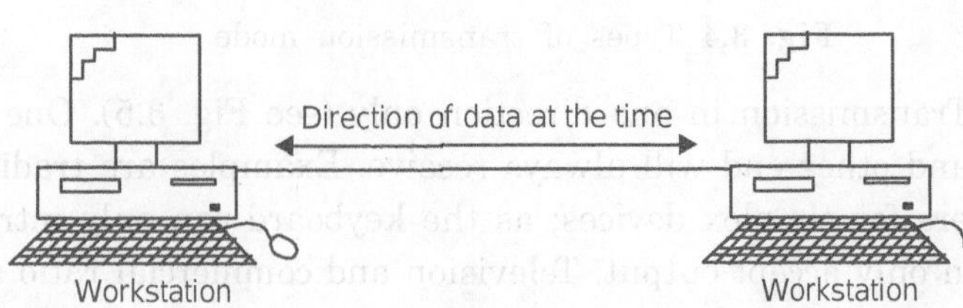

Fig. 3.7 Full duplex

The full-duplex mode is like a two-way street with traffic flowing in both directions at the same time. In full-duplex mode, signals going in either direction share the capacity of the link. This sharing can occur in two ways: either the link must contain two physically separate transmission paths, one for sending or the other for receiving, or the capacity of the channel is divided between signals travelling in opposite directions.

One common example of full-duplex communication is the telephone network. When two people are communicating by a telephone line, both can talk and listen at the same time.

3.3 TRANSMISSION MEDIA

- Media are what the message is transmitted over. In other words a communication channel is also called as a *medium.*
- Different types of transmission media is used for different data transfer rates and long distances. Bandwidth, noise, radiation and attenuation are considered while using the different transmission media.
- Higher bandwidth transmission media support higher data rates.
- Attenuation limits the usable distance that data can travel on the media. Noise is related to electrical signal noise that can cause distortion of the data signal and data errors.
- Radiation is the leakage of signal from the media cause by undesirable electrical characteristics of the transmission media.
- The *transmission medium* is the physical path between transmitter and receiver in a data transmission system. In transmission medium, communication is in the form of electromagnetic waves.
- The characteristics and quality of transmission are determined both by the characteristics of the medium and the characteristics of signal.

3.3.1 Classification of Transmission Media

- Figure 3.8 indicates the classification of transmission media.

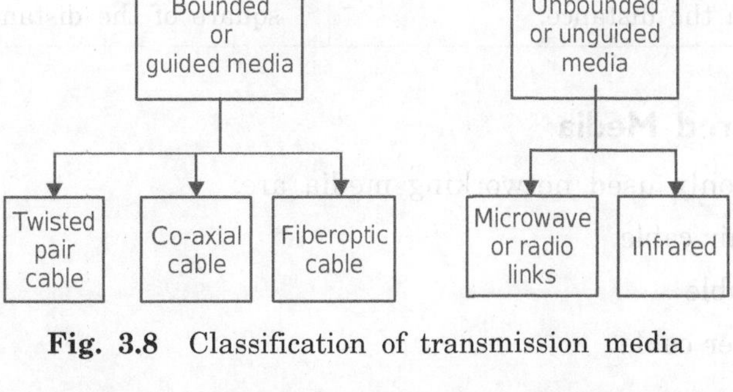

Fig. 3.8 Classification of transmission media

- The transmission medium can be mainly classified into two types.
  1. Bounded or Guided media
  2. Unbounded or unguided media.

(i) *Guided media:* Guided media is a communication medium, which allows the data to get guided along it. For this the media need to have a point-to-point physical connection.

- The examples of wired media are copper pair wires, coaxial cables and fiber optic cables.
- The wired media is used for point to point communication

(ii) *Unguided media:* The wireless media is also called as an unguided media.

- The examples of guided media are copper wires and fiber-optics. Similarly ratio and lasers through the air are examples of unguided media.

Comparison of Wired and Wireless Media

Comparison of media and wireless is given in Table 3.1.

Table 3.1 Comparison of wired and wireless media

Sr. No.	*Wired media*	*Wireless media*
1.	The signal energy is contained and guided within a solid medium.	The signal energy propagates in the form of unguided electromagnetic waves.
2.	Twisted pair wires, coaxial cable, optical fiber cables are the examples of wired media.	Radio and infrared light are the examples of wireless media.
3.	Used for point-to-point communication.	Used for ratio broadcasting in all directions.
4.	Wired media lead to discrete network topologies.	Wireless media leads to continuous network topologies.
5.	Additional transmission capacity can be procured by adding more wires.	It is not possible procure additional capacity.
6.	Installation is costly, time consuming and complicated.	Installation needs less time and money.
7.	Attenuation depends exponentially on the distance.	Attenuation is proportional to square of the distance.

3.3.2 Types of Wired Media

The most commonly used networking media are:

- Twisted pair cable
- Co-axial cable
- Optical fiber cable

1. Twisted Pair Cable

The most common form of wiring in data communication application is the twisted pair cable. As a voice grade medium (VGM), it is the basis for most internal office telephone wiring. It consists of two identical wires wrapped together in a double helix.

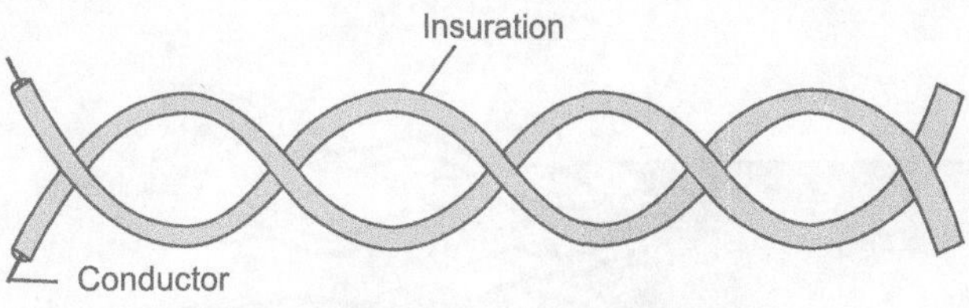

Fig. 3.9 Twisted pair cable

Uses

- TP may be used to transmit both analog and digital signals. For analog signals amplifiers are required about every 5 to 6 km. For digital signals, repeaters are required every 2 or 3 km.
- TP is most commonly used medium for in the telephone network. Compared to other commonly used transmission media, TP is limited in distance, bandwidth and data rate when two copper wires conduct electric signal in close proximity, a certain amount of electromagnetic interface occurs (EMI). This type of interference is called *cross talk.* Twisting the copper wire reduces cross talk.

Problems

Problems can occur due to differences in the electrical characteristics between the pair (*e.g.*, length, resistance, and capacitance). For this reason, LAN applications will tend to use a higher-quality cable known as data grade medium (DGM).

Advantage

The main advantages of twisted pair cable are its simplicity and ease of installation. It is physically flexible, has a low weight and can be easily connected.

Disadvantage

The data transmission characteristics are not so good. Because of high attenuation, it is incapable of carrying a signal over long distance without the use of *repeaters*. Its low bandwidth capabilities make it unsuitable for broadband applications. Fig. 3.9 shows a twisted pair cable.

Types of Twisted Pair Cables

A twisted pair cable comes in two varieties:

(*a*) Unshielded twisted pair (UTP) Cable

(*b*) Shielded twisted pair (STP) Cable.

(a) Unshielded Twisted Pair (UTP) Cable

(*i*) UTP is a set of twisted pairs of cable within a plastic sheet. UTP is an ordinary telephone wire this is the least expensive of all the transmission media commonly used for LAN, and is easily to work with and simple to install.

(*ii*) UTP is subject to external electromagnetic interference. Category 3 and Category 5 UTP are commonly used in computer networks. UTP can transfer data at 1 to 100 Mbps over a distance of 100 meters. The difference between cat3 & cat5 cable is the number of twist in the cable per unit distance cat5 is much more tightly twisted. Fig. 3.10 shows the UTP cable.

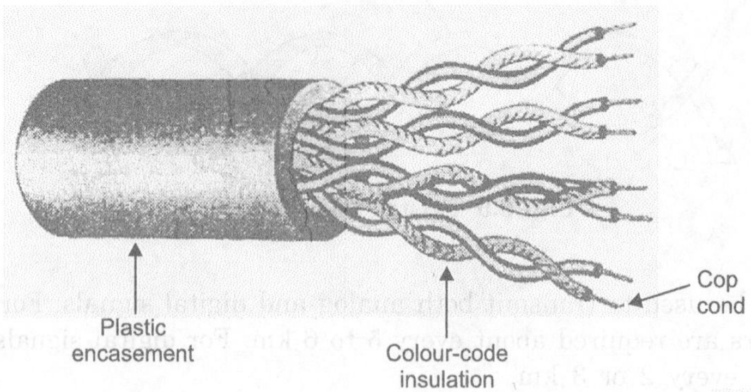

Fig. 3.10 Unshielded four pair cable

(*iii*) The Electronic Industries Association (EIA) has developed standard to grade UTP cable by quality. Category 1 (cat1) as the lowest quality and category 5 (cat5) as the highest quality. Use of each category cable is as follows.

Category 5. Used in local area network. It support up to 100 Mbps data transmission speed.

Category 4. It support transmission speed of 16 Mbps and three twist per foot.

Category 3. It support data transmission speed upto 10 Mbps. At least three twist peer feet and used in telephone system.

Category 2. It support data transmission speed upto 4 Mbps and suitable for voice data transmission.

Category 1. Mostly used in telephone system. Cat1 is suitable for voice and low speed data communication.

Characteristics of UTP

UTP has the following characteristics:

1. Transmission rate of 10-100 Mbps.
2. UTP is less expensive than FOC and coaxial cable.
3. Maximum cable segment of UTP is 100 meters.
4. UTP cable is very flexible and easy to work.
5. UTP uses RJ-45 connector.
6. Most susceptible to electrical interference or cross talk.

Advantages of UTP

1. UTP is easy to terminate.
2. Cost of installation is less.
3. High installed base.

Disadvantages of UTP

1. It is very noisy.
2. It covers less distance.
3. UTP suffers from interference.

(b) Shielded Twisted Pair (STP) Cable

- STP offers a protective sheathing around the copper wire. STP provides better performance at lower data rates. They are not commonly used in networks.

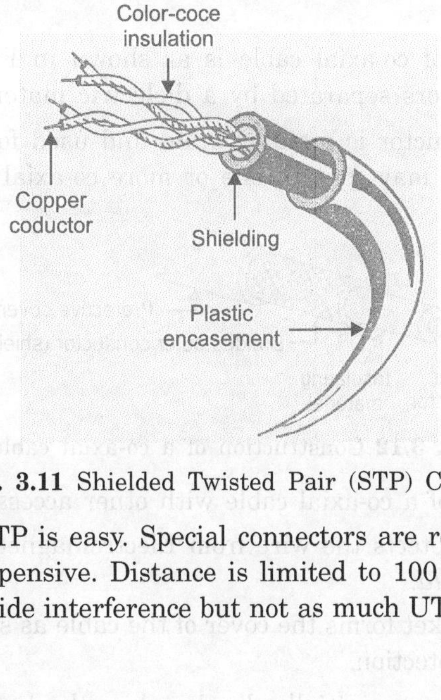

Fig. 3.11 Shielded Twisted Pair (STP) Cable

- Installation of STP is easy. Special connectors are required for installation. Cost is moderately expensive. Distance is limited to 100 meters for 500 meters. STP suffers from outside interference but not as much UTP. Shows the STP cable. (see Fig. 3.11)

Applications of TP Cable

1. Twisted pair cable used for both analog and digital signals.
2. Twisted pair cables are used in telephone network.
3. In LAN, TP wires are mainly use for low cost, low performance applications.

Comparison of UTP and STP

S.N.	*Parameter*	*UTP*	*STP*
1.	Data rate	10-100 Mbps	150 Mbps
2.	Cable length	100 meters max	500 meters max

3.	Electrical interference	Most susceptible to interference or cross-talk	Less susceptible to interference or cross-talk
4.	Installation	Easy to install	Very easy to install
5.	Cost	Lowest	Little costly
6.	Bandwidth capacity	1-155 mbps(typically 10 mbps)	1-155mbps(typically 16 mbps)
7.	Node capacity per segment	2	2
8.	Attenuation	High	High
9.	EMI	Very High	High

2. Co-axial Cables

- The construction of co-axial cable is as shown in Fig. 3.12. It consists of two concentric conductors separated by a dielectric material.
- The external conductor is metallic braid and used for the purpose of shielding. The co-axial cable may contain one or more co-axial pairs.

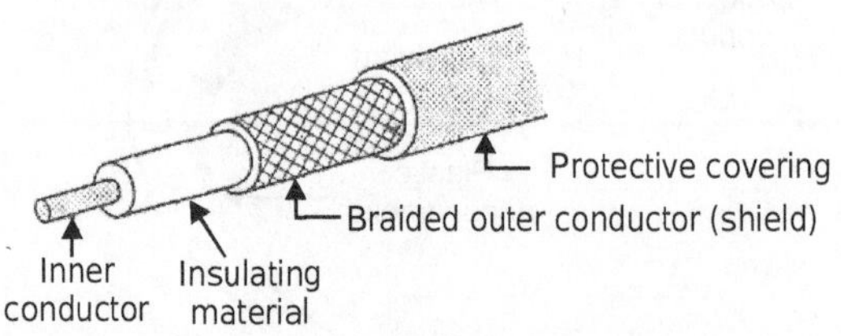

Fig. 3.12 Construction of a co-axial cable

- The construction of a co-axial cable with other accessories is shown in Fig. 3.13
- The wire mesh protects the wire from Electromagnetic Interference (EMI). It is often called a *shield.*
- A tough plastic jacket forms the cover of the cable as shown in Fig. 3.13 providing insulation and protection.
- The co-axial cable was initially developed as the backbone of analog telephone networks where a single telephone cable would be used to carry more than 10,000 voice channels at a time.
- The digital transmission systems using the co-axial cable were developed in 1970s. These systems operated in the range of 8.5 Mb/s to 565 Mb/s.
- The most popular application of a co-axial cable is in the cable TV system. The existing co-axial cable system has a range from 54 MHz to 500 MHz.
- Other important application is cable modem, with the cable modem termination system. (CMTS).
- One more application is Ethernet LAN using the co-axial cable. The co-axial cable is used for its large bandwidth and high noise immunity.

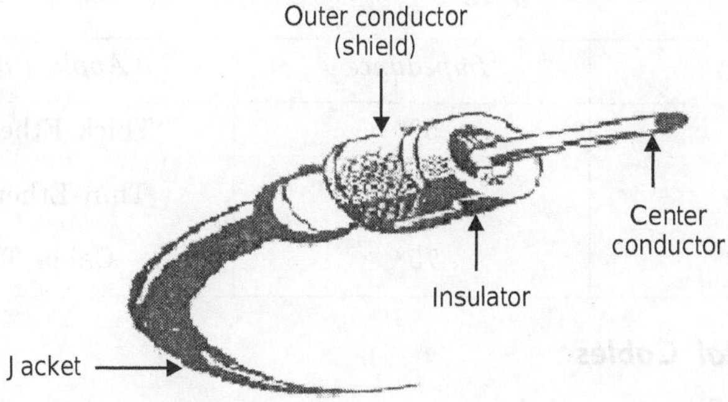

Fig. 3.13 Co-axial cable

Characteristics of Co-axial Cable

The important characteristics of a co-axial cable are as follows:

- Two types of cables having 75* and 50* impedance are available.
- Due to the shield provided, this cable has excellent noise immunity.
- It has a large bandwidth and low losses.
- 10 Mbps is the transmission rate.
- Maximum cable length for thin net is 185 meters and for thick net is 500 meters.
- Flexible and easy to work with thin net.
- Ethernet designation to 10 base 2 (thin net) or 10 base 5 (thick net).
- Less expensive than fiber optics cable but more expensive than twisted pair.
- Good resistance to electrical interference.

Advantages of Co-axial Cable

- Co-axial cable used both data transmission *i.e.*, analog and digital data transmission.
- It has higher bandwidth.
- Easy to handle and relatively inexpensive as compared to fiber optic cables.
- It uses for longer distances at higher data rates.
- Excellent noise immunity.

Disadvantages of Co-axial Cable

- Distance is limited.
- Number of node connection is limited.
- Proper connectors and termination is must.

Co-axial Cable Standards

Table 3.2 shows the co-axial cable standards. The co-axial cables are categorized by their RG ratings where RG stands for Radio Government.

Table 3.2 Categories of Co-axial Cables

Category	*Impedance*	*Application*
RG-11	50*	Thick Ethernet
RG-58	50*	Thin Ethernet
RG-59	75*	Cable TV

Applications of Co-axial Cables

1. Analog telephone networks.
2. Digital telephone network.
3. Cable TV.
4. Traditional Ethernet LANs.
5. Digital transmission.
6. Thick and thin Ethernet.

3. Optical Fiber Cable

- The constriction of an optical fiber cable is as shown in Fig. 3.14.
- It consists of an inner glass core surrounded by a glass cladding, which has a lower refractive index.
- Digital signals are transmitted in the form of intensity-modulated light signal, which is trapped in the glass core.
- Light is launched into the fiber using a light source such as a light emitting diode (LED) or laser.
- It is detected on the other side using a photo detector such as a phototransistor.
- The optical fiber cables are costlier than the other two types but they have many advantages over the other two types.

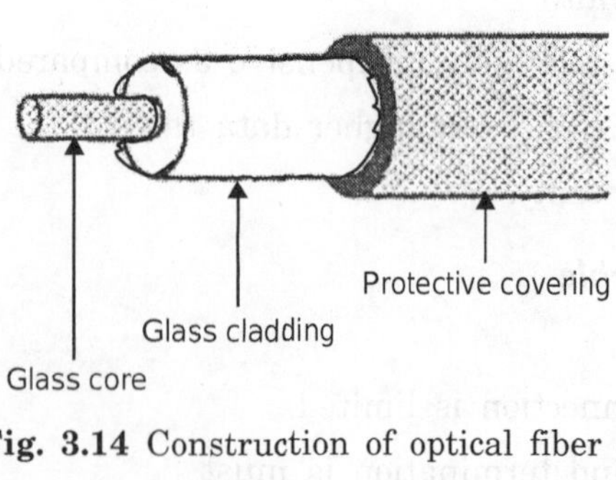

Fig. 3.14 Construction of optical fiber cable

Problems

The major problems with optical fibers are associated with installation. They are quite fragile and may need special care to make them sufficiently robust for an office environment.

Characteristics of Fiber Optic Cable

Fiber optic cable has the following characteristics:

1. Transmission rate of 100 Mbps.
2. Not affected by the electrical interference.
3. Most expensive cable.
4. FOC support cable length of 2 km or more.
5. It supports voice, video and data.
6. It provides most secured media.
7. Commonly used as backbones between buildings and token ring networks.
8. Not very flexible, difficult to work.

Advantages of Optical Fibers

Some of the advantages of fiber optic communication over the conventional means of communication are as follows:

1. *Small size and light weight.* The size (diameter) of the optical fibers is very small (it is comparable to the diameter of human hair). Therefore, a large number of optical fibers can fit into a cable of small diameter.
2. *Easy availability and low cost.* The material used for the manufacturing of optical fibers is "silica glass". This material is easily available. So the optical fibers cost lower than the cables with metallic conductors.
3. *No electrical or electromagnetic interference.* Since the transmission takes place in the form of light rays the signal is not affected due to any electrical or electromagnetic interference.
4. *Large Bandwidth.* As the light rays have a very high frequency in the GHz range, the bandwidth of the optical fiber is extremely large. This allows transmission of more number of channels. Therefore the information carrying capacity of an optical fiber is much higher than that of a co-axial cable.

Disadvantages of Fiber Systems

1. *High Initial Cost.* The initial installation or setting up cost is very high compared to all other systems.
2. *Maintenance and repairing cost.* The maintenance and repairing of fiber optic systems is not only difficult but expensive also.

Comparison of Wired Media

Sr.No.	*Twisted pair Cable*	*Co-axial Cable*	*Optical Fiber*
1.	Transmission of signals takes place in the electrical form over the metallic conducting wires.	Transmission of signals takes place in the electrical form over the inner conductor of the cable.	Signal transmission takes place in an optical form over a glass fiber.

2.	Noise immunity is low. Therefore more distortion.	Higher noise immunity than the twisted pair cable due to the presence of shielding conductor.	Highest noise immunity as the light rays are unaffected by the electrical noise.
3.	Affected due to external magnetic field.	Less affected due to external magnetic field.	Not affected by the external magnetic field.
4.	Short circuit between the two conductors is possible.	Short circuit between the two conductors is possible.	Short circuit is not possible.
5.	Cheapest.	Moderately expensive.	Expensive.
6.	Can support low data rates.	Moderately high data rates.	Very high data rates.
7.	Power loss due to conduction and radiation.	Power loss due to conduction.	Power loss due to absorption, scattering, dispersion and bending.
8.	Low bandwidth (3 MHz.)	Moderately high bandwidth (350 MHz.)	Very high bandwidth (2 GHz.)
9.	Node capacity per segment is 2.	Node capacity per segment is 30 to 100.	Node capacity per segment is 2.
10.	Attenuation is very high.	Attenuation is low.	Attenuation is very low.
11.	Installation is easy.	Installation is fairly easy.	Installation is difficult.
12.	Electromagnetic interference (EMI) can take place.	EMI is reduced due to shielding.	EMI is not present.
13.	Support low data rates (4 Mbps.)	Support moderately high data rates (500 Mbps.)	A data rate is very high (2 Gbps.)
14.	Repeater spacing 2-10 Km.	Repeater spacing is 1-10 Km.	Repeater spacing 10-100 Km.
15.	Support all radio frequencies.	It supports all radio frequencies.	Frequency range is 902 MHz to 928 MHz.

3.3.3 Types of Wireless Media

- It does not use an electrical or optical conductor. In most cases the earth's atmosphere is the physical path for the data.
- Wireless media is used when distance or obstruction make cable media difficult. There are three main types:

  1. Radio wave, 2. Microwave, 3. Infrared.

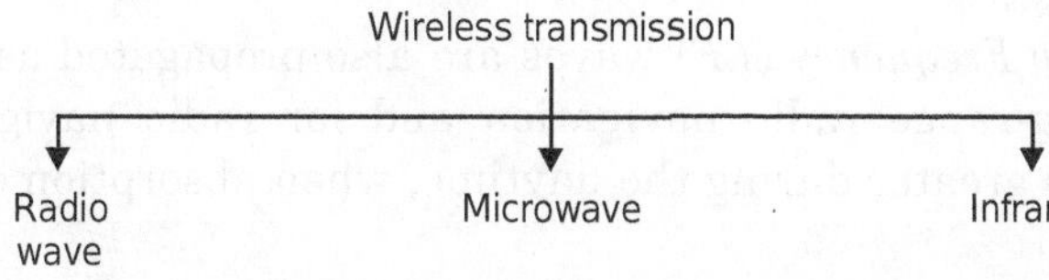

Classification of wireless media

I. Radio Transmission

- Radio waves have frequencies between 10 kilohertz (kHz) and 1 giga hertz (GHz). Radio waves include the following types:

  (*i*) Short Wave,

  (*ii*) Very high frequency (VHF) television and FM radio,

  (*iii*) Ultra high frequency (UHF) radio and television.

The range of frequency and type of medium used for their transfer is shown in Fig. 3.15.

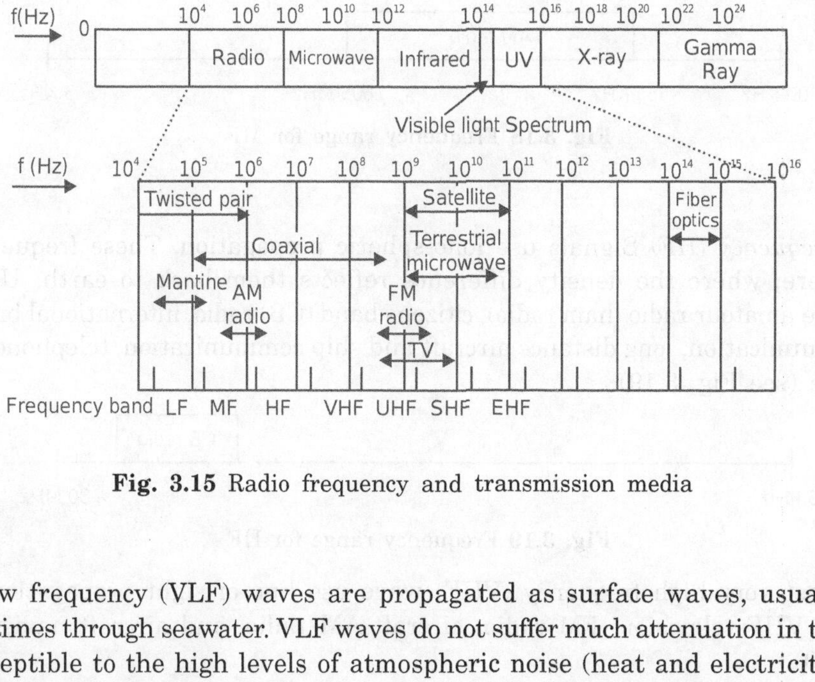

Fig. 3.15 Radio frequency and transmission media

VLF

Very low frequency (VLF) waves are propagated as surface waves, usually through air but sometimes through seawater. VLF waves do not suffer much attenuation in transmission but are susceptible to the high levels of atmospheric noise (heat and electricity) active at low altitudes. VLF waves are used mostly for long-range radio navigation and for submarine communication (see Fig. 3.16).

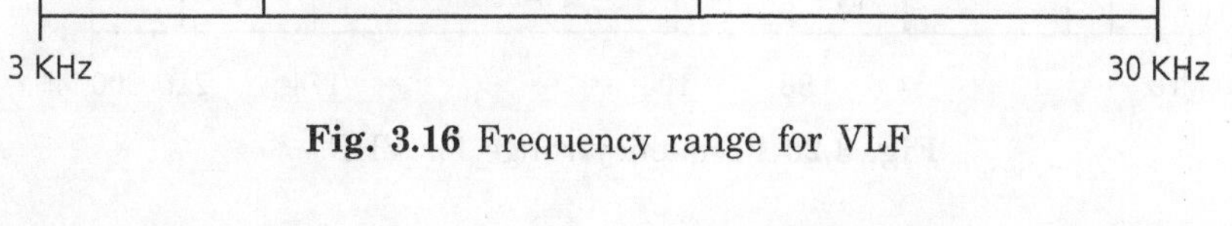

Fig. 3.16 Frequency range for VLF

LF

Similar to VLF, *Low Frequency (LF)* waves are also propagated as surface waves. LF waves are used for long-range radio navigation and for radio navigation locators (see Fig. 3.17). Attenuation is greater during the daytime, when absorption of waves by natural obstacles increases.

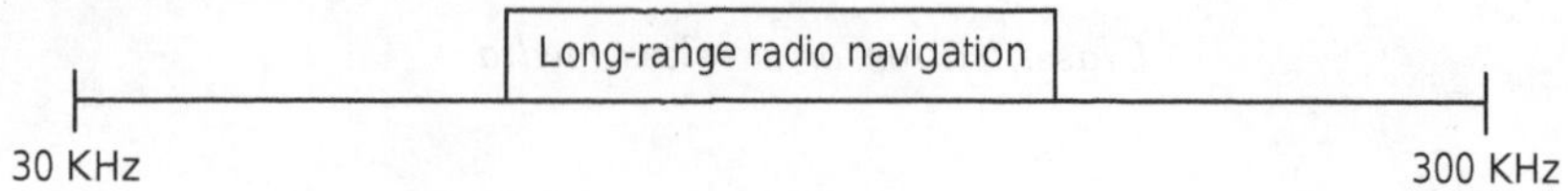

Fig. 3.17 Frequency range for LF

MF

Middle Frequency (MF) Signals are propagated in the troposphere. These frequencies are absorbed by the ionosphere. The distance they can cover is therefore, limited by the angle needed to reflect the signal within the troposphere without entering the ionosphere. Absorption increases during the daytime, but most MF transmissions rely on-line of-sight antennas to increase control and avoid the absorption problem altogether. Uses for MF transmission include AM radio, maritime radio, radio direction finding (RDF), and emergency frequencies (see Fig. 3.18).

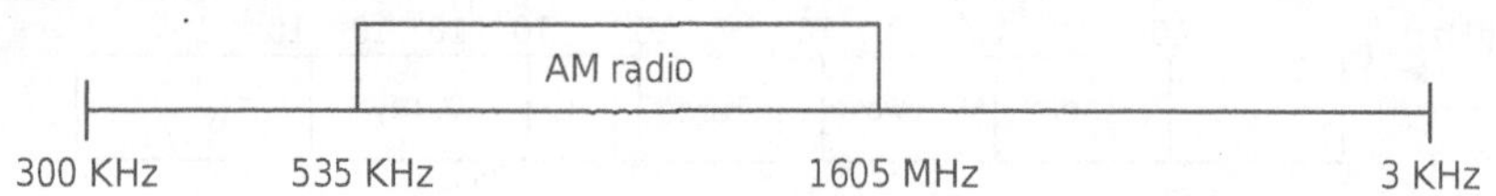

Fig. 3.18 Frequency range for MF

HF

High Frequency (HF) Signals use iono-spheric propagation. These frequencies move into ionosphere, where the density difference reflects them back to earth. Uses for HF signals include amateur radio (ham radio), citizens band (CB) radio, international broadcasting, military communication, long distance aircraft and ship communication, telephone, telegraph and facsimile (see Fig. 3.19).

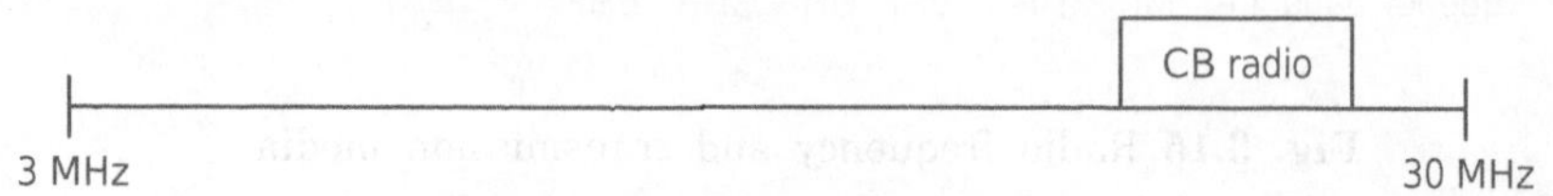

Fig. 3.19 Frequency range for HF

VHF Most very high frequency (VHF) wave use line of sight propagation. Uses for VHF include VHF television; FM radio, aircraft AM radio, and aircraft navigational aid (see Fig. 3.20).

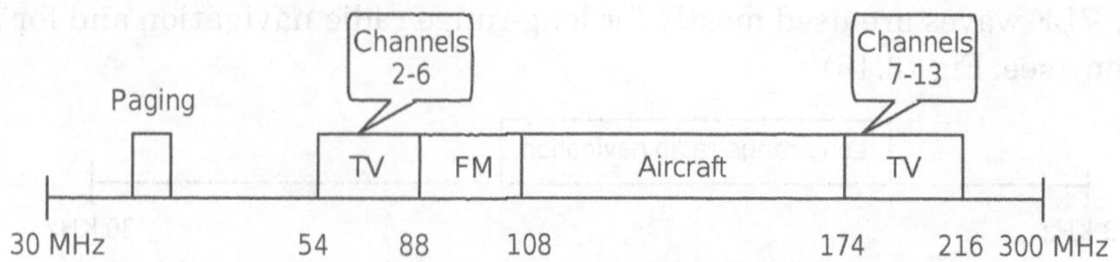

Fig. 3.20 Frequency range for VHF

UHF

Ultra High Frequency (UHF) Waves always use line of sight propagation. Uses for UHF include UHF televisions, Mobile Telephone, Cellular Radio, Paging, and Microwave links (see Fig. 3.21). Note that microwave communication begins at 1 GHz in the UHF band and continues into the SHF and EHF bands.

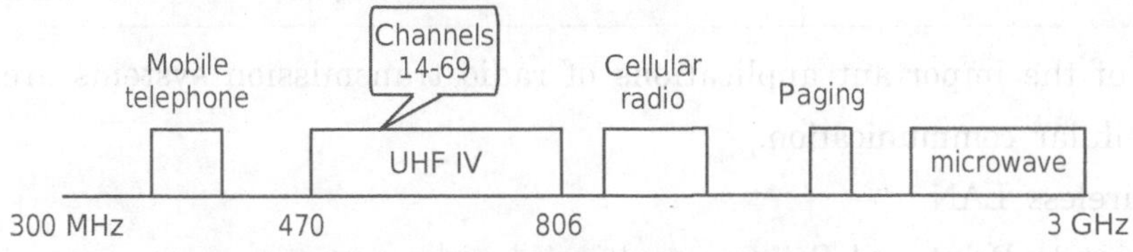

Fig. 3.21 Frequency range for UHF

SHF

Super High Frequency (SHF) waves are transmitted using mostly line of sight and some space propagation. Uses for SHF include terrestrial and satellite microwave and radar communication (see Fig. 3.22).

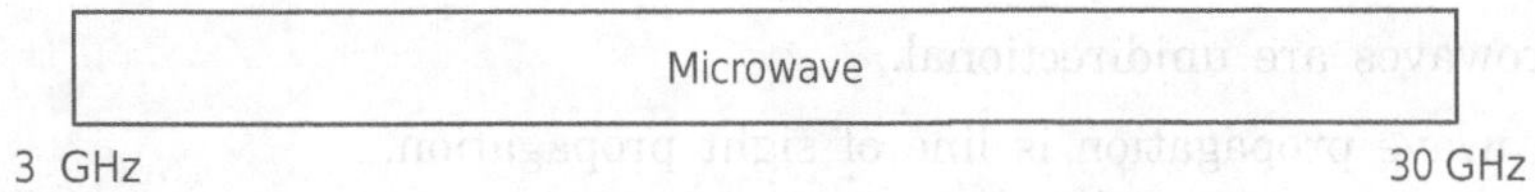

Fig. 3.22 Frequency range for SHF

EHF

Extremely High Frequency (EHF) waves use space propagation. Uses for EHF are predominantly scientific and include radar; satellite and experimental communication (see Fig. 3.23).

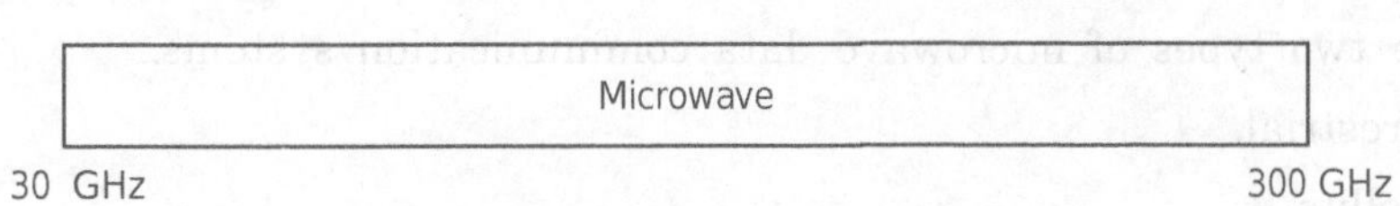

Fig. 3.23 Frequency range for EHF

Characteristics of Three Types of Radiowave

The characteristics of three types of radio waves are given in the following table:

Table 3.3

S.No.	*Factors*	*Low power single frequency*	*High Power single Frequency*	*Spread Spectrum*
1.	Frequency range	All radio frequencies	All radio frequencies	All radio frequencies (typically 902 to 928 MHz)
2.	Bandwidth capacity	1-10 Mbps	1-10 Mbps	2-6 Mbps

3.	Attenuation	High	Low	High
4.	EMI	Poor	Poor	Fair
5.	Installation	Simple	High	Moderate
6.	Cost	Low	Higher	Moderate

- Some of the important applications of radio transmission systems are:
  - (*i*) Cellular communication.
  - (*ii*) Wireless LAN.
  - (*iii*) Point to Point and Point to multipoint radio systems.
  - (*iv*) Satellite communication.

2. Microwaves

1. Microwaves are basically electromagnetic waves having frequencies between 1 and 300 GHz.
2. Microwaves are unidirectional.
3. Microwave propagation is line of sight propagation.
4. The microwave band is wide (299 GHz) so it is possible to allot wider sub-bands. Therefore it can support high data rates.

Microwave Transmission System

It makes use of the lower gigahertz frequencies of the electromagnetic spectrum. These frequencies are higher than the RF and they produce better throughput and performance.

There are two types of microwave data communication systems.

(*a*) Terrestrial.

(*b*) Satellite.

Terrestrial Microwave

Microwaves do not follow the curvature of the earth and therefore require line-of-sight transmission and reception equipment. The distance coverable by a line-of-sight signal depends to a large extent on the height of the antenna; the taller the antennas, the longer the sight distance. Height allows the signal to travel farther without being stopped by the curvature of the planet and raises the signal above many surface obstacles, such as low hills and tall buildings that would otherwise block transmission. Typically, antennas are mounted on towers that are in turn often mounted on hills or mountains.

Microwave signals propagate in one direction at a time, which means that two frequencies are necessary for two-way communication such as telephone conversation. One frequency is reserved for *microwave transmission* in one direction and the other for transmission in the other. Each frequency requires its own transmitter and receiver. Today, both pieces of equipment usually are combined in a single piece of equipment called a transceiver, which allows a single antenna to serve both frequencies and functions.

Repeaters. To increase the distance served by *terrestrial microwave*, a system of repeaters can be installed with each antenna. A signal received by one antenna can be converted back into transmittable form and relayed to the next antenna (see Fig. 3.24). The distance required between repeaters varies with the frequency of the signal and the environment in which the antennas are found. A repeater may broadcast the regenerated signal either at the original frequency or at a new frequency, depending on the system.

Terrestrial microwave with repeaters provides the basis for most contemporary telephone systems world wide.

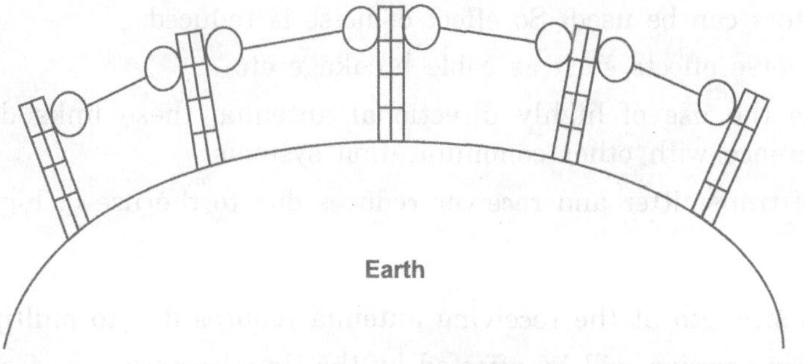

Fig. 3.24 Terrestrial microwave

Satellite Communication

Satellite transmission is much like line-of-sight microwave transmission in which one of the stations is a satellite orbiting the earth. The principle is the same as terrestrial microwave, with a satellite acting as a super tall antenna and repeater (see Fig. 3.25). Although in satellite transmission signals must still travel in straight lines, the limitations imposed on distance by the curvature of the earth are reduced. In the way, satellite relays allow microwave signals to span continents and oceans with a single bounce.

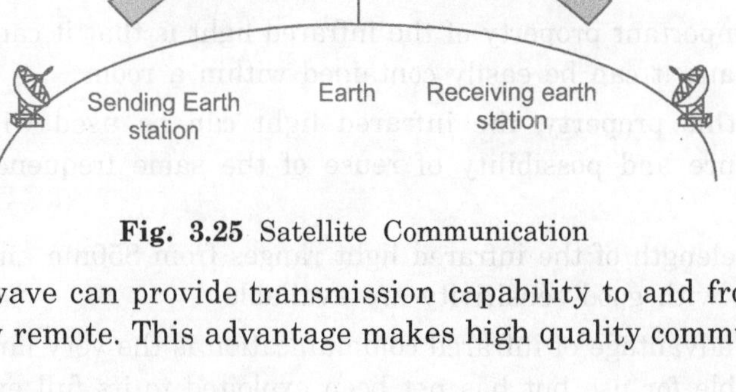

Fig. 3.25 Satellite Communication

Satellite microwave can provide transmission capability to and from any location on earth, no matter how remote. This advantage makes high quality communication available to underdeveloped parts of the world without requiring a huge investment in ground based infrastructure. Satellites themselves are extremely expensive, of course, but leasing time or frequencies on one can be relatively cheap.

Advantages of microwave link

Some of the important advantages are as follows:

(*i*) Installation of towers and associated equipments is cheaper than laying down a cable of 100 km. length.

(*ii*) Less maintenance as compared to cable.

(*iii*) Repeaters can be used. So effect of noise is reduced.

(*iv*) No adverse effects such as cable breakage etc.

(*v*) Due to the use of highly directional antenna, these links do not make any interference with other communication systems.

(*vi*) Size of transmitter and receiver reduces due to the use of high frequency.

Disadvantages

1. Signal strength at the receiving antenna reduces due to multipath reception.
2. The transmission will be affected by the thunderstorms, and other atmospheric phenomenons.

Applications of Microwave Communication

Microwave communication is mostly used in following applications.

1. Mobile telephone network uses microwave communication.
2. Wireless LAN.
3. Point to point communication between stations.
4. Line-of-sight communication.

3. Infrared Transmission

(*a*) The electromagnetic waves having frequencies from 300 GHz to 400 THz (wave lengths from 1mm to 770 nm) are known as infrared waves.

(*b*) IR uses line-of-sight propagation.

(*c*) Infrared light is a communication medium whose properties are significantly different from those of the radio frequencies.

(*d*) A very important property of the infrared light is that it cannot penetrate walls. That means it can be easily contained within a room.

(*e*) Due to this property, the infrared light can be used with a much reduced interference and possibility of reuse of the same frequency band in different rooms.

(*f*) The wavelength of the infrared light ranges from 850nm and 900nm, where the receivers with good sensitivity are available.

(*g*) Another advantage of infrared communication is the very large bandwidth which is available for use but has not been exploited to its full extent.

(*h*) The major disadvantage is that the sun generates radiation in the infrared band. This can cause a lot of interference with the IR communication.

(*i*) The infrared can be used in development of very high speed wireless LANs in future.

Applications of Infrared Transmission

1. In remote control of home appliances: *e.g.* TV, VCR, VCD and DVD players.
2. Indoor wireless LANs.
3. Communication between in house electronic gadgets such as keyboard, mouse, printers, scanners and for controlling fan, air conditions.

Applications of Infrared

1. Very High data rates can be supported, due to very high bandwidth (approximately 400 THz).
2. For communication between keyboard mouse PCs and printers.

3.4 INTRODUCTION TO SWITCHING

- It is an important technique that can determine how connections are made and how data movement is handled in wide area network (WAN).
- Data sent across the public switched telephone network or other internet works can travel along different paths from sender to receiver.
- Switching sends data along different routes. There are three switching techniques:
  1. Circuit switching
  2. Message switching
  3. Packet switching

Different types of switching techniques are employed to provide communication between two computers. These are: circuit switching, message switching and packet switching.

3.4.1 Circuit Switching

In this technique, first, the complete physical connection between two computers is established and then data are transmitted from the source computer to the destination computer. That is, when a computer places a telephone call, the switching equipment within the telephone system seeks out a physical copper path all the way from sender telephone to the receiver's telephone. The important property of this switching technique is to set up an end-to-end path (connection) between computers before any data can be sent.

Advantages

1. The major advantage of circuit switching is that the dedicated transmission channel the computers establish provides a guaranteed data rate.

2. In circuit switching because of the dedicated path there is no delay in data flow.
3. Fixed bandwidth, guaranteed capacity.
4. Low variance end to end delay.

Disadvantages

(*a*) The disadvantage of circuit switching is that, since the connection is dedicated it cannot be used to transmit any other data even if the channel is free.

(*b*) Dedicated channels require more bandwidth.

(*c*) It takes long time establish connection.

(*d*) Connection setup and tear down introduces extra overhead.

(*e*) User pay for circuit, even when not sending data.

(*f*) Other user cannot use circuit even if it is free of traffic.

3.4.2 Message Switching

In this technique, the source computer sends data for the message to the switching office first, which stores the data in its buffer. It then looks for a free link to another switching office and then sends the data to this office. This process is continued until the data are delivered to the destination computers. Owing to its working principle, it is also known as **store and forward.** That is, store first (in switching office), forward later, one jump at a time.

Advantages

1. It provides efficient traffic management by assigning priorities to the message to be switched.
2. Reduces network traffic congestion because it is able to store message until a communication channel becomes available.
3. In message switching, the network devices share the data channels.
4. Provides asynchronous communication across time zones.

Disadvantages

1. Storing and forwarding introduces delay hence cannot be used for real time applications like voice and video.
2. Intermediate devices require a large storing capacity since it has to store the message unless a free path is a available.

3.4.3 Packet Switching

With message switching, there is no limit on block size, in contrast, packet switching places a tight upper limit on block size. A fixed size of packet which can be transmitted across the network is specified. Another point of its difference from message switching is that data packets are stored on the disk in message switching whereas in packet switching, all the packets of fixed size are stored in main memory. This improves the performance as the access time (time taken to access a data packet) is reduced, thus, throughput (measure of performance) of the network is improved.

Advantages

1. It increases the bandwidth of the network by allowing many devices to communicate through the same network channel.
2. A switching node can route the packet as and when required.
3. Because of the small size packets the transmission delay is reduced, as the switching node does not write the packet into its memory before forwarding it.

Disadvantages

1. Switching nodes for packet switching require large amount of RAM to handle large quantities of packets.
2. The switching node requires more processing power because the packet switching protocols are more complex.
3. Packets are more easily lost on their route; hence sequence numbers are required to identify the missing packets.

3.4.4 Comparison of Packet Switching, Message Switching and Circuit Switching

Sr. No.	*Circuit Switching*	*Packet Switching*	*Message Switching*
1.	There is physical connection between transmitter and receiver.	No physical path is established between transmitter and receiver.	No physical path is set in advance between transmitter and receiver.
2.	All the packet uses same path.	Packet travels independently.	Packets are stored and forward.
3.	Needs an end-to-end path before the data transmission.	No needs of end-to-end path before data transmission.	Same as packet switching.
4.	Reverses the entire bandwidth in advance.	Does not reserve the bandwidth in advance.	Same as packet switching.
5.	Charge is based on distance and time, but not on traffic.	Charge is based on both number of bytes and connect time.	Charge is based on number of bytes and distance.
6.	Waste of bandwidth is possible.	No waste of bandwidth.	No waste of bandwidth.
7.	Congestion occurs for per minute.	Congestion occurs for per packet.	No congestion or very less congestion.
8.	It cannot support store and forward transmission.	It supports store and forward transmission.	It also supports store and forward transmission.
9.	Not suitable for handling interactive traffic.	Suitable for handling interactive traffic.	Same as circuit switching.
10.	Recording of packet can never happen with circuit switching.	Recording of packet is possible.	Same as packet switching.

3.5 MULTIPLEXING

A *multiplexer* is a device that allows a single communication channel to carry simultaneously data transmitted from many terminals. Thus, the channel can be shared among multiple users. The multiplexer combines two or more separate signals into one signal that can be transmitted over a single communication channel or line as shown in Fig. 3.26

In a multiplexed system, n devices share the capacity of one link. Fig. 3.27 shows the basic format of a multiplexed system. The four devices on the left direct their transmission streams to a *multiplexer (MUX),* which combines them into a single stream (many to one). At the receiving end, that stream is fed into a demultiplexer (DEMUX), which separates the stream back into its component transmissions (one to many) and directs them to their intended receiving devices.

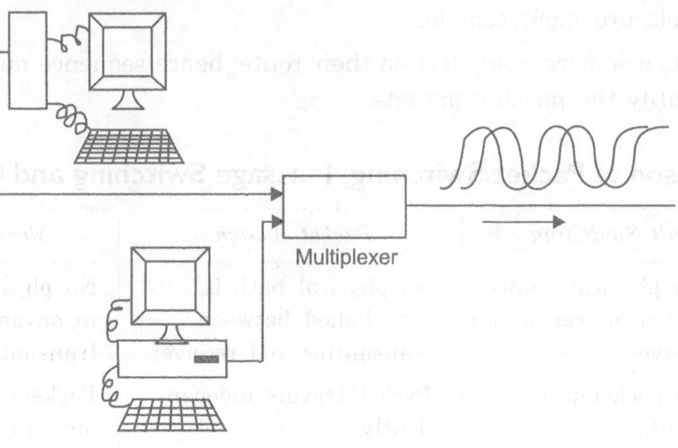

Fig. 3.26 Multiplexer

In Fig. 3.27 the word *path* refers to the physical link. The word channel refers to a portion of a path that carries a transmission between a given pair of devices. One path can have many (n) channels.

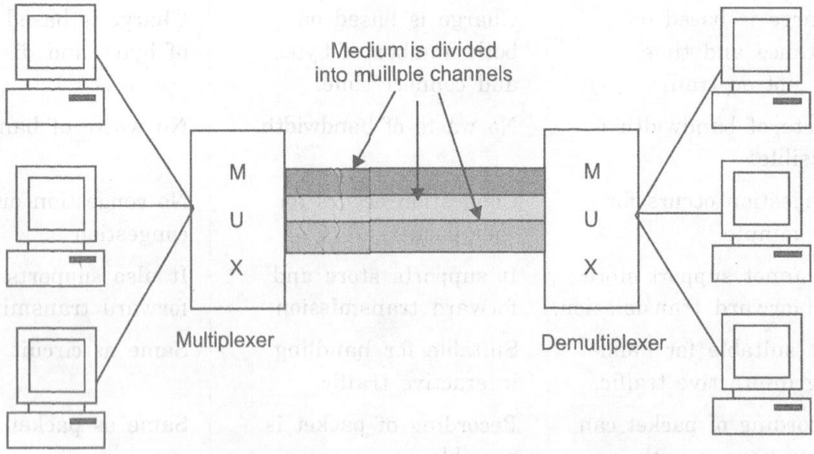

Fig. 3.27 Multiplexing and de multiplexing

3.5.1 Benefits of Multiplexing

The benefits of multiplexing are manifold. First of all its combines the transmission and facilitates the transmission via single line thus saving the money. Less number of physical lines and less number of modems are required. Another benefit is that it combines many low speed transmissions into high-speed transmission.

3.5.2 Methods of Multiplexing

Multiplexing can be done using different methods. Two main multiplexing methods are:

1. Frequency Division Multiplexing (FDM)
2. Time Division Multiplexing (TDM)

1. *Frequency Division Multiplexing.* FDM divides the available transmission band into separate frequencies to establish multiple channels within the transmission medium. Each frequency belongs to a separate terminal that is used to transmit data of that terminal as shown in Fig 3.28.

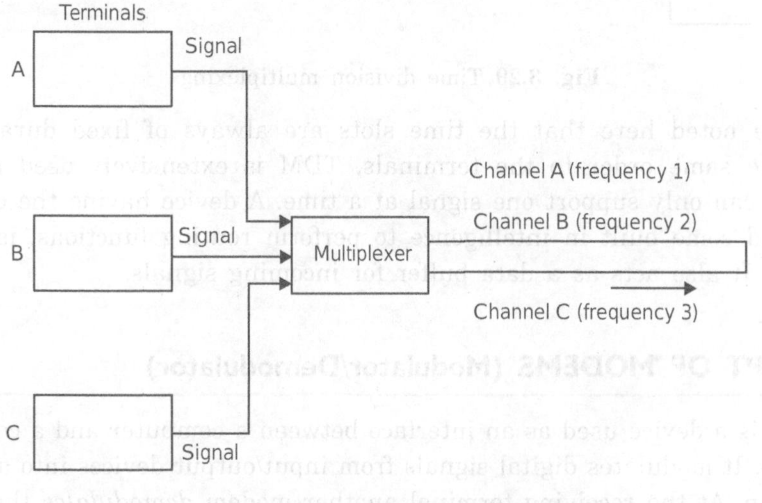

Fig. 3.28 Frequency division method

We are familiar with this technique used in public telephones. *Frequency Division Multiplexing (FDM)* is also used in the cable TV system, where a single cable carries multiple video signals from different channels or stations up to your TV set. With the remote control, we essentially activate the electronics in the television to select a specify frequency band or a channel. This is how we see a specific program on the TV. The signals from other programs also actually transverse to your TV set on the same cable, but they *lie idle* at your TV set for you to choose from.

For example, in broad band systems such as radio transmission, each radio station is assigned a separate frequency range. The radio receiver gets signals from all the stations. However, the tuner in the radio isolates the required signal for the listener.

2. *Time Division Multiplexing.* Time Division Multiplexing (TDM) is a digital process that can be applied when the data rate capacity of the transmission medium is greater than the data rate required by the sending and receiving devices. In such a case, multiple transmissions can occupy a single link by sub dividing them and inter-leaving the portions.

TDM divides the channel into short time slots of fixed intervals. The various terminals time share the channel. The total transmission time is divided into time slots and each terminal transmits the data during its allotted slot (Fig. 3.29).

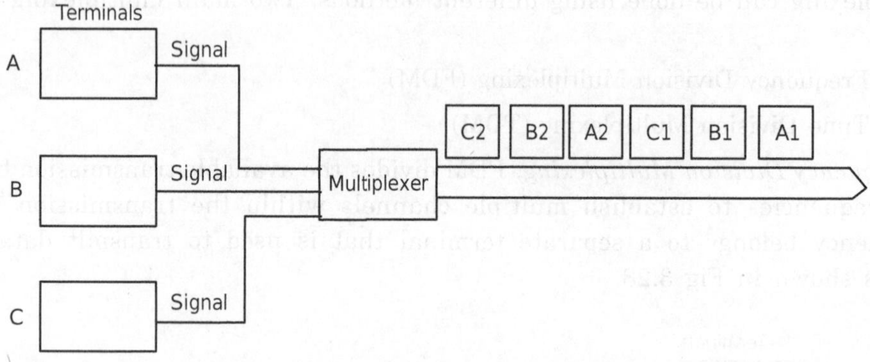

Fig. 3.29 Time division multiplexing

It may be noted here that the time slots are always of fixed duration and are assigned in the same order to the terminals. TDM is extensively used in base band systems which can only support one signal at a time. A device having the capabilities of multiplexer and some built in intelligence to perform routing functions, is known as a **concentrator.** It also acts as a data buffer for incoming signals.

3.6 CONCEPT OF MODEMS (Modulator/Demodulator)

A modem is a device used as an interface between a computer and a communication channel or line. It modulates digital signals from input/output devices into analog signals for transmission. At the receiving terminal another modem *demodulates* the transmitted signal back to digital. Thus the modem can act both as modulator and demodulator. Modems produced by AT&T are trade named *Data sets.*

Modems are also useful in a situation when an input signal is not powerful enough to travel the required distance over a transmission line. It amplifies the signals before the transmission.

Now a days *fiber optic modems* are also available which convert digital signals into pulses of light for the transmission over the glass fiber. Generally, for long distance computer communication, the communication channel is telephone.

A 25 pin connector or RS-232 C interface is a common standard that is used to connect a computer to a modem.

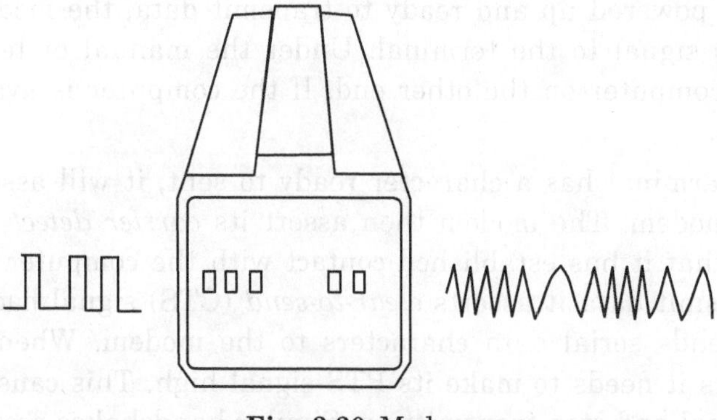

Fig. 3.30 Modem

Now a days, modems are also available as add on cards for personnel computers. Such cards do not require an external connector.

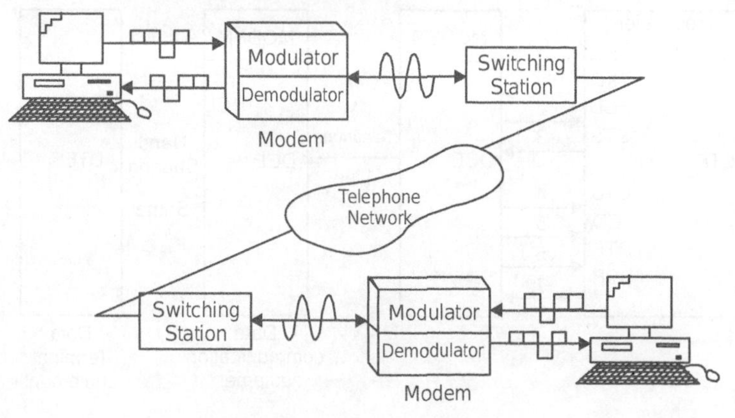

Fig. 3.31 Modem Concept

Fig. 3.31 shows the relationship of modems to a communication link. The two PCs at the ends are the DTEs; the modems are the DCEs. The DTE creates a digital signal and relays it to the modem via an interface (like the EIA-232). The modulated signal is received by the demodulation function of the second modem. The demodulator takes the ASK, FSK, PSK or QAM signal and decodes it into whatever format its computer can accept. It then relays the resulting digital signal to the receiving computer via an interface. Each DCE must be compatible with both its own DTE and with other DCEs.

3.6.1 Working of Modem

Modem converts digital signals to A/F (Audio Frequency) tones which are in the frequency range that the telephone lines can transmit and also it can convert transmitted tones back to digital information.

Figure 3.32 illustrates the working of the modem.

After the power is turned on in DTE (Data Terminal Equipment) and DCE (Data Communication Equipment), the terminal runs for self check, it asserts the *data terminal ready* (DTR) signal to tell the modem that it is ready.

When modem is powered up and ready to transmit data, the modem will assert the data set ready (DSR) signal to the terminal. Under the manual or terminal control the modem dials up the computer on the other end. If the computer is available it will send back a specified tone.

Now when the terminal has a character ready to sent, it will assert *request to send* (RTS) signal to the modem. The modem then assert its *carrier detect* (CD) signal to the terminal to indicate that it has established contact with the computer. When the Modem is fully ready to transmit data it asserts *clear-to-send* (CTS) signal back to the terminal. The terminal then sends serial data characters to the modem. When the terminal has sent all the characters it needs to make its RTS signal high. This causes the MODEM to un assert its CTS signal and stop transmitting. Similar handshakes occur between Modem and computers on other side also.

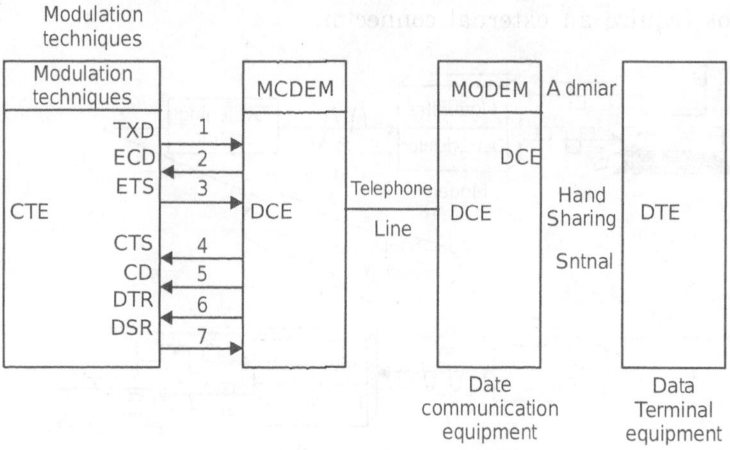

Fig. 3.32 The working of modem

3.6.2 Modulation Techniques

To understand the functioning of a modem at a conceptual level is very easy. Modulation basically user a coding scheme or a convention. This coding can be achieved using basically the three properties of a signal viz. Amplitude. Frequency and Phase. Depending upon the technique used, it is called *Amplitude Shift Keying (ASK), Frequency Shift Keying (FSK)* or *Phase Shift Keying (PSK).* In all these techniques, we choose a carrier signal with given amplitude, frequency and phase, and then choose form of encoding.

Amplitude Shift Keying (ASK). In amplitude shift keying or *amplitude modulation,* we do not alter the frequency or phase of the carrier signal. However, we specify different amplitudes, *i.e.*, shift the amplitude values, to represent a binary 1 and a binary 0. Fig. 3.33 illustrates this. It is clearly a coding scheme.

The figure shows a bit string 10011010011 modulated as an analog signal. Note that only the amplitudes of the signal change as per the values 0 and 1, but the phase and the frequency for the signals for both 0 and 1 are same and the frequency is between 0 and 4000 Hz. Therefore, the signal can be sent over the telephone lines.

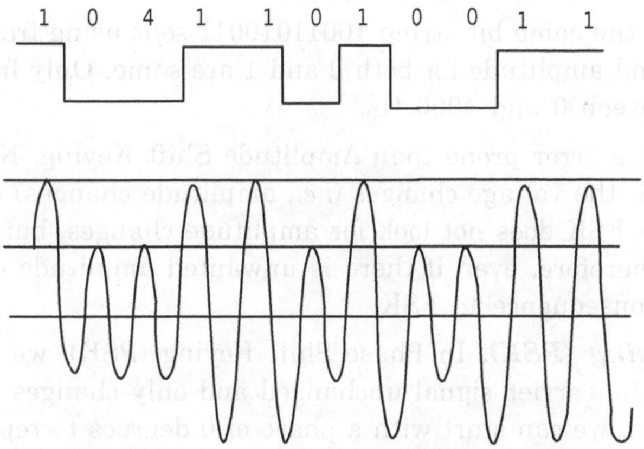

Fig. 3.33 Amplitude shift keying (ASK)

At receiving end, the modem working on this principle basically measures amplitudes at regular intervals to *decode* them as 0s and 1s and then generates a digital signal. The binary bits then can be stored at the destination node. This technique is normally used for transmitting data over optical fiber. However, on the other lines; it is a very inefficient technique due to the noise. Since amplitude is the only aspect of ASK encoding technique, noise is a major problem. Noise usually affects the amplitude of a signal. Therefore, ASK is highly susceptible to noise.

Frequency Shift Keying (FSK). In Frequency Shift Keying (FSK) or *frequency modulation* technique, we keep the amplitude and the phase of the carrier signals unaltered. We assign a certain frequency f_1 to denote 1 and f_2 to denote 0. The frequency of the carrier signal is varied to represent binary 1 (using f_1) and binary 0 (f_2). Both f_1 and f_2 must be in the bandwidth of the channel *i.e.* between 0 and 400 Hz which can be easily carried by the telephone wires.

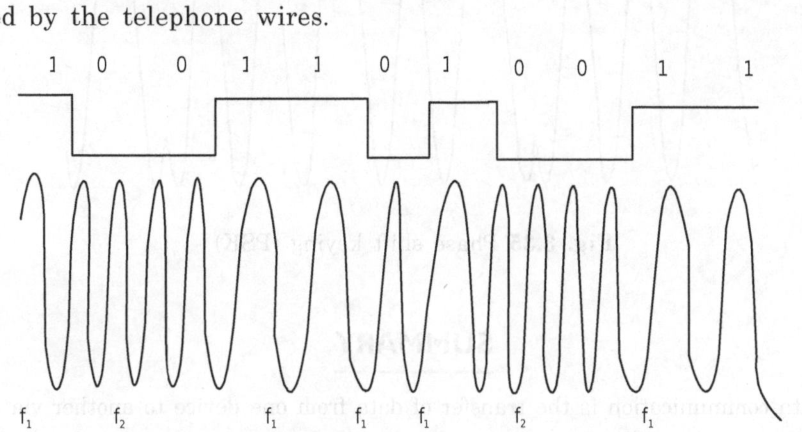

Fig. 3.34 Frequency shift keying (FSK)

Fig. 3.34 depicts this. The signal component with slower cycle is f_1, and the signal component that shows rapid cycle portions is f_2. The two respectively represent 1 and 0 of the input digital signal. It is obvious that the modem at the destination *decodes* these signals into 0s and 1s by measuring the frequencies of the received signals at regular predefined time interval.

The figure shows the same bit string 10011010011 sent using frequency shift keying. Note that the phase and amplitude for both 0 and 1 are same. Only frequency varies. But both f_1 and f_2 are between 0 and 4000 Hz.

This scheme is less error prone than Amplitude Shift Keying. Noise is not an issue with FSK. Unlike ASK, the voltage changes (*i.e.*, amplitude changes) are ignored by FSK. This is simply because FSK does not look for amplitude changes, but it looks for varying frequency patterns. Therefore, even if there is unwanted amplitude changes (*i.e.*, noise), they are not of any consequence to FSK.

Phase Shift Keying (PSK). In Phase Shift Keying (PSK), we keep the amplitude and the frequency of the carrier signal unchanged and only changes the phase to denote 0s and 1s. For instance, we can start with a phase of 0 degrees to represent binary 0 and then change the phase to 180 degrees to represent binary 1. In PSK, we change the timing of the carrier wave abruptly to encode data. After a phase shift happens, the carrier wave still continues to oscillate, but it immediately jumps to a new point in its cycle. The phase of the signal during each bit duration is constant and its value depends on whether it is 0 or 1. Fig. 3.35 depicts this.

The figure 3.35 indicates that the 0 bit indicates no phase change at all. This is true even if the preceding bit is either 0 or 1. However, a bit 1 represents a phase shift of 180°. Again this is true irrespective of whether the previous bit is 0 or 1.

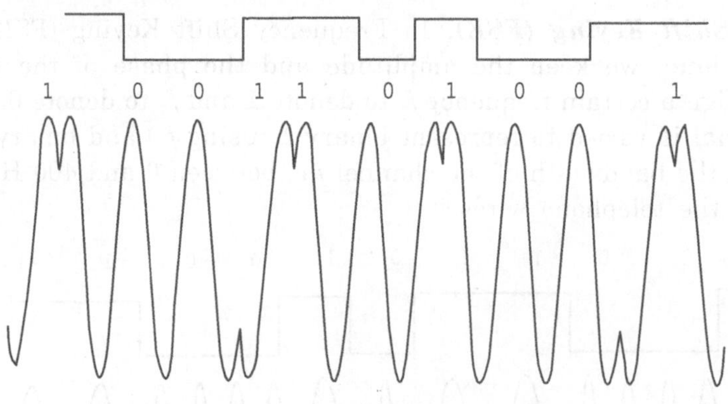

Fig. 3.35 Phase shift keying (PSK)

SUMMARY

- Data communication is the transfer of data from one device to another via some form of transmission media.
- A data communication system must transmit data to the correct destination in an accurate and timely manner.
- The five basic components of a data communication system are the message, the sender, the receiver, the medium and the protocol.
- Data communication depends on three fundamental characteristics: delivery, accuracy and timeliness.

- Communication between two devices can occur in one of three transmission modes: simplex, half-duplex, or full-duplex.
- Simplex transmission means that data flows in one direction only.
- Half-duplex transmission allows data to flow in both directions, but not at the same time.
- Full-duplex transmission allows data to flow in both directions at the same time.
- Signals travel from transmitter to receiver via a path. This path, called the medium can be guided or unguided.
- A guided medium is contained within physical boundaries, while an unguided medium is boundless.
- The most popular types of guided media are of the following:
  (*a*) Twisted Pair Cable (metallic)
  (*b*) Coaxial Cable (metallic)
  (*c*) Optical fiber (glass or plastic).
- The most popular types of unguided media are the following:
  (*a*) Radio Transmission
  (*b*) Microwave Transmission
  (*c*) Infra-red Transmission.
- Switching is a method in which multiple communication devices are connected to one another efficiently.
- There are three fundamental switching methods: circuit switching, packet switching and message switching.
- In circuit switching, packets from a single device travel on dedicated links to the destination.
- Packet switching is generally more efficient than circuit switching for non-voice communication.
- There are two popular approaches to packet switching: the datagram approach and the virtual circuit approach.
- In the datagram approach, each packet (called a datagram) is treated independently from all other packets.
- In the virtual circuit approach, all packets of a message follow the exact same route.
- Virtual circuit packet switching is implemented in two forms:
  (*a*) Switched virtual circuit (SVC)
  (*b*) Permanent Virtual Circuit (PVC).
- In message switching (also Known as store and forward), a node receives a message, stores it, and then sends it.
- In circuit switching, the different segments of a message follow a dedicated path. In virtual approach to packet switching, the segments follow a created route, the links of which may be shared by other connections.
- Multiplexing is the simultaneous transmission of multiple signals across a single data link.
- Two types of multiplexing are Frequency Division Multiplexing (FDM) and Time-Division Multiplexing (TDM).

- A modem is a DCE that modulates and demodulates signals.
- Modem changes digital signals to analog signals using ASK, FSK, PSK, or QAM modulation.
- The most popular modems today have surpassed the capabilities of the older Bell modems and are based on standards (the V series) defined by the ITU-T.
- An intelligent modem contains software to perform functions in addition to modulation and demodulation.
- 56 K modems are asymmetrical: they download at a rate of 56 Kbps and send data at 33.6 Kbps.

EXERCISE

1. Identify the five components of a data communication system.

2. What are the advantages of distributed processing?

3. What are the three fundamental characteristics that determine the effectiveness of a data communication system?

4. What do you understand by data communication?

5. What are the different characteristics of data communication?

6. Explain the main components of data communication.

7. Draw the general block diagram of communication model.

8. Describe the key elements of the communication model.

9. What are the different methods of the transmission?

10. Write short note on:

(*a*) Simplex mode,

(*b*) Half duplex,

(*c*) Full duplex.

11. What is the main difference between TWA and TWS?

12. What is transmission media?

13. What are two types of transmission media?

14. Compare between wired and wireless media.

15. Write short note on:

(*a*) co-axial cable,

(*b*) Twisted pair cable,

(*c*) Optical fiber cable.

16. Explain the difference between UTP and STP.

17. Compare different types of cables with its factors.

18. What are the categories of co- axial cable?

19. Construct the optical fiber cables.

20. Describe the advantages of optical fiber cables.

21. Describe the comparison of wired media.

22. Explain the three types of radio.

23. Write shot note on:

(*a*) Circuit switching,

(*b*) Packet switching,

(*c*) Message switching.

24. What is the use of infrared light for transmission?

25. Describe the comparison of circuit switching, packet switching and message switching.

26. Explain the working of the multiplexer.

27. Compare between the FDM and TDM.

28. What is modem? Explain with diagram.

29. Explain the key various elements of the data communication.

30. What are the differences between simplex, half and full duplex?

31. Explain the co-axial cable and twisted pair cable with their advantages and disadvantages.

32. What are microwaves and explain microwave transmission system with its types?

33. Explain the key various elements of the data communication.

34. What do you mean by switching? And what different types of switching techniques are employed between two computers?

Chapter 4

FRAMING AND ERROR CONTROL

4.1 FRAMING TECHNIQUES

Framing

- To service the network layer, data link layer uses the service provided to it by the physical layer.
- Physical layer accepts the raw bit stream and delivers it to the destination. This bit stream may contain error *i.e.*, number of bits received may not be equal to number of bits transmitted.
- The data link layer breaks the stream into discrete frames and computes the checksum for each frame.
- At the destination the checksum is recomputed.
- The breaking of bit stream by inserting spaces or time gaps is called framing. Since it is difficult and risky to count on timing and mark the start and end of each frame, various simple methods used for framing are:
  1. Character count.
  2. Starting and ending characters, with character stuffing.
  3. Starting and ending flags, with bit stuffing.

1. Character Count

- This framing method uses a field in the header of frame to specify the number of characters in the frame. Fig 4.1 illustrates such framing for four frames of sizes 5, 5, 8, 8 characters respectively.
- A disadvantage with his framing is that the count can be garbled by transmission error. E.g. if a character count of 5 in the first frame becomes 7, the destination will go out of synchronization and will be unable to locate the exact start of next frame. [Fig 4.2 illustrates this type of error.]

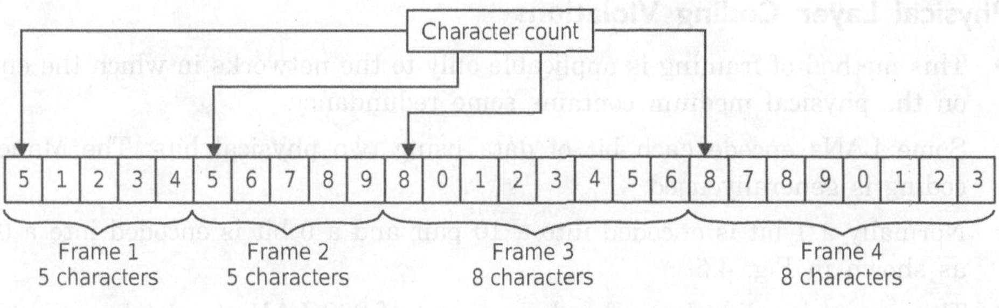

Fig. 4.1 Character count framing

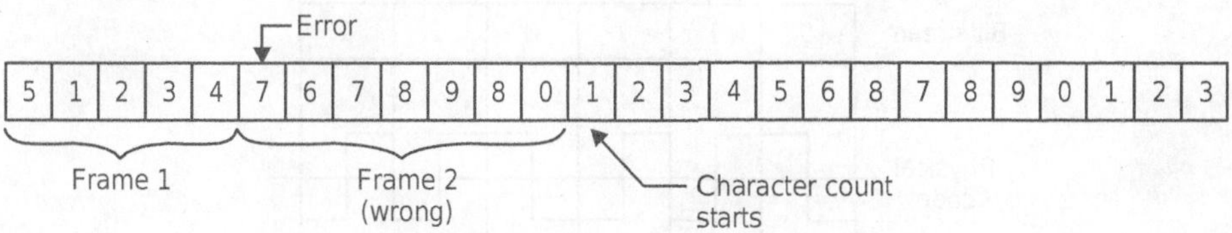

Fig. 4.2 Character count framing with error

2. *Character Stuffing*

- In character stuffing, the special character Data Link Escape (DLE) is stuffed in front of control character when it appears as apart of data. The frame format is as follows:

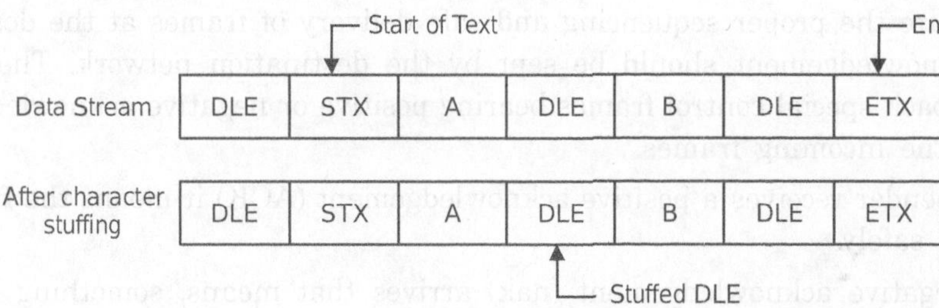

Fig. 4.3 Character stuffing

3. *Bit Stuffing*

- In bit stuffing a specific bit is stuffed into the outgoing character stream. The format is as follows:

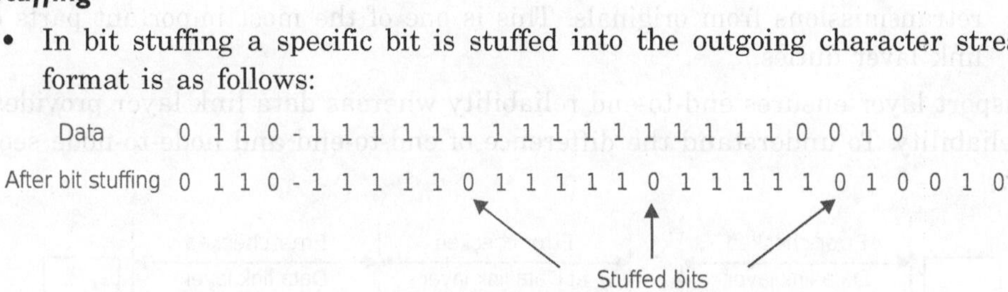

Fig. 4.4 Bit stuffing

- Each frame begins and ends with a special bit pattern, 01111110 called a flag byte. When five consecutive 1's are encountered in the data, it automatically stuffs a '0' bit into outgoing bit stream.

4.1.1 Physical Layer Coding Violations

- This method of framing is applicable only to the networks in which the encoding on the physical medium contains some redundancy.
- Some LANs encode each bit of data using two physical bits. The Manchester coding is generally used.
- Normally a 1 bit is encoded into a 10 pair and a 0 bit is encoded into a 01 pair as shown in Fig. 4.5.
- This use of invalid physical code is a part of 802 LAN standards.

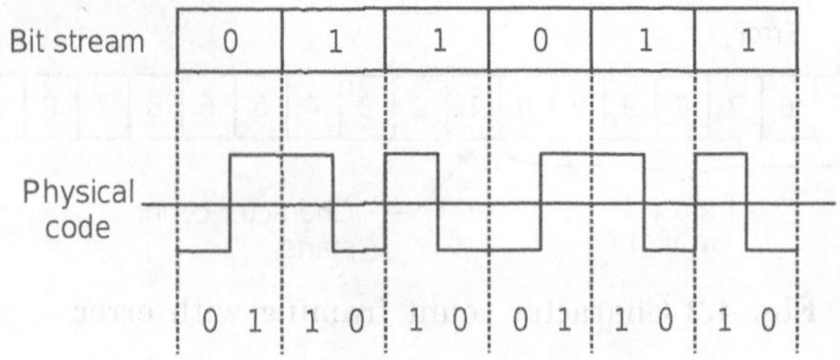

Fig. 4.5 Manchester Coding

4.2 ERROR CONTROL

- To ensure the proper sequencing and safe delivery of frames at the destination, an acknowledgement should be sent by the destination network. The receiver sends back special control frames bearing positive or negative acknowledgements about the incoming frames.
- If the sender receives a positive acknowledgement (ACK) it means the frame has arrived safely.
- If a negative acknowledgement (nak) arrives that means, something has gone wrong and the frame is to be retransmitted.
- A timer at sender's and receiver's end is introduced. Also sequence numbers to the outgoing frames are maintained so that the receiver can distinguish retransmissions from originals. This is one of the most important parts of data link layer duties.

Transport layer ensures end-to-end reliability whereas data link layer provides node-to-node reliability. To understand the difference of end-to-end and node-to-node see figure 4.6 below.

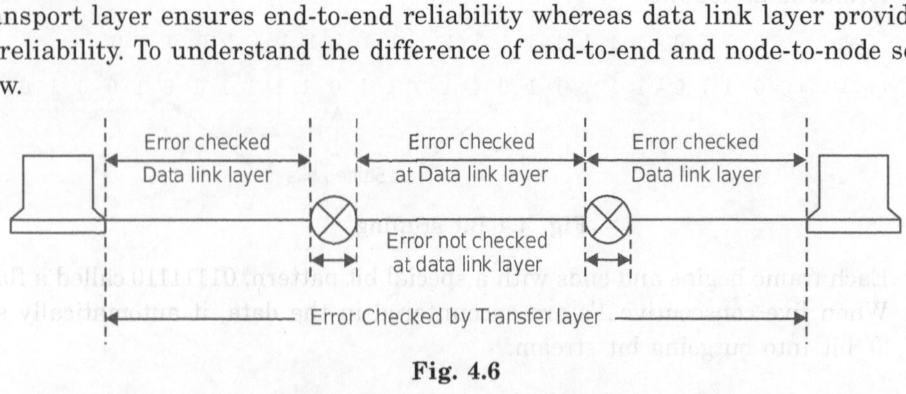

Fig. 4.6

In above figure the data link layer in taking care of error between nodes and that why it is taking care of error between DTE and Router and Router to Router also. But an error is introduced as the packet is processed inside one of the routers that's why this error will not be traced by the data link layer which takes case node to node only and not at any node. To avoid this type of errors Transport layer must do its own checking end to end to make sure that the packet has arrived at destination properly.

4.3 ERROR DETECTION AND CORRECTION

In digital transmission systems, an error occurs when a bit is altered between transmission and reception; that is, a binary 1 is transmitted and a binary 0 is received, or a binary 0 is transmitted and a binary 1 is received. Two general types of error can occur: Single bit errors and burst errors.

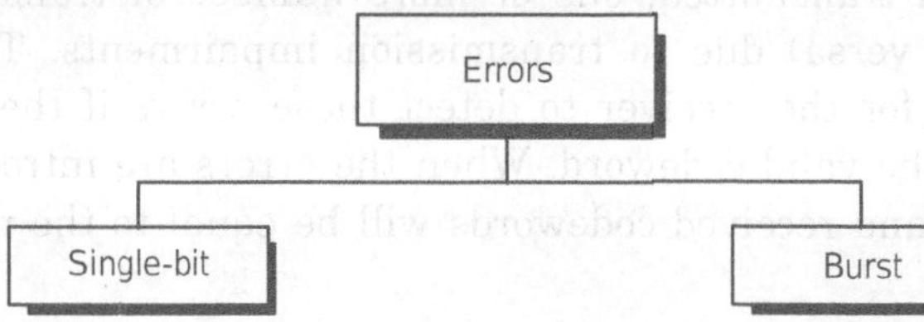

Fig. 4.7 Types of errors

Single Bit Error

A single bit error is an isolated error condition that alters one bit but does not affect nearby bits.

OR

"In a single bit error, only one bit in the data unit has changed."

That means only bit will change from 1 to 0 or 0 to 1 as shown in Fig 4.8 below:

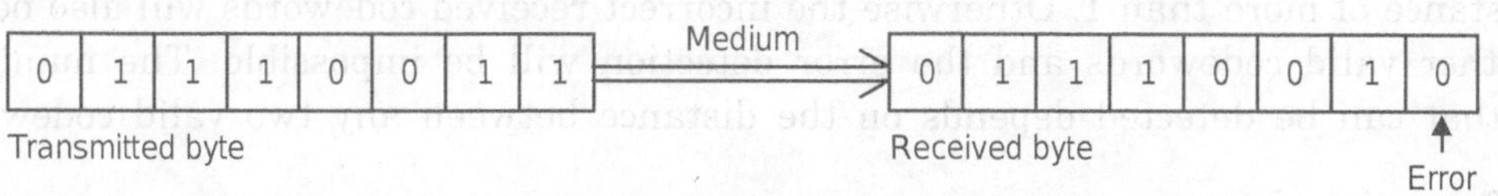

Fig. 4.8 Single bit error

A single bit error can occur in the presence of white noise, when a slight random deterioration of the signal-to-noise ratio is sufficient to confuse the receiver's decision of a single bit.

Burst Error

The term burst error means that two or more bits in the data unit have changed from 1 to 0 or from 0 to 1. The length of the burst is measured from the first corrupted bit to the last corrupted bit. Some of the bits in between may not have been corrupted. Burst errors are illustrated in Fig. 4.9.

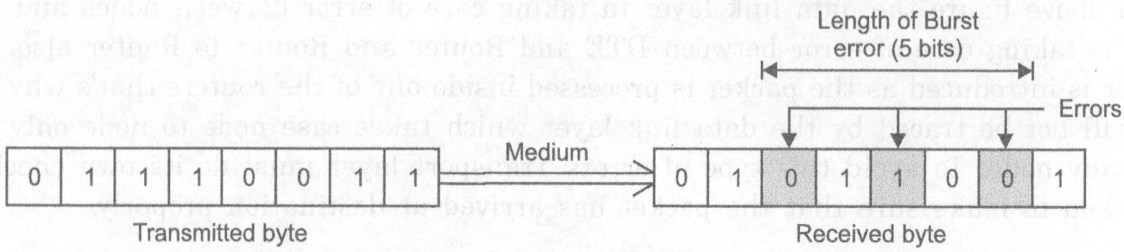

Fig. 4.9 Burst errors

Burst errors are more common and more difficult to deal with. Burst errors can be caused by impulse noise.

4.3.1 Error Detection

When a codeword is transmitted, one or more number of transmitted bits will be reversed (0 to 1 or vice versa) due to transmission impairments. Thus errors will be introduced. It is possible for the receiver to detect these errors if the received codeword (corrupted) is not one of the valid codeword. When the errors are introduced, the distance between the transmitted and received codewords will be equal to the number of errors as illustrated in Fig. 4.10.

Transmitted code word	10101100	11101011	00100101
Received code word	1①101100 (Error)	⓪11①1011 (Error)	①01①0⓪01 (Error)
Number of errors	1	2	3
Distance	1	2	3

Fig. 4.10

Hence to detect the errors at the receiver, the valid codewords should be separated by a distance of more than 1. Otherwise the incorrect received codewords will also become some other valid codewords and the error detection will be impossible. The number of errors that can be detected depends on the distance between any two valid codewords.

Error Detection Process

For a given frame of bits additional bits that constitute an error-detecting code are added by the transmitter. This code is calculated as a function of the other transmitted bits Typically, for a data block of k bits, the error-detection algorithm yields an error detection code of $n - k$ bits, where $(n - k) < k$. The error-detection code, also referred to as the **check bits,** is appended to the data block to produce a frame of n bits, which is then transmitted. The receiver separates the incoming frame into the k bits of data and $(n - k)$ bits of the error-detection code. The receiver performs the same error-detection calculation on the data bits and compares this value with the value of the incoming error-detection code. A detected error occurs if and only if there is a mismatch. Thus P_3 is the probability that a frame contains errors and that the error-detection scheme will detect that fact. P_2 is known as the residual error rate and is the probability that an error will be undetected despite the use of an error-detection scheme.

The error detection process is shown in the following figure 4.11:

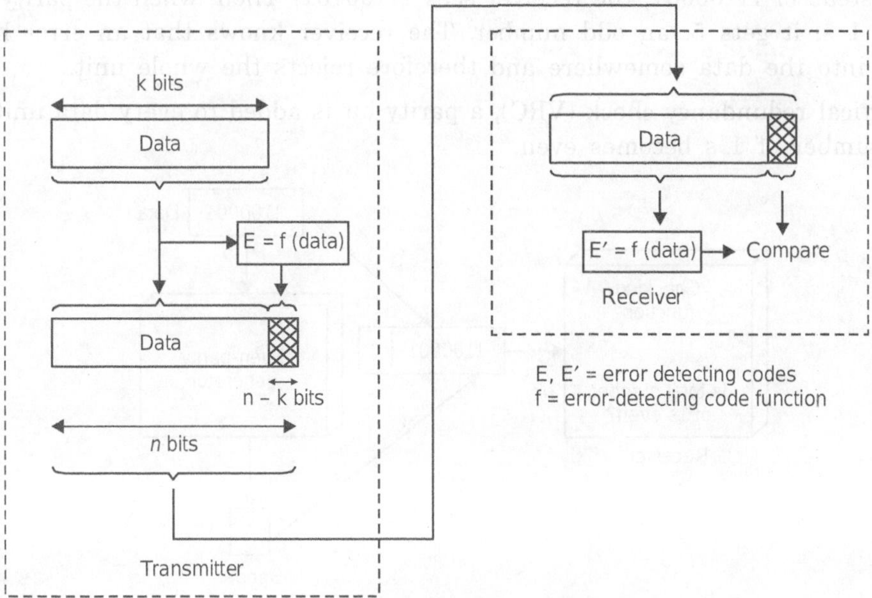

Fig. 4.11 Error Detection Process

4.4 ERROR DETECTION METHODS

Some of the most important error deduction methods are as follows:

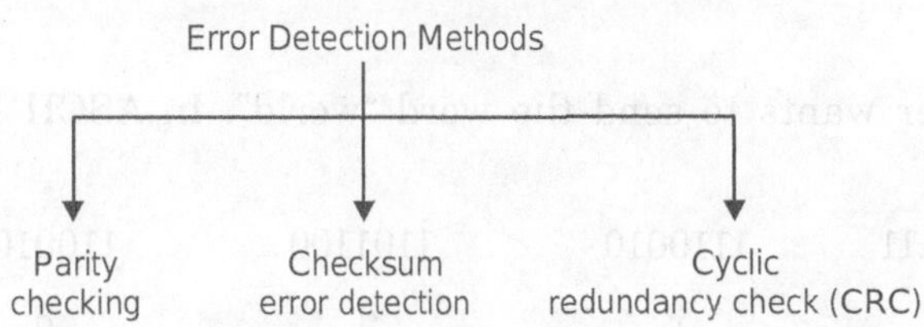

4.4.1 Vertical Redundancy Check (VRC)

The most common and least expensive mechanism for error detection is the *vertical redundancy check, (VRC),* often called **a parity check**. In this technique, a redundant bit, called a **party bit**, is appended to every data unit so that the total number of 1s in the unit (including the parity bit) becomes even.

Suppose we want to transmit the binary data unit 1100001 [ASCII a (97)]; see Figure 4.12. Adding together the number of 1s gives us 3, an odd number. Before transmitting, we pass the data unit through a parity generator. The parity generator counts the 1s and appends the parity bit (a 1 in this case) to the end. The total number of 1 s is now four, an even number. The system now transmits the entire expended unit across the network link. When it reaches its destination, the receiver puts all eight bits through an **even-parity** checking function. If the receiver sees 11100001, it counts four 1 s, an even number, and the data unit passes. But what if the data unit has been damaged in transit? What if, instead of 11100001, the receiver sees 11100101? Then, when the parity checker counts the 1 s, it gets 5, an odd number. The receiver knows that an error has been introduced into the data somewhere and therefore rejects the whole unit.

In vertical redundancy check (VRC), a parity bit is added to every data unit so that the total number of 1 s becomes even.

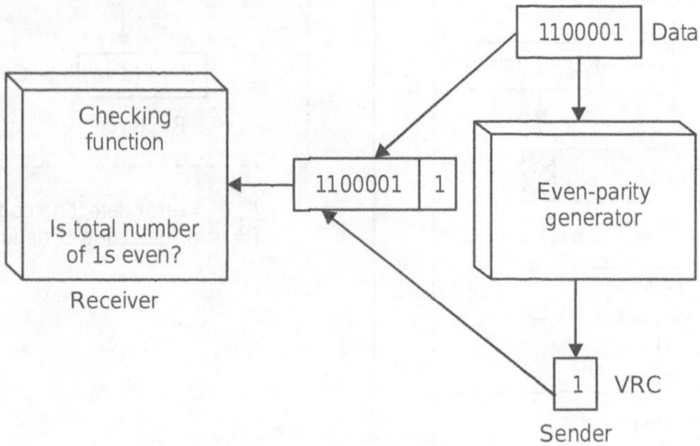

Fig. 4.12 Even parity VRC concept

Note that for sake of simplicity, we are discussing here even-parity checking, where the number of 1s should be an even number. Some systems may use **odd-parity** checking, where the number of 1s should be odd. The principle is the same; the calculation is different.

Example 4.1

Imagine the sender wants to send the word "world". In ASCII , the five characters are coded as

1110111	1101111	1110010	1101100	1100100
w	o	r	l	d

Each of the first four characters has an even number of 1s, so the parity bit is a 0. The last character ("d"), however, has three 1s (an odd number), so the parity bit is a 1 to make the total number of 1s even. The following shows the actual bits sent (the parity bits are underlined).

1110111<u>0</u> 1101111<u>0</u> 1110010<u>0</u> 1101100<u>0</u> 1100100<u>1</u>

Example 4.2

Now suppose the word "world", in the previous example, is received by the receiver without being corrupted in transmission

1110111<u>0</u> 1101111<u>0</u> 1110010<u>0</u> 1101100<u>0</u> 1100100<u>1</u>

The receiver counts the 1s in each character and comes up with even numbers (6, 6, 4, 4, and 4). The data would be accepted.

Example 4.3

Now suppose the word "world", in example 4.1, is received by the receiver but corrupted during transmission.

11111110 11011110 11101100 11011000 11001001

The receiver counts the 1s in each character and comes up with even and odd numbers (7, 6, 5, 4, 4). The receiver knows that the data are corrupted, discards them, and asks for retransmission.

4.4.2 Longitudinal Redundancy Check (LRC)

In *longitudinal redund-ancy check (LRC),* a block of bits is organized in a table (rows and columns). For example, instead of sending a block of 32 bits, we organize them in a table made of four rows and eight columns, as shown in Figure 4.13. We then calculate the parity bit for each column and create a new row of eight bits, which are the parity bits for the whole block. Note that the first parity bit in the fifth row is calculated based on all first bits. The second parity bit is calculated based on all second bits, and so on. We then attach the eight parity bits to the original data and send them to the receiver.

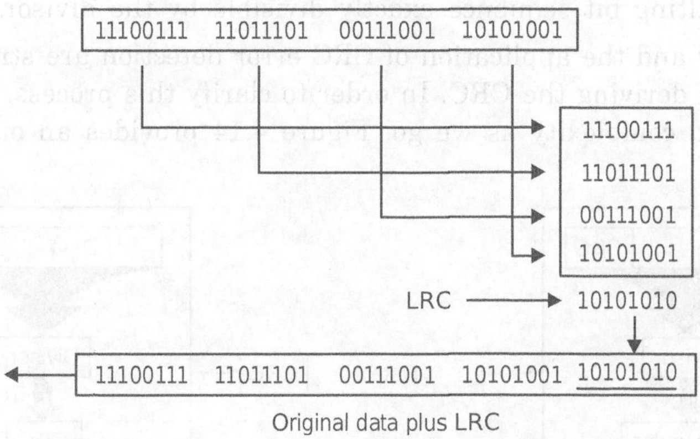

Fig. 4.13 LRC

In longitudinal redundancy check (LRC), a block of bits is divided into rows and a redundant row of bits is added to the whole block.

Example 4.4

Suppose the following block is sent:

10101001 00111001 11011101 11100111 10101010
(LRC)

However it is hit by a burst noise of length eight and some bits are corrupted.

10100011 10001001 11011101 11100111 10101010
(LRC)

When the receiver checks the LRC, some of the bits do not follow the even-parity rule and the whole block is discarded (the non-matching bits are shown in bold).

10100011 10001001 11011101 11100111 10101010
(LRC)

4.4.3 Cyclic Redundancy Check (CRC)

The third and most powerful of the redundancy checking techniques is the *cyclic redundancy check (CRC).* Unlike VRC and LRC, which are based on addition, CRC is based on binary division. In CRC, instead of adding bits together to achieve a desired parity, a sequence of redundant bits, called the CRC or the CRC remainder, is appended to the end of a data unit so that the resulting data unit becomes exactly divisible by a second, predetermined binary number. At its destination, the same number divides the incoming data unit. If at this step there is no remainder, the data unit is assumed to be intact and is therefore accepted. A remainder indicates that the data unit has been damaged in transmit and therefore must be rejected.

The redundancy bits used by CRC are derived by dividing the data unit by a predetermined divisor, the remainder is the CRC. To be valid, a CRC must have two qualities: it must have exactly one less bit than the divisor, and appending it to the end of the data string must make the resulting bit sequence exactly divisible by the divisor.

Both the theory and the application of CRC error detection are straightforward. The only complexity is in deriving the CRC. In order to clarify this process, we will start with an overview and add complexity as we go. Figure 4.14 provides an outline of the three basic steps.

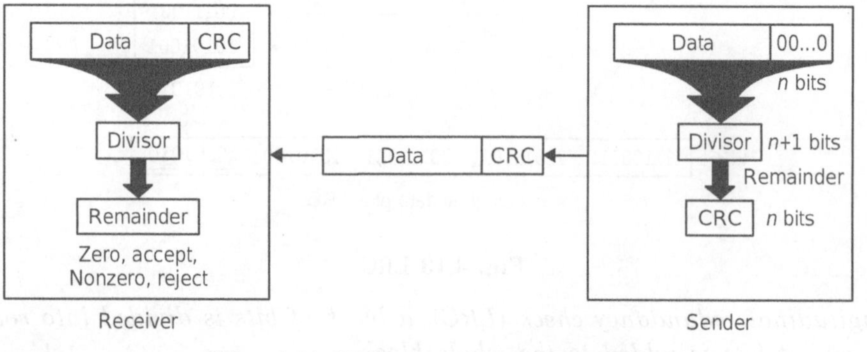

Fig. 4.14 CRC generator and checker

First a string of n 0s is appended to the data unit. The number n is one less than the number of bits in the predetermined divisor, which is $n + 1$ bits.

Second, the newly elongated data unit is divided by the divisor using a process called binary division. The remainder resulting from this division is the CRC.

Third, the CRC of n bits derived in step 2 replaces the appended 0s at the end of the data unit. Note that the CRC may consist of all 0s.

The data unit arrives at the receiver data first, followed by the CRC. The receiver treats the whole string as a unit and divides it by the same divisor that was used to find the CRC remainder.

If the string arrives without error, the CRC checker yields a remainder of zero and the data unit passes. If the string has been changed in transit, the division yields a non-zero remainder and the data unit does not pass.

The CRC Generator

A CRC generator uses modulo-2 division. Figure 4.15 shows this process. In the first step, the four-bit divisor is subtracted from the first four bits of the dividend. Each bit of the divisor is subtracted from the corresponding bit of the dividend without disturbing the next higher bit. In our example, the divisor, 1101, is subtracted from the first four bits of the dividend, 1001, yielding 100 (the leading 0 of the remainder is dropped off).

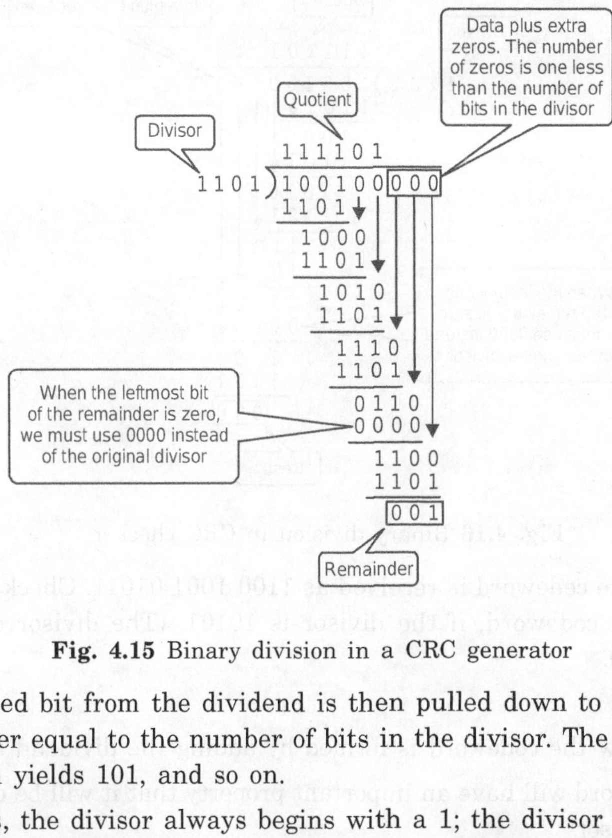

Fig. 4.15 Binary division in a CRC generator

The next unused bit from the dividend is then pulled down to make the number of bits in the remainder equal to the number of bits in the divisor. The next step, therefore, is 1000-1101, which yields 101, and so on.

In this process, the divisor always begins with a 1; the divisor is subtracted from a portion of the previous dividend/remainder that is equal to it in length; the divisor can only be subtracted from a dividend/remainder whose leftmost bit is 1. Anytime the leftmost bit of the dividend/remainder is 0, a string of 0s, of the same length as the divisor, replaces the divisor in that step of the process. For example, if the divisor is four bits long, it is replaced by four 0s. (Remember, we are dealing with bit patterns, not with quantitative values; 0000 is not the same as 0). This restriction means that, at any step, the leftmost subtraction will be either 0-0 or 1-1, both of which equal 0. So, after subtraction, the leftmost bit of the remainder will always be a leading zero, which is dropped off, and the next unused bit of the dividend is pulled down to fill out the remainder. Note that only the first bit of the remainder is dropped—if the second bit is also 0, it is retained, and the dividend/remainder for the next step will begin with 0. This process repeats until the entire dividend has been used.

The CRC Checker

A CRC checker functions exactly like the generator. After receiving the data appended with the CRC, it does the same modulo-2 division. If the remainder is all 0s, the CRC is dropped and the data accepted; otherwise, the received stream of bits is discarded and data are resent. Figure 4.16 shows the same process of division in the receiver. We assume that there is no error. The remainder is therefore all 0s and the data are accepted.

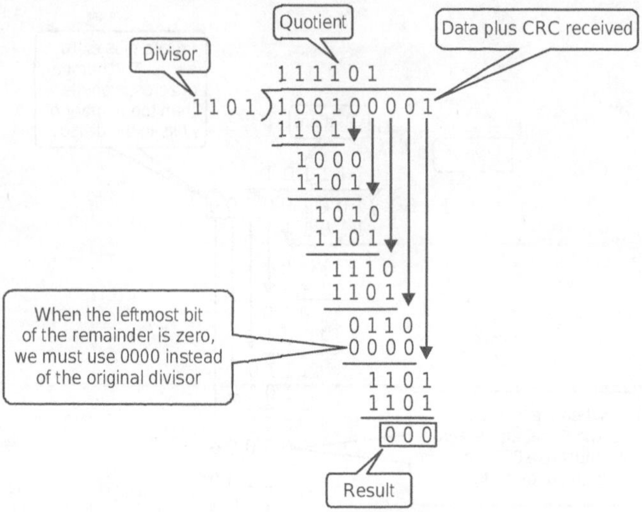

Fig. 4.16 Binary division in CRC checker

Example 4.5. The codeword is received as 1100 1001 01011. Check whether there are errors in the received codeword, if the divisor is 10101. (The divisor corresponds to the generator polynomial).

Solution:

- As we know the codeword is formed by adding the dividend and the remainder.
- This codeword will have an important property that it will be completely divisible by the divisor.
- Thus at the receiver we have to divide the received codeword by, the same divisor and check for the remainder.
- If there is no remainder then there are no errors. But if there is remainder after division, then there are errors in the received codeword.
- Let us use this technique and find if there are errors.

Data word: 1100 1001 01011
Divisor: 10101

```
                1111100001
   ┌→10101)11001001011011  ← Received codeword
   │       ⊕10101
 Divisor   011000
            ⊕10101
 MOD-2      011010
 additions  ⊕10101
             011111
             ⊕10101
              010100
              ⊕10101
               000011011
                   10101
                   01110  ← Remainder
```

The non-zero remainder shows that there are errors in the received codeword.

Generation of CRC code

The generation of CRC code is clear after solving the following example.

Example 4.6. Generate the CRC code for the data word of 1100 10101. The divisor is 10101.

Solution:

Given: Data word : 110010101

Divisor : 10101

The number of data bits = m = 9

The number of bits in the codeword = N

Dividend = Data word number of zeros.

```
| 1 1 0 0 1 0 1 0 1 | 0 0 0 0 0 |
      Data word       5 additional
                         zeros
```

Carry out the division as follows:

```
                11111001111     ← Quotient
   ┌→10101)1100101010 0000  ← Dividend
   │       10101
 Divisor   ⊕⊕⊕⊕⊕
           011000
            10101
            011011
             10101
             011100
              10101
               10011
               10101
                11000
                10101
                 11010
                 10101
                  11110
                  10101
                   10110
                   10101
                   00110  ← Remainder
```

Codeword

In CRC the required codeword is obtained by writing the data word followed by the remainder.

$$
\begin{array}{rl}
 & 1\,1\,0\,0\,1\,0\,1\,0\,1\,0\,0\,0\,0\,0 \\
 & 1\,1\,0 \\
\hline
\text{Codeword} = & 1\,1\,0\,0\,1\,0\,1\,0\,1\,0\,0\,1\,1\,0
\end{array}
$$

4.4.4 Checksum

The error detection method used by the higher-layer protocols is called **checksum.** Like VRC, LRC, and CRC, checksum is based on the concept of redundancy.

Checksum Generator

In the sender, the checksum generator subdivides that the data unit into equal segments of n bits (usually 16). These segments are added together using **one's complement** arithmetic in such a way that the total is also n bits long. That total (sum) is then complemented and appended to the end of the original data unit as redundancy bits, called the **checksum field.** The extended data unit is transmitted across the network. So if the sum of the data segment is T, the checksum will be – T (see figures 4.17 and 4.18).

Checksum Checker

The receiver subdivides the data unit as above and adds all segments together and complements the result. If the extended data unit is intact, the total value found by adding the data segments and the checksum field should be zero. If the result is not zero, the packet contains an error and the receiver rejects it.

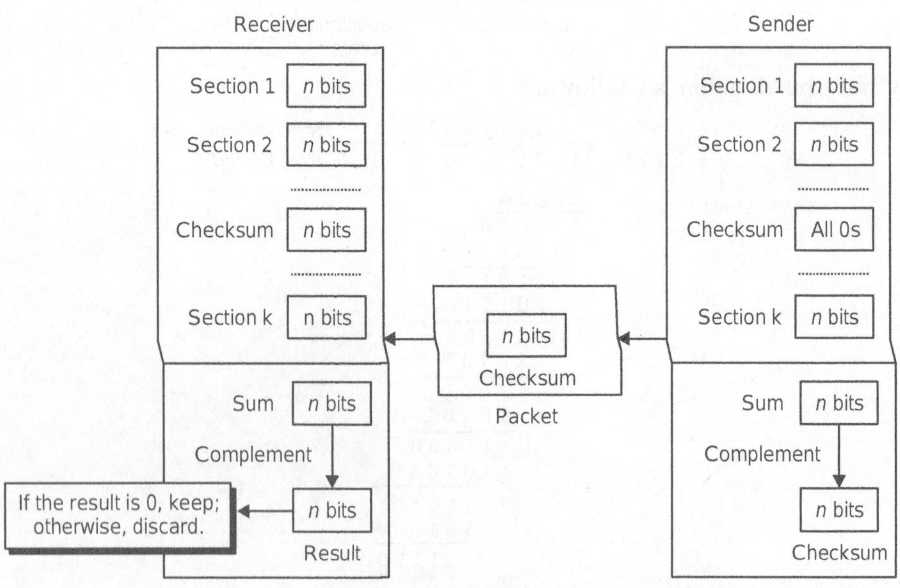

Fig. 4.17 Checksum

The sender follows these steps:

- The unit is divided into k sections, each of n bits.
- All sections are added together using one's complement to get the sum.
- The sum is complemented and becomes the checksum.
- The checksum is sent with the data.

The receiver follows these steps:

- The unit is divided into k sections, each of n bits.
- All sections are added together using one's complement to get the sum.
- The sum is complemented.
- If the result is zero, the data are accepted: otherwise, they are rejected.

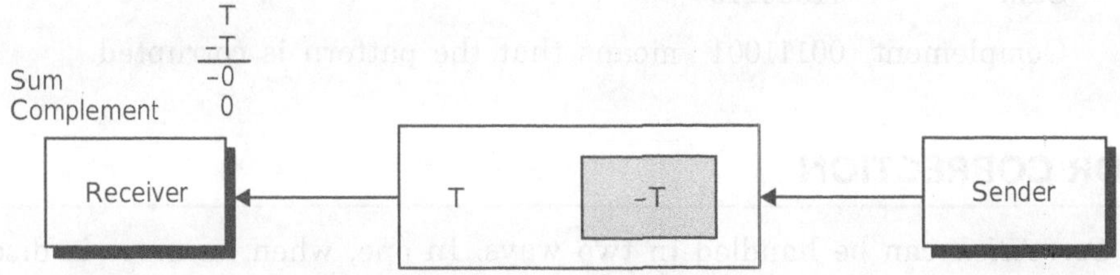

Fig. 4.18 Data unit and checksum

Example 4.7

Suppose the following block of 16 bits is to be sent using a checksum of 8 bits.

10101001 00111001

The numbers are added using one's complement arithmetic

```
           10101001
           00111001
       Sum 11100010
  Checksum 00011101
```

The pattern sent is:

10101001 00111001 00011101

Checksum

Example 4.8

Now suppose the receiver receives the pattern sent in Example 4.7 and there is no error.

10101001 00111001 00011101

When the receiver adds the three sections together, it will get all 1s, which, after complementing is all 0s and shows that there is no error.

```
             10101001
             00111001
             00011101
         Sum 1111111
  Complement 0000000   means that the pattern is OK.
```

Example 4.9

Now suppose there is a burst error of length five that affects four bits.

10101*111* <u>1</u>1111001 00011101

When the receiver adds the three sections together, it gets

	10101111
	11111001
	00011101
Result 1	11000101
Carry	1
Sum	11000110
Complement	00111001 means that the pattern is corrupted.

4.5 ERROR CORRECTION

Error Correction can be handled in two ways. In one, when an error is discovered, the receiver can have the sender retransmit the entire data unit. In the other, a receiver can use an error-correcting code, which automatically corrects certain errors.

4.5.1 Single-Bit Error Correction

The concept underlying error correction can be most easily understood by examining the simplest case : single-bit errors.

Single-bit errors can be detected by the addition of a redundant (parity) bit to the data unit (VRC). A single additional bit can detect single - bit errors in any sequence of bits because it must distinguish between only two conditions: error or no error. A bit has two states (0 and 1). These two states are sufficient for this level of detection.

Two states are enough to detect an error but not to correct it. An error occurs when the receiver reads a 1 bit as a 0 or a 0 bit as a 1. To correct the error, the receiver simply reverses the value of the altered bit. To do so, however, it must know which bit is in error. The secret of error correction, therefore, is to locate the invalid bit or bits.

For example, to correct a single-bit error in an ASCII character, the error correction code must determine which of the seven bits has changed. In this case, we have to distinguish between eight different states: no error, error in position 1, error in position 2, and so on, up to error in position 7, to do so requires enough redundancy bits to show all eight states.

Redundancy Bits

To calculate the number of redundancy bits (r) required to correct a given number of data bits (m), we must find a relationship between m and r. Figure 4.19 shows m bits of data with r bits of redundancy added to them. The length of the resulting code is $m + r$.

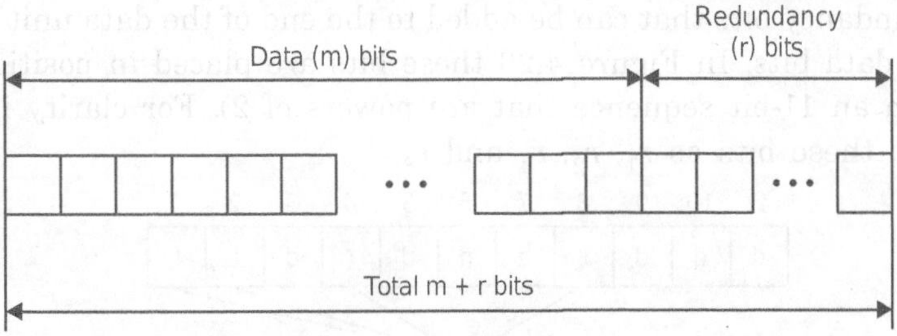

Fig. 4.19 Data and redundancy bits

If the total number of bits in a transmittable unit is $m + r$, then r must be able to indicate at least $m + r + 1$ different state. Of these, one state means no error and $m + r$ states indicate the location of an error in each of the $m + r$ positions.

So, $m + r + 1$ state must be discoverable by r bits; and r bits can indicate 2^r different states. Therefore, 2^r must be equal to or greater than $m + r + 1$:

$$2^r > m + r + 1$$

The value of r can be determined by plugging in the value of m (the original length of the data unit to be transmitted). For example, if the value of m is 7 (as in a seven-bit ASCII code), the smallest r value that can satisfy this equation is 4:

$$2^4 > 7 + 4 + 1$$

Table 4.1 shows some possible m values and the corresponding r-values.

Table 4.1 Relationship between data and redundancy bits

Number of Data Bits (m)	*Number of Redundancy Bits (r)*	*Total Bits (m + r)*
1	2	3
2	3	5
3	3	6
4	3	7
5	4	9
6	4	10
7	4	11

Hamming Code

So far, we have examined the number of bits required to cover the entire possible single-bit error states in a transmission. But how do we manipulate those bits to discover which state has occurred? A technique developed by R. W. Hamming provides a practical solution.

Positioning the Redundancy Bits

The **Hamming code** can be applied to data units of any length and uses the relationship between data and redundancy bits discussed above. For example, a seven-bit ASCII code requires four redundancy bits that can be added to the end of the data unit on interspersed with the original data bits. In Figure 4.20 these bits are placed in positions 1, 2, 4, and 8 (the positions in an 11-bit sequence that are powers of 2). For clarity in the examples below, we refer to these bits as r_1, r_2, r_4 and r_8.

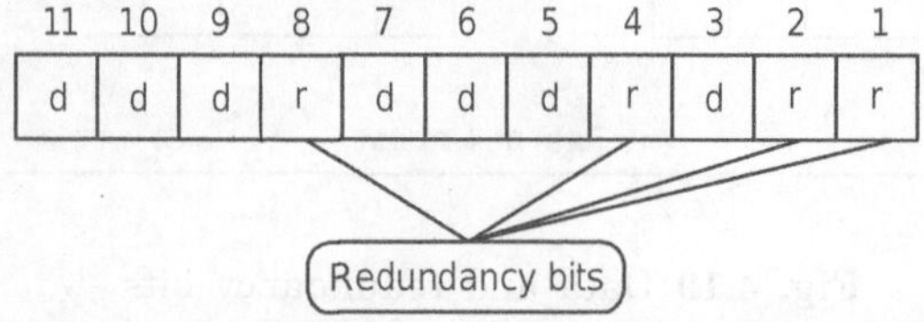

Fig. 4.20 Positions of redundancy bits in Hamming code

In the hamming code, each r bit is the VRC bit for one combination of data bits: r_1 is the VRC bit for one combination of data bits; r_2 is the VRC bit for another combination of data bits, and so on. The combination used to calculate each of the four r values for a seven-bit data sequence are as follows:

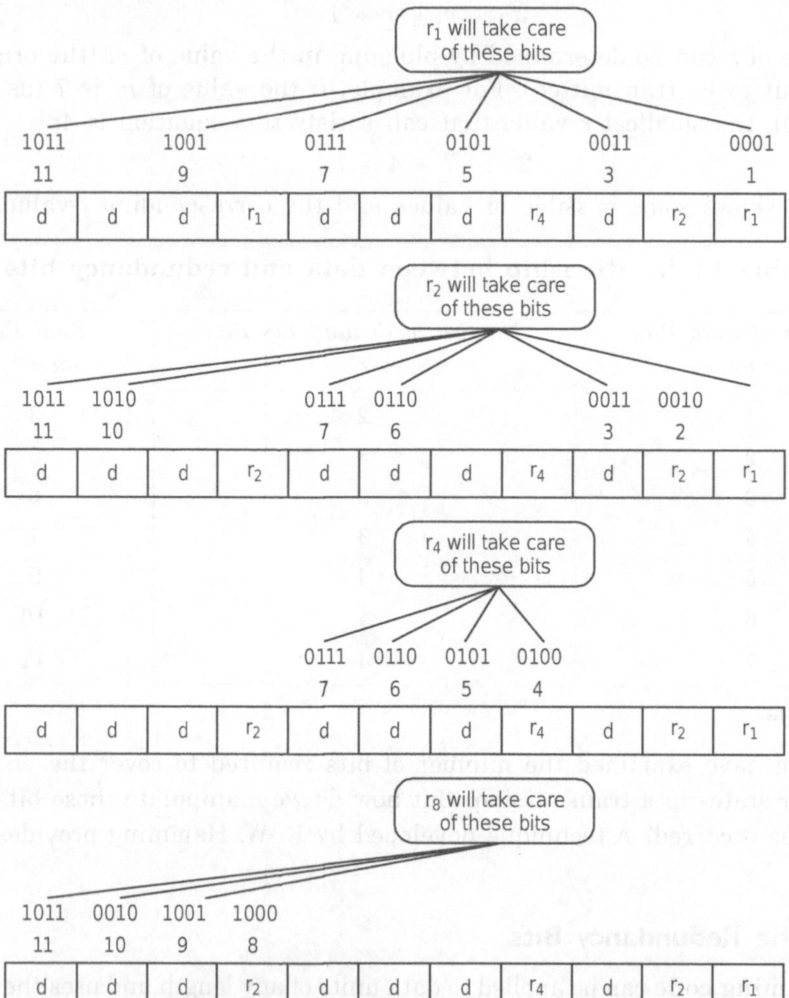

Fig. 4.21 Redundancy bits calculation

r_1 : bits 1, 3, 4, 5, 7, 9, 11

r_2 : bits 2, 3, 6, 7, 10, 11

r_4 : bits 4, 5, 6, 7

r_8 : bits 8, 9, 10, 11

Each data bit may be included in more than one VRC calculation. In the sequences above, for example, each of the original data bits is included in at least two sets, while the r bits are included in only one.

To see the pattern behind this strategy, look at the binary representation of each bit position. The r_1 bit is calculated using all bit positions whose binary representation includes a 1 in the rightmost position. The r_2 bit is calculated using all bit positions with a 1 in the second position, and so on (see Fig. 4.21).

Calculating the *r* Values

Figure 4.22 shows a Hamming code implementation for an ASCII character. In the first step, we place each bit of the original character in its appropriate position in the 11-bit unit. In the subsequent steps, we calculate the even parities for the various bit combinations. The parity value for each combination is the value of the corresponding r bit. For example, the value of r_1 is calculated to provide even parity for a combination of bits 3, 5, 7, 9, and 11. The value of r_2 is calculated to provide even parity with bits 3, 6, 7, 10, and 11, and so on. The final 11-bit code is sent through the transmission line.

Error Detection and Correction

Now imagine that by the time the above transmission is received, the number 7 bit has been changed from 1 to 0 (see Fig. 4.23).

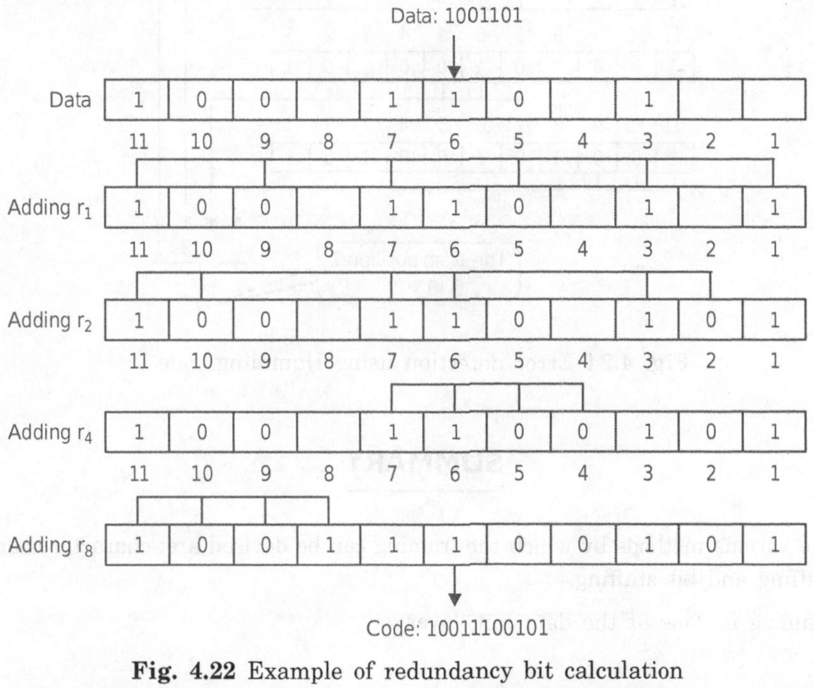

Fig. 4.22 Example of redundancy bit calculation

The receiver takes the transmission and recalculates four news VRCs using same sets of bits used by the sender plus the relevant parity (r) bit for each set (see Figure 4.24). Then it assembles the new parity values into a binary number in order of r position (r_8, r_4, r_2, r_1). In our example, this step gives us the binary number 0111 (7 in decimal), which is the precise location of the bit in error. Once the bit is identified, the receiver can reverse its value and correct the error.

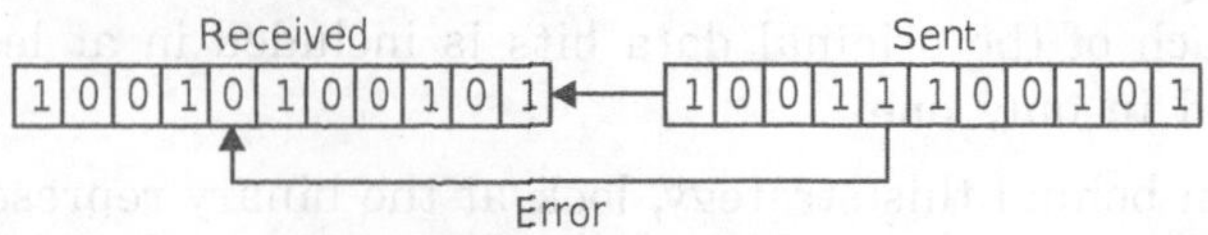

Fig. 4.23 Single-bit errors

4.5.2 Burst Error Correction

A Hamming code can be designed to correct burst errors of certain lengths. The number of redundancy bits required to make these corrections, however, is dramatically higher than that required for single-bit errors. To correct double-bit errors, for example, we must take into consideration that the two bits can be a combination of any two bits in the entire sequence. Three-bit correction means any three bits in the entire sequence, and so on. So the simple strategy used by the Hamming code to correct single-bit errors must be redesigned to be applicable for multiple-bit correction.

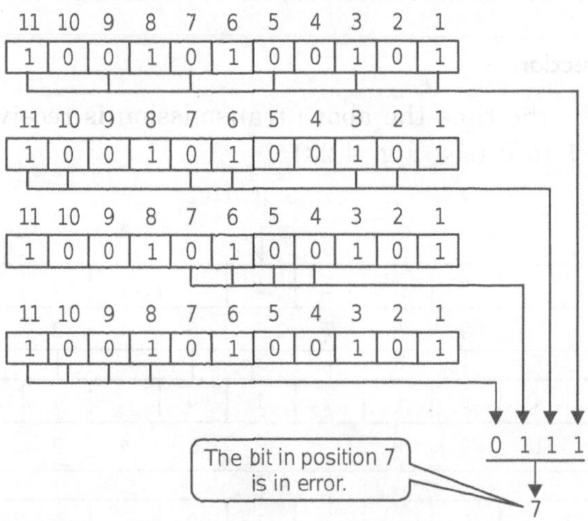

Fig. 4.24 Error detection using Hamming code

SUMMARY

- The various methods by which the framing can be devised are: character count, character stuffing and bit stuffing.
- Framing is done at the data link layer.

- The task of the data link layer is to convert the raw bit stream offered by the physical layer into a stream of frames for use by the network layer.
- Error control is provided by the data link protocols to retransmit damaged or lost frames.
- Transmission errors are usually detected at the physical layer of the OSI model.
- Transmission errors are usually corrected at the data link layer of the OSI model.
- Errors can be categorized as follows:

  (*a*) Single-bit: one bit error per data unit

  (*b*) Burst: two or more bit errors per data unit.
- Redundancy is the concept of sending extra bits for use in error detection.
- Four common methods of error detection are the following:

  (*a*) Vertical redundancy check (VRC)

  (*b*) Longitudinal redundancy check (LRC)

  (*c*) Cyclic redundancy check (CRC)

  (*d*) Checksum.
- In VRC an extra bit(parity bit) is added to the data unit.
- VRC can detect only an odd number of errors: it cannot detect an even number of errors.
- In LRC a redundant data unit follows n data units.
- CRC, the most powerful of the redundancy checking techniques, is based on binary division.
- Checksum is used by the higher-layer protocols (TCP/IP) for error detection.
- To calculate a checksum:

  (*a*) Divide the data into sections.

  (*b*) Add the sections together using one's complement arithmetic.

  (*c*) Take the complement of the final sum; this is the checksum.
- At the receiver, when using the checksum method, the data and checksum should add up to zero if there are no errors present.
- The Hamming code is a single-bit error correction method using redundant bits. The number of bits is a function of the length of the data bits.
- In the Hamming code, for a data unit of m bits, use the formula $2r^{\circ}\ m + r + 1$ to determine r, the number of redundant bits needed.

EXERCISE

1. What do you understand by framing?
2. Explain different methods used for framing.
3. What is the different between character count and character stuffing?
4. What is bit stuffing?
5. Explain physical layer coding violations.
6. Describe the operation of the error control.

7. Explain the error detection and correction.
8. What is the different between single bit error and burst error? Explain it with the help of example.
9. Explain the error detection processes.
10. What are different methods of error detection?
11. Compare between VRC and CRC.
12. What are the three basic steps of CRC?
13. What are the functions of the CRC checker?
14. Define checksum in brief.
15. Explain the working of the checksum generator and checksum checker.
16. What do you understand by error correction?
17. Explain single bit error correction with example.
18. Describe the hamming code with diagram.
19. What is burst error correction?
20. Explain the error detection using hamming code.
21. Explain the steps, which are followed in order to generate Hamming code from the given data bits with the help of an example.
22. Explain the different techniques, which are used for framing a packet of data?
23. Explain the concepts of error control.
24. What are the different error detection methods? Explain anyone in detail.
25. What is the difference between single bit error correction and burst error correction?

Chapter 5

DATA LINK CONTROL

5.1 ELEMENTARY DATA LINK PROTOCOL

- This protocol is the simplest possible protocol.
- Data are transmitted in one direction only.
- It is assumed that, both the transmitting and receiving network layers are always ready.
- It is also assumed that the processing time can be ignored and infinite butter space is available.
- The communication channel is imagined to be noise free so it dose not damage or lose any frames.
- The communication channel between the date link layers never damages or loses frames.
- All this is highly unrealistic. This protocol is called as "Utopia".
- This protocol consists of two distinct procedures, namely a sender and receiver.
- The sender runs in the data link layer of the sender machine whereas the receiver runs in the data link layer of the receiver machine.
- No sequence numbers or acknowledgments are used.

5.1.1 A Simplex Stop and Wait Protocol

- The most unrealistic restriction in the previous protocol is the assumption that the receiving network layer can process the data with zero processing time.
- In this protocol it is assumed that a finite processing time is essential.
- However like the first protocol, the communication channel is assumed to be noise free and the communication is simplex *i.e.*, only in one direction.

- This protocol deals with an important problem *i.e.*, how to prevent the sender from flooding the receiver with data faster than its processing speed.
- In this protocol, a small dummy frame is sent back from the receiver to the transmitter to indicate that it can send the next frame.
- The transmitter sends one frame and then waits for the dummy frame called acknowledgement.
- Once the acknowledgement is received, it sends the next frame. Hence the name **stop-and-wait.**
- The best thing about this protocol is that the incoming frame is always an acknowledgement.

5.1.2 A Simplex Protocol for Noisy Channel

- This is the third protocol in which we go one step ahead and assume that the communication channel is noisy and can introduce errors in the data travelling over it.
- Frames may either be damaged or lost completely.
- In this protocol, the sender waits for a positive acknowledgement before advancing to the next data item.
- So it is called as PAR (Positive Acknowledgement with Retransmission) or automatic repeat request (ARQ).
- Note that due to retransmission, there is always a possibility of duplication of frames at the receiver.
- To avoid this, the sender puts a sequence number in the header of each frame it sends.
- The receiver can check the sequence number of each arriving frame to check the possible duplication. If a frame is duplication then receiver will discard it.
- The operation can be divided into two modes.
  1. Normal operation and
  2. Time out.

1. Normal operation

- After transmitting one packet, the sender waits for an ***acknowledgement*** **(ACK)** from the receiver before transmitting the next one.
- In this way, the sender can recognize that the previous packet is transmitted successfully and we could say "stop and wait" guarantees reliable transfer between nodes.
- To support this feature, the sender keeps a record of each packet it sends.
- Also, to avoid confusion caused by delayed or duplicated ACKs, "stop-and-wait" sends each packet with unique sequence numbers and receives that numbers in each ACKs.

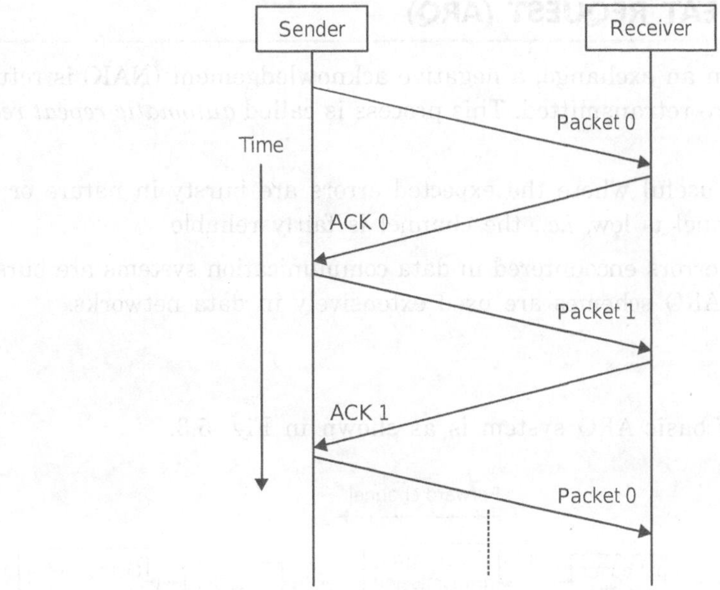

Fig. 5.1 Positive acknowledgement with retransmission

2. *Timeout*

- If the sender does not receive ACK for previous sent packet after a certain period of time, the sender ***times out*** and ***retransmit*** that packet again.
- There are two cases when the sender does not receive ACK; one is when the ACK is lost and the other is when the frame itself is not transmitted.
- To support this feature, the sender keeps timer for each packet.
- We have already discussed that a timer is introduced in the data link layer.

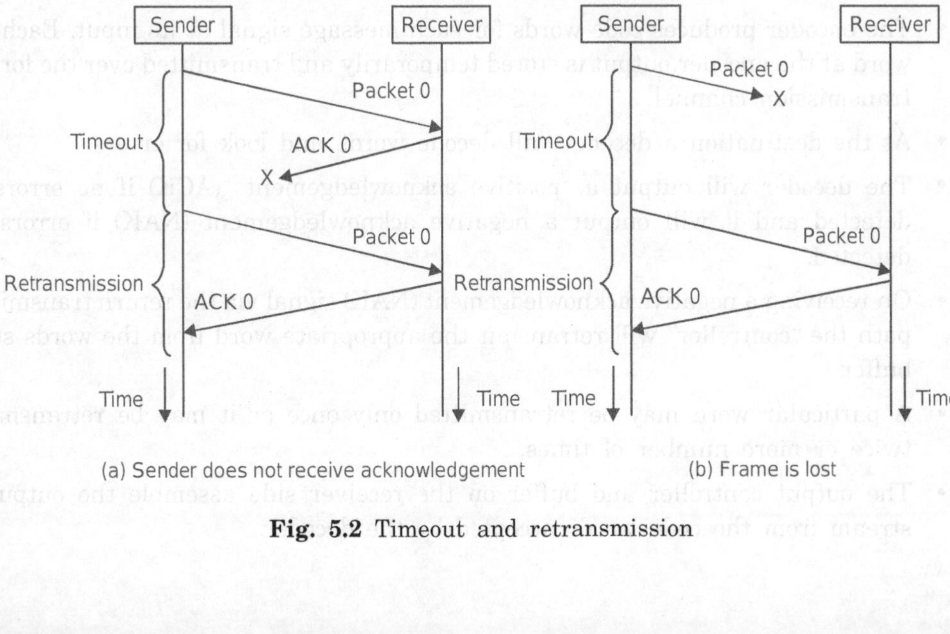

Fig. 5.2 Timeout and retransmission

5.2 AUTOMATIC REPEAT REQUEST (ARQ)

An error is detected in an exchange, a negative acknowledgement (NAK) is returned and the specified frames are retransmitted. This process is called *automatic repeat request (ARQ).*

- ARQ system is useful where the expected errors are bursty in nature or error rate of the channel is low, *i.e.*, the channel is fairly reliable.
- Most often, the errors encountered in data communication systems are bursty in nature. Hence, ARQ schemes are used extensively in data networks.

Basic ARQ System

The block diagram of basic ARQ system is as shown in Fig. 5.3.

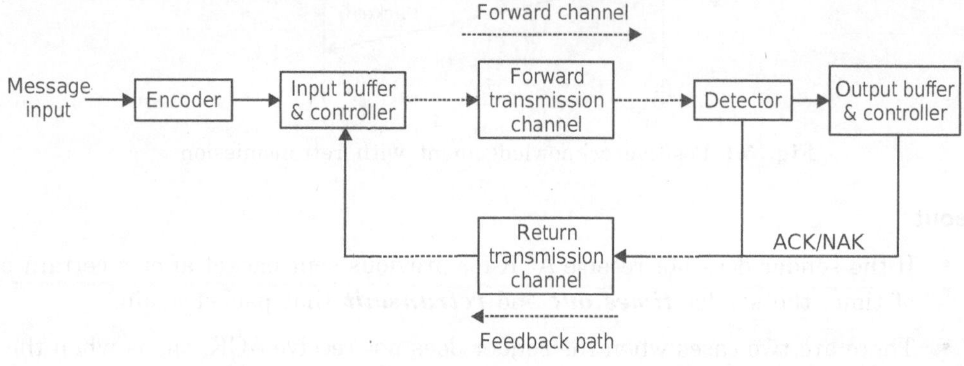

Fig. 5.3 Block diagram of the basic ARQ system

Operation of ARQ System

- The encoder produces code words for each message signal at its input. Each code word at the encoder output is stored temporarily and transmitted over the forward transmission channel.
- At the destination a decoder will decode words and look for errors.
- The decoder will output a "positive acknowledgement "(ACK) if no errors are detected and it will output a negative acknowledgement (NAK) if errors and detected.
- On receiving a negative acknowledgement (NAK) signal via the return transmission path the "controller" will retransmit the appropriate word from the words stored buffer.
- A particular word may be retransmitted only once or it may be retransmitted twice or more number of times.
- The output controller and buffer on the receiver side assemble the output bit stream from the code words accepted by the decoder.

5.3 CATEGORIES OF ERROR CONTROL

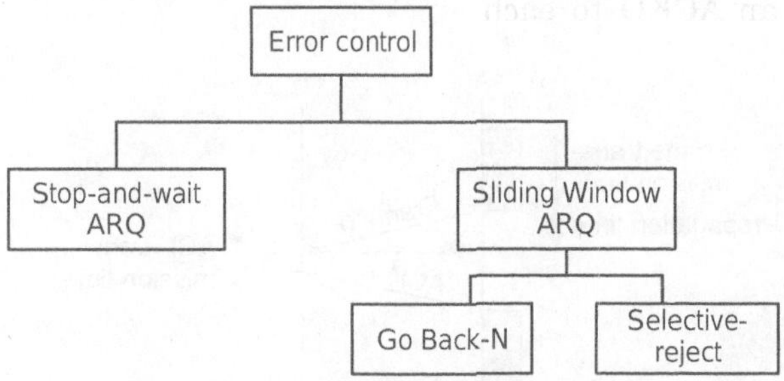

Fig. 5.4 Categories of error control

Three version of ARQ have been standardized

- Stop and wait ARQ.
- Go-back-N ARQ.
- Selective- reject ARQ.

5.3.1 Stop-and-Wait ARQ

Stop-and-wait ARQ is based on the stop-and-wait flow control technique outline previously. The source station transmits a single frame and then must a wait and acknowledgement (ACK). No other data frames can the send until the destination station's reply arrives at the source station.

Two sorts of the errors could occur. First, the frames that arrive at the destination could be damaged. The receiver detects this by using the error-detection technique referred to earlier and simply discard the frame. To account for this possibility, the source station is equipped with a timer. After a frame is transmitted, the source station waits for an acknowledgement. If no acknowledgement is received by the time that the timer expires, then the same frame is sent again. Note that this method requires that the transmitter maintain a copy of a transmitted frame until an acknowledgement is received for that frame.

The second sort of error is a damaged acknowledgement. Consider the following situation. Station A sends a frame. The frame is received correctly by station B, which responds with an acknowledgement (ACK). The ACK is damaged in transit and is not recognizable by A, which will therefore time out and resend the same frame. This duplicate frame arrives and is accepted by B. B has therefore accepted two copies of the same frame as if they were separate. To avoid this problem, frames are alternately labeled with 0 or 1, and positive acknowledgements are of the form ACK0 and ACK1. In keeping with the sliding-window convention, an ACK0 acknowledges receipt of a frame numbered 1 and indicated that the receiver is ready for a frame numbered 0.

Figure 5.5 gives an example of the use of stop-and-wait ARQ, showing the transmission of a sequence of frames from source A to destination B. The figure shows the two types of errors just described. The third frame transmitted by A is lost or damaged and therefore no ACK is returned by B. A times out and retransmits the frame. Later, A transmits a frame labeled 1 but the ACKO for that frame is lost. A times out and retransmits the same frame. When B receives two frames in a row with the same label, it discards the second frame but sends back an ACKO to each.

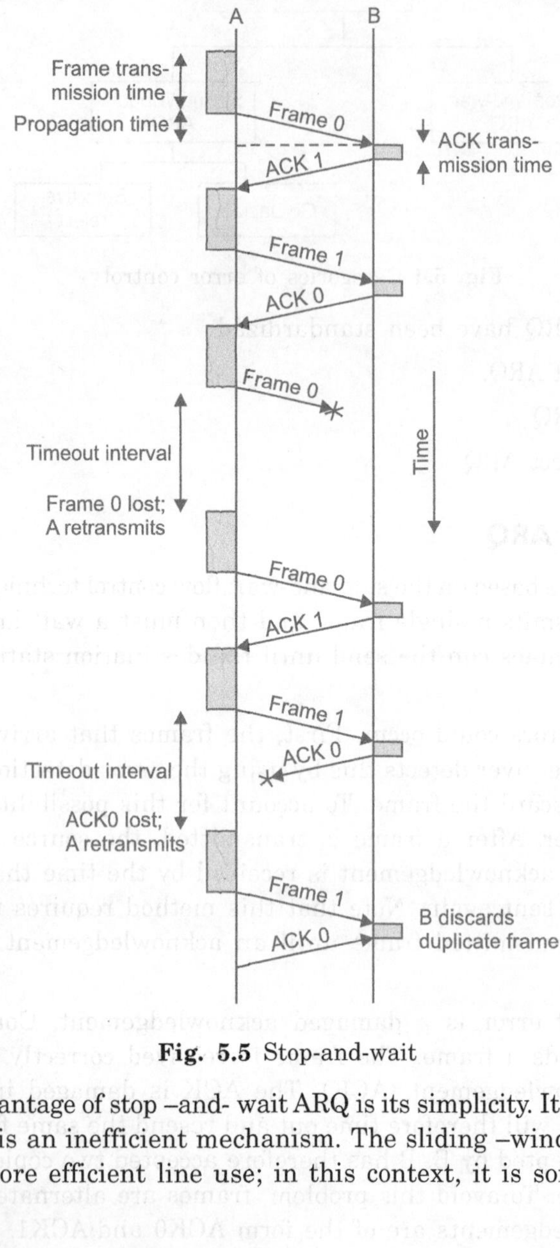

Fig. 5.5 Stop-and-wait

The principal advantage of stop –and- wait ARQ is its simplicity. Its principal disadvantage is that stop-and-wait is an inefficient mechanism. The sliding –window flow control can be adapted to provide more efficient line use; in this context, it is sometimes referred to as continuous ARQ.

5.3.2 Go-Back-N ARQ

The form of error control based on sliding window flow control that is most commonly used is called Go-Back-N ARQ. In this method, a station may send a series of frames sequentially numbered modulo some maximum value. The number of unacknowledged frames outstanding is determined by window size, using the sliding-window flow control technique. While no errors occur, the destination will acknowledge incoming frame as usual (RR = receive ready, or piggybacked acknowledgement). If the destination station detects an error in a frame, it may send a negative acknowledgement (REJ = reject) for that frame, as explained in the following rules, the destination station will discard that frame and all future incoming frames until the frame in error is correctly received. Thus, the source station, when it receives a REJ, must retransmit the frame in error plus all succeeding frames that were transmitted in interim.

Suppose that station A is sending frames to station B. After each transmission, A sets an acknowledgement timer for the frame just transmitted. Suppose that B has previously successfully received frame $(i - 1)$ and A has just transmitted frame i. the go-back-N technique takes into account the following contingencies:

1. Damaged frame

If the receiver frame is invalid (*i.e.*, B detects an error, or the frame is so damaged that B does not even perceive that it has received a frame), B discards the frame and takes no further action as the result of that frame. There are two sub cases:

(*a*) Within a reasonable period of time, A subsequently sends frame $(i + 1)$. B receives frame $(i + 1)$ out of order and sends a REJ i. A must retransmit frame i and all subsequent frames.

(*b*) A does not soon send additional frames. B receives nothing and returns neither an RR nor a REJ. When A's timer expires, it transmits an RR frame that includes a bit known as the P bit, which is set to 1. B interprets the RR frame with a P bit of 1 as a command that must be acknowledged by sending an RR indicating the next frame that it expects, which is frame i. When A receives the RR, it retransmits frame i. Alternatively, A could just retransmit frame i, when its timer expires.

2. Damaged RR

There are two sub cases:

(*a*) B receives frame i and sends RR $(i + 1)$, which suffers an error in transit. Because acknowledgment are cumulative (*e.g.*, RR 6 means that all frames though 5 are acknowledged), it may be that A will receive a subsequent RR to a subsequent frame and that it will arrive before the timer associated with frame i expires.

(*b*) If A's timer expires, it transmits an RR command as in Case 1b. It sets another timer, called the P-bit timer. If B fails to respond to the RR command, or if its response suffers an error in transit, then A's P-bit timer will expire. At this point, A will try again by issuing a new RR command and restarting the P-bit timer. This procedure is tried for a number of iterations. If A fails to obtain an acknowledgement after some maximum number of attempts, it initiates a reset procedure.

3. Damaged REJ

If a REJ is lost, this is equivalent to Case 1b. Figure 5.6a is an example of the frame flow for go-back-N ARQ. Because of the propagation delay on the line, by the time that an acknowledgement (positive or negative) arrives back at the sending station, it has already sent at least one additional frame beyond the one being acknowledged. In this example, frame 4 is damaged. Frames 5 and 6 are received out of order and are discarded by B. When frame 5 arrives, B immediately sends a REJ 4. When the REJ to frame 4 is received, not only frame 4 but frames 5 and 6 must be retransmitted. Note that the transmitter must keep a copy of all unacknowledged frames.

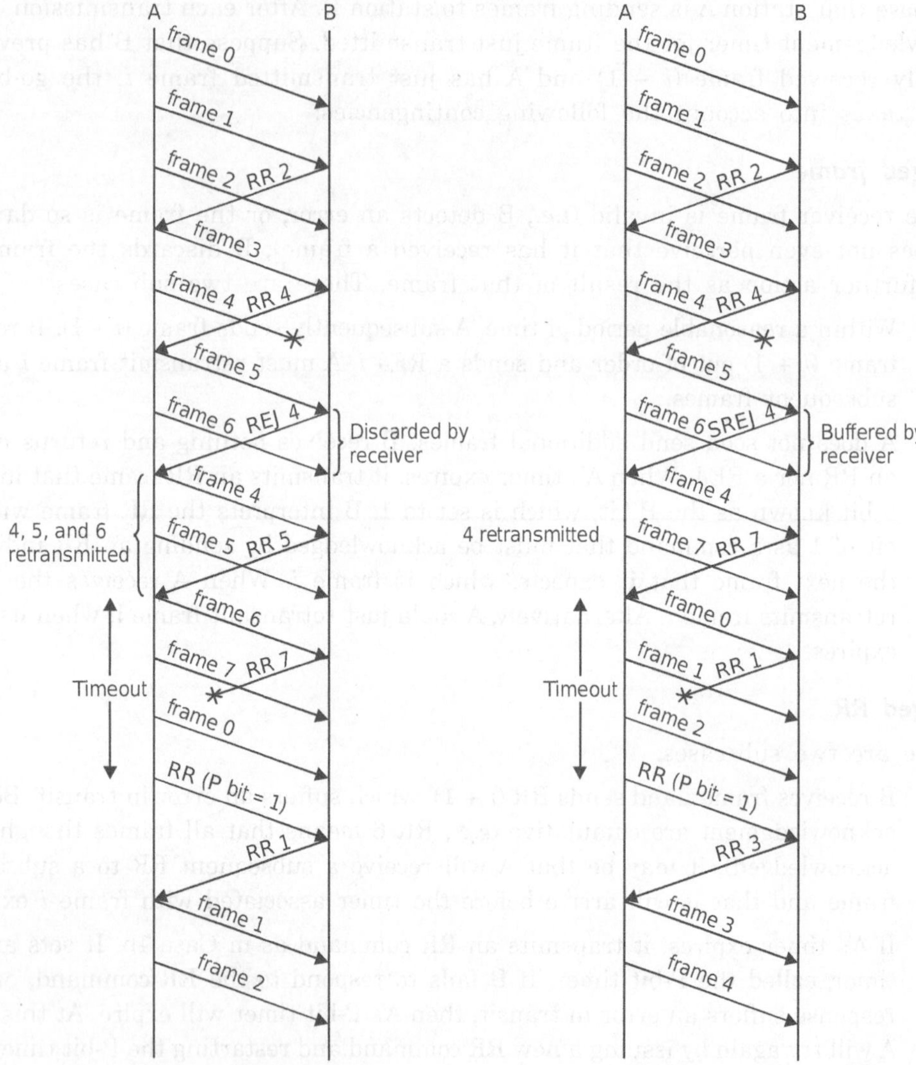

Fig. 5.6 Sliding window ARQ protocols

We mentioned that for a k-bit sequence number field, which provides a sequence number range of $2k$, the maximum window size is limited to $2k - 1$. This has to do with the interaction between error control and acknowledgement. Consider that if data are being exchanged in both directions, station B must send piggybacked acknowledgement to station A's frames in the data frames being transmitted by B, even if the acknowledgement has already been sent. As we have mentioned, this is because B must put some number in the acknowledgement field of its data frame. As an example, assume a 3-bit sequence number (sequence number space = 8). Suppose a station sends frame 0 and gets back an RR 1, and then sends frame 1, 2, 3, 4, 5, 6, 7, 0 and gets another RR 1. This could mean that all eight frames were received correctly and the RR 1 is a cumulative acknowledgement. It could also mean that all eight frames were damaged or lost in transit, and receiving station is repeating its previous RR 1. The problem is avoided if the maximum window size is limited to $7(2^3 - 1)$.

5.3.3 Selective-Reject ARQ

With selective-reject ARQ, the only frames retransmitted are those that receive a negative acknowledgement, in this case called SREJ, or those that time out. Figure 5.6b illustrates this scheme. When frame 5 is received out of order, B sends a SREJ 4, indicating that frame 4 has not been received. However, B continues to accept incoming frames and buffer them until a valid frame 4 is received. At that point, B can place the frames in the proper order for delivery to higher-layer software.

Selective reject would appear to be more efficient than go-back-N, because it minimizes the amount of retransmission. On the other hand, the receiver must maintain a buffer large enough to save post-SREJ frames until the frame in error is retransmitted and must contain logic for reinserting that frame in the proper sequence. The transmitter, too, requires more complex logic to be able to send a frame out of sequence. Because of such complications, select-reject ARQ is much less widely used than go-back-N ARQ. Selective reject is a useful choice for a satellite link because of the long propagation delay involved.

The window size is limitation is more restrictive for selective-reject than for go-back-N, consider the case of a 3-bit sequence number size for selective-reject. Allow a window size of seven, and consider the following scenario [TANE03]:

1. Station A sends frames 0 through 6 to station B.
2. Station B receives all seven frames and cumulatively acknowledges with RR 7.
3. Because of a noise burst, the RR 7 is lost.
4. A times out and retransmits frame 0.
5. B has already advanced it's receive window to accept frame 7, 0, 1, 2, 3, 4 and 5. Thus it assumes that frame 7 has been lost and that this is a new frame 0, which it accepts.

The problem with the foregoing scenario is that there is an overlap between the sending and receiving windows. To overcome the problem, the maximum window size should be no more than half the range of sequence numbers. In the preceding scenario, if only four unacknowledged frames may be outstanding, no confusion can result. In general for a k-bit sequence number field, which provides a sequence number range of 2^k, the maximum window size is limited to 2^{k-1}.

5.4 FLOW CONTROL (TCP WINDOW MANAGEMENT)

Flow control defines the amount of data a source can send before receiving an acknowledgement from the destination. In an extreme case, a transport-layer protocol could send 1 byte of data and wait for an acknowledgement before sending the next byte. But this would be an extremely slow process. If the data are traveling a long distance, the source is idle while it wants for an acknowledgement.

At the other extreme, a transport layer transport-layer protocol can send all the data it has without worrying about acknowledgement. This speeds up the process, but it may overwhelm the receiver. Besides, if some part of the data is lost, duplicated, received out of order, or corrupted, the source will not know until all data have been check by the destination.

TCP has a solution that stands somewhere in between. It defines a window that is imposed on the buffer of the data delivered from the application program and is ready to be sent. TCP sends as many data as are defined by the sliding window protocol.

5.4.1 Sliding Window Protocol

To accomplish flow control, TCP uses a sliding protocol. With this method, both hosts use a window for each connection. The window spans a portion of the buffer containing bytes that a host can send before worrying about an acknowledgement from the other host. The window is called a *sliding window* because it can slide over the buffer as data and acknowledgement are sent and received.

Figure 5.7 shows the sender buffer. However, instead of a circular buffer, we have shown a flat for simplicity. Note that if we connect the two ends of the buffer, we get the circular buffer.

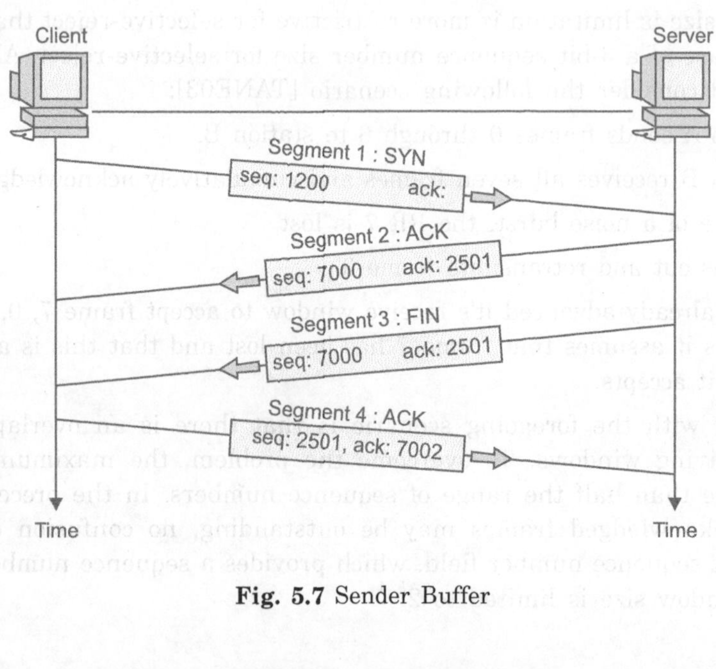

Fig. 5.7 Sender Buffer

In figure 5.8, the bytes before 200 have been sent and acknowledgement. The sender can reuse these locations. Bytes 200 to 202 have been sent, but not acknowledged. The sender has to keep these bytes in the buffer in case they are lost or damaged. Bytes 203 to 211 are in the buffer (produced in the process) but have not yet been sent.

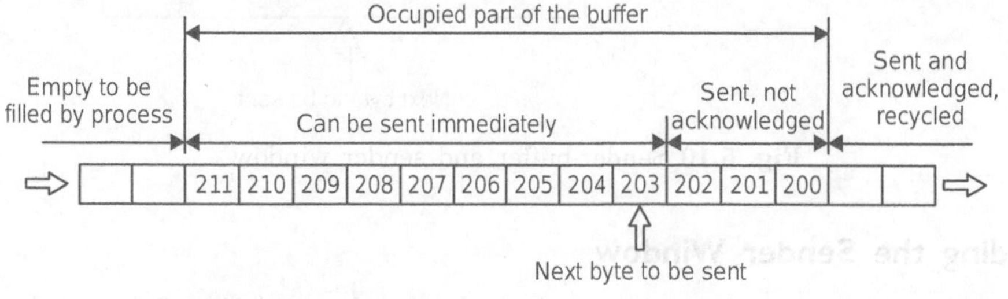

Fig. 5.8 Sender Buffer

Let's examine the situation in which there is no sliding window protocol. In this case, the sender can go ahead and send all the bytes (up to 211) in is buffer, with out regard to the condition of the receiver. The receiver's buffer, with its limited size, could completely fill up because the receiving process is not consuming data fast enough. The excess bytes discarded by the receiver will require retransmission. The sender must adjust it self to the number of location available at the receiver site.

5.4.2 Receiver Window

Figure 5.9 shows the receiver buffer. Note that the next byte to be consumed by the process is byte 194. The receiver expects to receiver byte 200 from the sender (which has been sent but not received). How many more bytes can the receiver store? If the total size of the receiving buffer is N and M locations are already occupied, then only N-M more bytes can be received. This value is called the receiver window. For example, if N=13 and M=6, this means that the value of the receiver window is 7'.

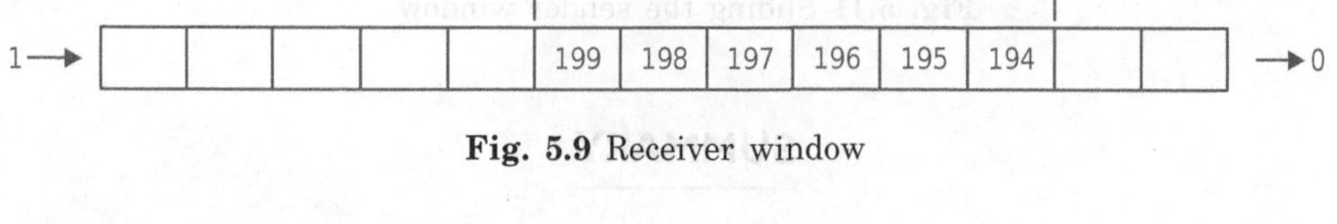

Fig. 5.9 Receiver window

5.4.3 Sender Window

We have flow control if the sender creates a window-the **sender window**-with a size less than or equal to the size of receiver window. This window includes the bytes sent and acknowledged and those that can be sent. Figure 5.10 shows the sender buffer with the sender window.

Note that the size of the sender window is equal to the size of the receiver window (7 in our example). However, this does not mean that the sender can send 7 more bytes; it can send only 4 more bytes because it has already sent 3 bytes.

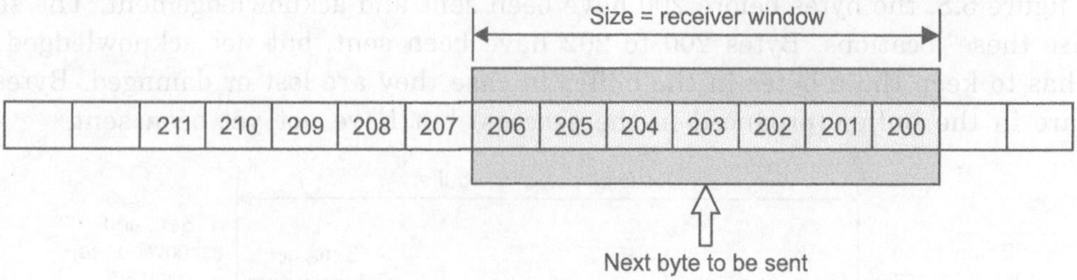

Fig. 5.10 Sender-buffer and sender window

5.4.4 Sliding the Sender Window

Let's see how messages from the receiver change the position of the sender window. In our example, suppose the sender 2 more bytes and an acknowledgement is received from the receiver (expecting byte 203) with no change in the size of the receiver window (still 7). The sender can now slide its window, and the locations occupied by bytes 200 to 202 can be received. Figure 5.11 shows the position of the sender buffer and the sender window before and after this event. In part B of the figure, the sender can now send bytes 205 to 209 (5 more bytes).

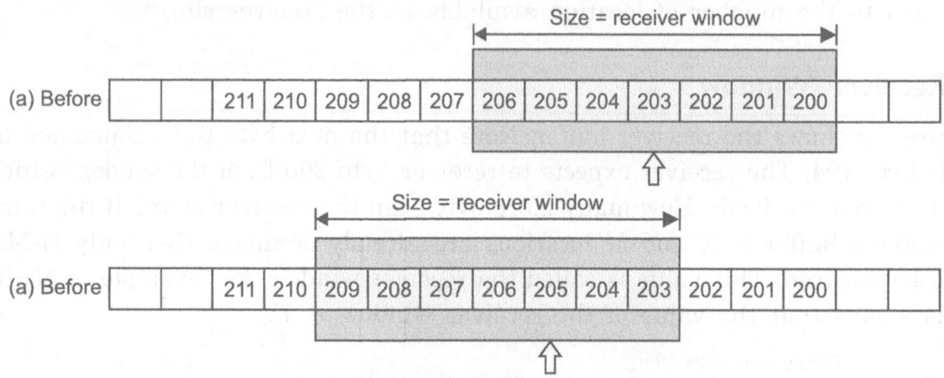

Fig. 5.11 Sliding the sender window

SUMMARY

- In elementary data link control protocols data are transmitted in one direction only.
- It is assumed that, in elementary data link control protocols both the transmitting and receiving network layers are always ready.
- In elementary data link control protocols it is also assumed that the processing time can be ignored and infinite butter space is available.
- The two elementary data link control protocols are:

(*a*) A Simplex Stop And Wait Protocol.

(*b*) A Simplex Protocol for Noisy Channel.

- In Simplex Stop And Wait Protocol it is assumed that a finite processing time is essential.
- In Simplex Protocol for Noisy Channel assume that the communication channel is noisy and can introduce errors in the data traveling over it.
- Simplex Protocol for Noisy Channel is also called as PAR (Positive acknowledgement with retransmission) or automatic repeat request (ARQ).
- ARQ system is useful where the expected errors are bursty in nature or error rate of the channel is low, *i.e.* the channel is fairly reliable.
- The three categories of error control are
  (*a*) Stop and wait ARQ.
  (*b*) Go-back-N ARQ.
  (*c*) Selective- reject ARQ.
- Stop-and-wait ARQ is based on the stop-and-wait flow control technique.
- In Stop-and-wait ARQ the source station transmits a single frame and then must a wait and acknowledgement (ACK).
- In Stop-and-wait ARQ two sorts of the errors could occur. First, the frames that arrive at the destination could be damaged. The second sort of error is a damaged acknowledgement.
- The form of error control based on sliding window flow control that is most commonly used is called Go-Back-N ARQ.
- In Go-Back-N ARQ method, a station may send a series of frames sequentially numbered modulo some maximum value.
- With selective-reject ARQ, the only frames retransmitted are those that receive a negative acknowledgement.
- Flow control defines the amount of data a source can send before receiving an acknowledgement from the destination.
- TCP uses a sliding protocol to accomplish flow control.
- In Sliding Window Protocol Method, both hosts use a window for each connection. The window spans a portion of the buffer containing bytes that a host can send before worrying about an acknowledgement from the other host.
- The window is called a **sliding window** because it can slide over the buffer as data and acknowledgement are sent and received.

EXERCISE

1. Write a short note on elementary data link protocols.
2. What are the various assumptions made in a simplex stop and wait protocol?
3. Explain a simplex protocol for noisy channel
4. Discuss the two modes of operations in which a simplex protocol for noisy channel is divided.
5. What do you mean by the term automatic repeat request (ARQ)? Draw the schematic diagram of Basic ARQ system and explain its operation.

6. Write a short note on the following:
   (*a*) A simplex stop and wait protocol.
   (*b*) A simplex protocol for noisy channel.
7. Explain the different categories of error control.
8. Explain Stop-and-Wait ARQ technique of error control with the help of a suitable diagram.
9. Explain with the help of a suitable diagram Go-Back-N ARQ technique of error control.
10. What are the different categories of error control? Explain any one of them.
11. Write in brief the concept of flow control with reference to TCP window management.
12. Explain the detailed concept of Sliding Window Protocol with the help of a suitable diagram.

Chapter 6

Medium Access Control and LAN

6.1 MEDIUM ACCESS CONTROL (MAC) SUB-LAYER

The role of Medium Access Control (MAC) sub layer is to resolve the contention for the shared media between adjacent nodes. MAC sub layer is lower sub layer of Data link layer. It contains the synchronization, flag flow physical address of next station and error control specifications necessary to move information from one place to another. MAC protocols are specific for each LAN using them (*e.g.*, Token Bus, Token Ring, Ethernet etc.)

- The basic functions of MAC sub layer are the media access control, error detection and station addressing. The physical transmission medium of a LAN is shared by the stations connected on the LAN.
- Media access control procedures are implemented to ensure that every station gets a fair chance to transmit and collision do not take place.
- There are several methods of media access control in LANs. Each method is applicable to specific LAN topology. In addition to the basic access procedures, the MAC layer also handles the frame delimiting, address recognition and error checking functions.

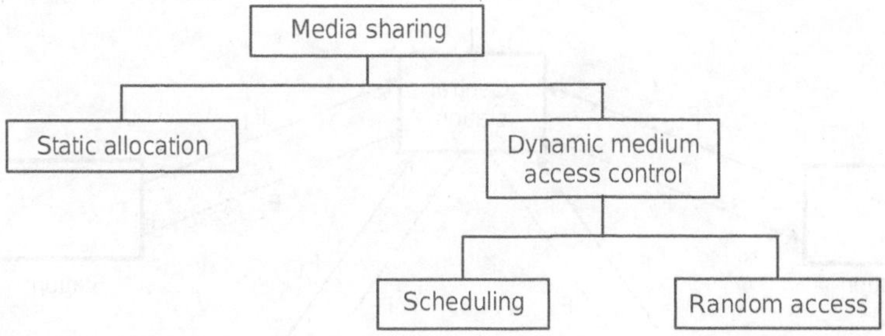

Fig. 6.1 Sharing a transmission medium

- When a number of user stations share a single transmission medium. This is called as *multiple access communication.* The transmission medium is broadcast in nature, so all other attached stations to the medium can receive the transmission from any given station.

- The two basic approaches to medium access control are random access and scheduling. Fig. 6.1 illustrates the various approaches to sharing a transmission medium.

6.2 ALOHA

Basics

As the name suggests, the ALOHA random access scheme had its origins in the Hawaiian Islands. The University of Hawaii needed a means to interconnect terminals at causes located on different islands to the host computer on the main campus. The solution is brilliant in its simplicity. A radio transmitter is attached to the terminals, and messages are transmitted as soon as they become available, thus producing the smallest possible delay. From time to time, frame transmission will collide, but these can be treated as transmission errors, and recovery can take place by retransmission. When traffic is very light, the probability of collision is very small, and so retransmissions need to be carried out infrequently. Consequently, under light traffic the frame transfer delay will be low.

The ALOHA system has two Versions:

1. Pure ALOHA—does not require global time synchronization.
2. Slotted ALOHA—requires time synchronization.

6.2.1 Pure ALOHA

- A station can transmit whenever they have data to send. To determine whether a transmission was successful, a sender waits for an acknowledgement from the receiver for a time period. If no acknowledgement is received, the message will be sent again.

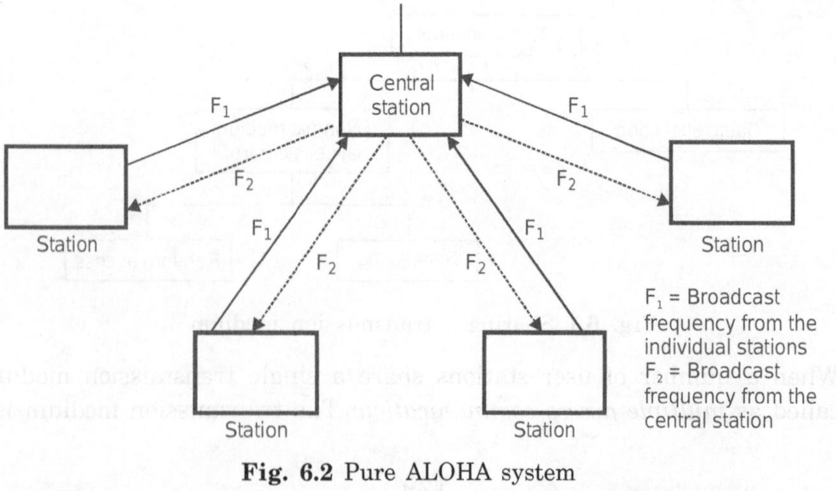

Fig. 6.2 Pure ALOHA system

- Collisions are easily detected, as shown in Fig. 6.2. When the central station receives a frame it sends and acknowledgement on a different frequency.
- If a user station receives an acknowledgement it assumes that the transmitted frame was successfully received and if it does get an acknowledgement it assumes that collision had occurred and is ready to retransmit.
- The advantage of pure ALOHA is its simplicity in implementation but its performance becomes worse as the data traffic on the channel increases.
- If a station starts to transmit when another transmission is already in progress, collisions will occur. A mechanism to detect the collision is established. Messages are sent in the form of packets. Each packet contains parity bits for error detection.
- Let all the packets have the same length. And each requires one time unit for transmission (t_p). Consider any user to send packet A at time t_o. If any other user B has generated a packet between time t_o and $t_o + t_p$, the end of packet B will collide with the beginning of packet A. Since in pure ALOHA packet, a station does not listen to the channel before transmitting, it has no way of knowing that above frame was already under way.
- Fig. 6.3 shows vulnerable periods during which packets can collide.

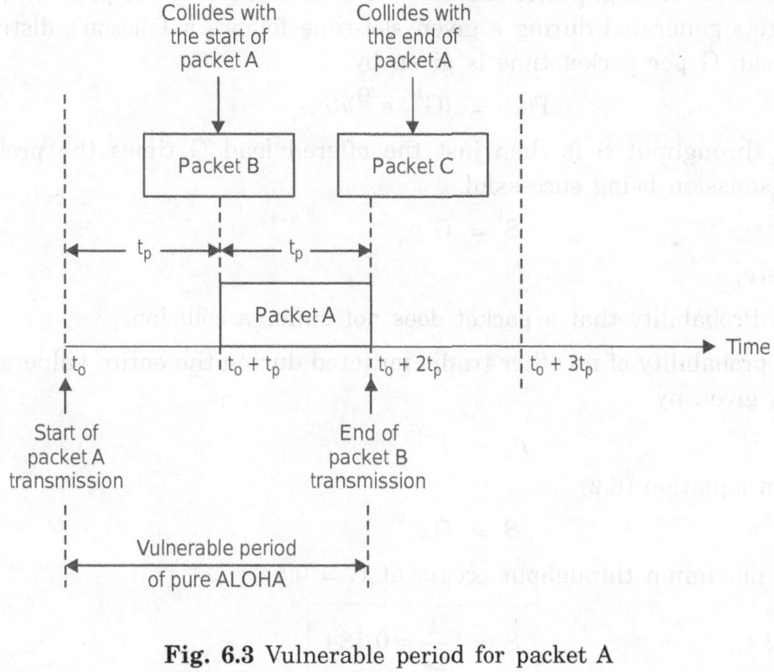

Fig. 6.3 Vulnerable period for packet A

- Similarly if another user wants to transmit between $(t_o + t_p)$ and $(t_o + 2t_p)$ *i.e.*, packet C, the beginning of packet C will collide with the end of packet A. Thus if two packets overlap by even the smallest amount in the vulnerable period both packets will be corrupted and need to be retransmitted.

Throughput of pure ALOHA channel

1. *Throughput*

- The throughput S is defined as average successful traffic transmitted between stations per unit time. The unit of time is slot-time, which is the time required to transmit a frame.
- Assuming all packets or frames is of same size. Since only one packet per slot can be transmitted, the maximum value of S is 1. When collision occurs, some of the packets are lost and part of available channel time is wasted. The resulting value of S is less than 1.

2. *Offered traffic*

- The offered traffic is the average number of packets per slot time which are presented to the network for transmissions by users. It is denoted by G. The throughput is expressed in terms of offered load or traffic G. Practically G can have any value between 0 to infinity.

3. *Channel capacity*

- The maximum achievable throughput for a particular type of access scheme is called the *capacity of the channel.*
- To find the throughput of channel, let us assume that the probability (p_k) that k packets generated during a given slot-time follows a Poisson's distribution with a mean G per packet time is given by

$$P(k) = (G^k \cdot e^{-G})/(k!) \qquad ...(6.1)$$

The throughput S is then just the offered load G times the probability of a transmission being successful.

$$S = G\,p_o \qquad ...(6.2)$$

Where,

p_o = Probability that a packet does not suffer a collision.

The probability of no other traffic initiated during the entire vulnerable period is thus given by

$$p_o = e^{-2G} \qquad ...(6.3)$$

From equation (6.2)

$$S = G.e^{-2G} \qquad ...(6.4)$$

The maximum throughput occurs at G = 0.5,

i.e.,

$$\boxed{S = \frac{1}{2e} = 0.184}$$

- This means that the best channel utilization that can be achieved is around 18% for pure ALOHA method.
- The advantage of pure Aloha protocol is its simplicity, which can result in low cost user stations no synchronization is required between stations in the system. Each

station transmits a packet whenever its buffer has one. The disadvantage is somewhat inefficient channel utilization *i.e.*, maximum channel utilization is only 18.4% of the available capacity.

6.2.2 Slotted ALOHA

- In slotted ALOHA, the channel time is divided into time slots and the stations are allowed to transmit at specific instance of time. These time slots are exactly equal to the packet transmission time. All users are then synchronized to these time slots, so that whenever a user generates a packet it must synchronize exactly with the next possible channel slot. Consequently the wasted time due to collisions can be reduced to one packet time or vulnerable period is reduced to half.
- Transmission attempts for four network user and random retransmission delays for colliding packets in slotted ALOHA is shown in Fig. 6.4.

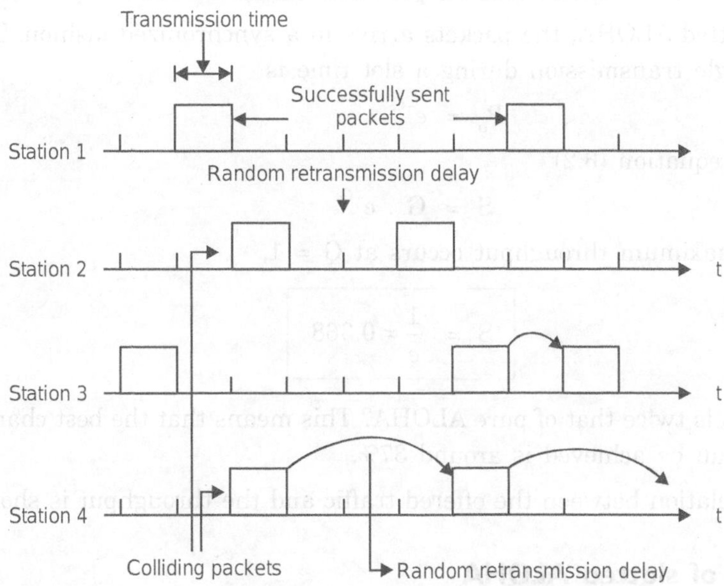

Fig. 6.4 Transmission attempts and random retransmission delays for colliding packets in slotted ALOHA

Assumptions

1. All frames are of same size.
2. Time is divided into equal sized slots; a slot equals the time to transmit one frame.
3. Nodes start to transmit frames only at beginning of slots.
4. Nodes are synchronized.
5. If two or more nodes transmit in a slot, all nodes detect collision before the slot ends.

Throughput of slotted ALOHA channel

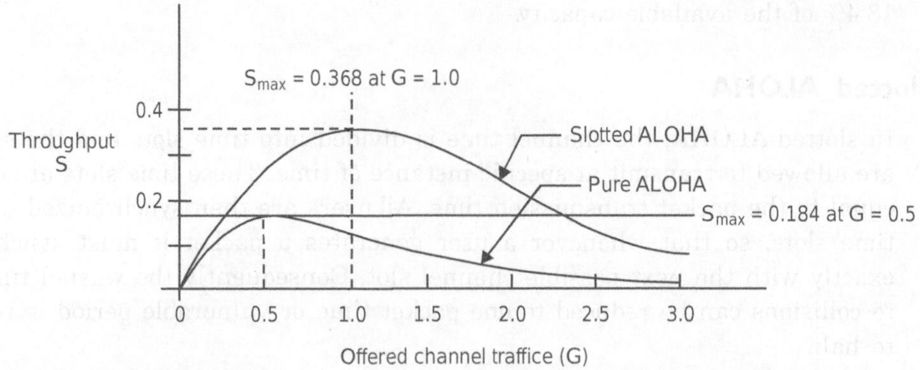

Fig. 6.5 Comparison of the throughput as a function of Offered load for pure and slotted ALOHA

- In slotted ALOHA, the packets arrive in a synchronized fashion. The probability of single transmission during a slot time is

$$P_o = e^{-G} \quad \text{...(6.5)}$$

From equation (6.2)

$$S = G \cdot e^{-G} \quad \text{...(6.6)}$$

The maximum throughput occurs at G = 1,

$$\boxed{S = \frac{1}{e} = 0.368}$$

Which is twice that of pure ALOHA? This means that the best channel utilization that can be achieved is around 37%.

- The relation between the offered traffic and the throughput is shown in Fig. 6.5.

Pros and Cons of slotted ALOHA

Pros

1. Single active node can continuously transmit at full rate of channel.
2. Highly decentralized, each node independently decides when to retransmit.
3. Simple to implement.

Cons

1. Collisions waste slots.
2. Idle slots.

Example 6.1. *Given that radio system uses a 9600 bps channel for call setup request messages to a base station. Suppose that frames are 120 bits long. What is the maximum throughput possible with ALOHA and with slotted ALOHA?*

Solution. The system transmits frames at a rate of 9600 bits/second 1 frame/120 bits = 80 frames/second. The maximum throughput for ALOHA is then 80(0.184) 15 frames/second. The maximum throughput for slotted ALOHA is then frames/second.

Example 6.2. *Calculate the throughput S for a pure ALOHA network if the offered traffic G is 0.75.*

Solution. For pure ALOHA, throughput S is given by

$$S = G.\ e^{-2G}$$

$$S = 0.75 * e^{-2 * 0.75} = 0.1673$$

Or $$S = 16.73\%$$

Example 6.3. *A slotted ALOHA channel has an average 10% of the slots idle.*

(a) What is the offered traffic G?

(b) What is the throughput?

(c) Is the channel overloaded or under loaded?

Solution. For slotted ALOHA channel,

(*a*) Probability of single transmission during a slot time is = e^{-G}.

$$10\% = e^{-G}$$

$$0.1 = e^{-G}$$

$$-G = -2.3$$

$$G = 2.3$$

(*b*) $$S = G * e^{-G}$$

$$= 2.3 * e^{-(2.3)}$$

$$= 0.23$$

(*c*) For slotted ALOHA, S is maximum at G = 1.

Here $$G = 2.3 \text{ and}$$

$$S = 0.23$$

It is beyond G = 1, hence it is **overloaded.**

6.3 CARRIER SENSE MULTIPLE ACCESS

(i) Need of Carrier Sense Multiple Access

The low maximum throughput of the ALOHA schemes is due to the wastage of transmission bandwidth because of frame collisions. This wastage can be reduced by avoiding transmissions that are certain to cause collisions. By sensing the medium for the presence of a carrier signal from other stations, a station can determine whether there is an on going transmission. The class of **carrier sensing multiple access (CSMA)** MAC schemes uses this strategy.

In Fig. 6.6, we show how the vulnerable period is determined in a CSMA system. At time t = 0, station A begins transmission at one extreme end of a broadcast medium. As the signal propagates through the medium, stations become aware of the transmission from station A. At time $t - t_{prop}$, the transmission from. Station A reaches the other end of the medium. By this time all station are aware of the transmission from station A. Thus the vulnerable period consists of the propagation delay, and if no other station initiates a transmission during this period, station A will effect capture the channel because no other stations will transmit thereafter.

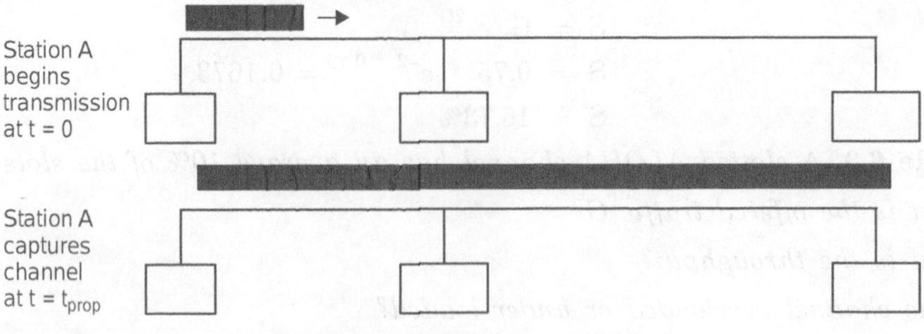

Fig. 6.6 CSMA random access scheme

(ii) 1-Persistent CSMA

CSMA schemes differ according to the behaviour of stations that have a frame to transmit when the channel is busy. In **1-Persistent CSMA**, stations with a frame to transmit sense the channel. If the channel is busy, they sense the channel continuously, waiting until the channel becomes idle. As soon as the channel is sensed idle, they transmit their frames. Consequently if more than one station is waiting, a collision will occur. In addition, stations that have a frame arrive within t_{prop} of the end of the preceding transmission will also transmit and possibly be involved in a collision. Stations that are involved in a collision perform the back off algorithm to schedule a future time for recsensing the channel. In a sense, in 1-Persistent CSMA stations act in a "greedy" fashion, attempting to access the medium as soon as possible. As a result, 1-Persistent CSMA has a relatively high collision rate.

(iii) Non-Persistent CSMA

Non-Persistent CSMA attempts to reduce the incidence of collisions. Stations with a frame to transmit sense the channel. If the channel is busy, the stations immediately run the back off algorithm and reschedule a future resensing time. If the channel is idle, the stations transmit. By immediately rescheduling a resensing time and not persisting, the incidence of collisions is reduced relative to 1-Persistent CSMA. This immediate rescheduling also results in longer delays than are found in 1-Persistent CSMA.

(iv) p-Persistent CSMA

The class of **p-Persistent CSMA** schemes combines elements of the above two schemes. Stations with a frame to transmit sense the channel, and if the channel is busy, they persist with sensing until the channel becomes idle, as shown in figure 6.7. If the channel is idle, the following occurs with probability p, the station transmits its frame, with probability (1 – p) the station decides to wait an additional propagation delay t_{prop} before again sensing the channel. This behavior is intended to spread out the transmission attempts by the stations that have been waiting for a transmission to be completed and hence to increase the likelihood that a waiting station successfully seizes the medium.

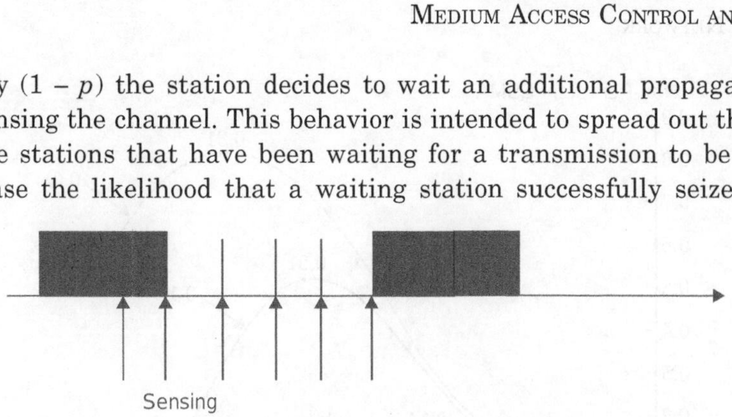

Fig. 6.7 p-Persistent CSMA random access scheme

(v) Throughput S versus Load G

All of the variation of CSMA is sensitive to the end-to-end propagation delay of the medium that constitutes the vulnerable period. An analysis of the throughput S versus load G for CSMA is beyond the scope of this text. Figure 6.8 shows the throughput S versus load G for 1-Persistent and Non-Persistent CSMA for three values of a. It can be seen that the throughput of 1-Persistent CSMA drops off much sharply with increased G. It can also be seen that the normalized propagation delay $a = t_{prop}/X$ has a significant impact on the maximum achievable throughput. Non-Persistent CSMA achieves a higher throughput than 1-Persistant CSMA does over a broader range of load values G. For very small values of a, Non-Persistent CSMA has a relatively high maximum achievable throughput. However, as an approaches 1, both 1-Persistent and Non-Persistent CSMA have maximum achievable throughputs that are even lower than the ALOHA schemes.

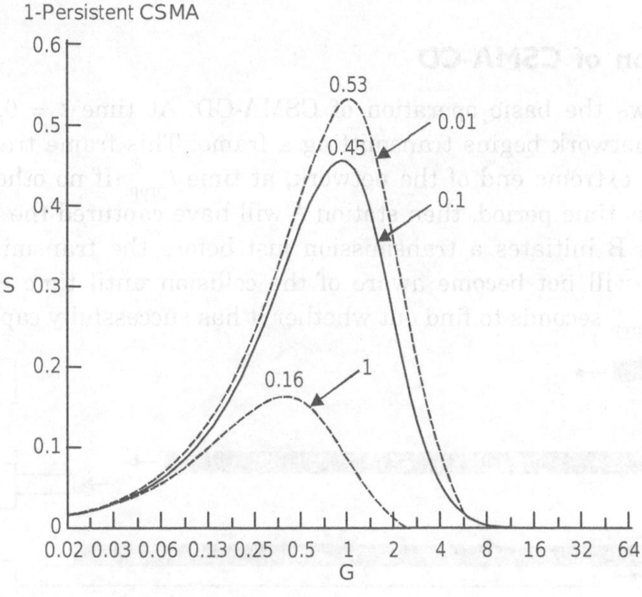

Fig. 6.8(a)

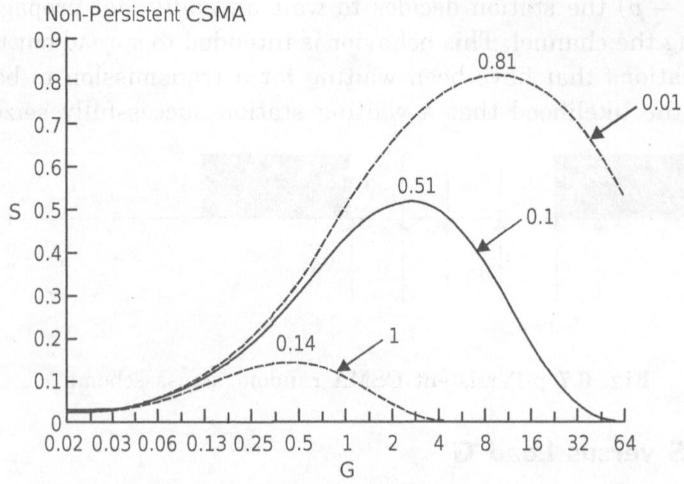

Fig. 6.8(b)

6.4 CARRIER SENSE MULTIPLE ACCESS WITH COLLISION DETECTION

(i) Basics

The CSMA schemes improve over the ALOHA schemes by reducing the vulnerable period from one or two-frame transmission times to a single propagation delay t_{prop}. In both ALOHA and CSMA schemes, collisions involve entire frame transmissions. If a station can determine whether a collision is taking place, then the amount of wasted bandwidth can be reduced by aborting the transmission when a collision is detected. The **carrier sensing multiple access with collision detection (CSMA-CD)** schemes use this approach.

(ii) Basic Operation of CSMA-CD

Figure 6.9 shows the basic operation of CSMA-CD. At time $t = 0$, station A at one extreme end of the network begins transmitting a frame. This frame transmission reaches station B at another extreme end of the network, at time $t_{prop.}$ If no other station initiates a transmission in this time period, then station A will have captured the channel. However, suppose that station B initiates a transmission just before the transmission arrival from station A. Station A will not become aware of the collision until time = $2t_{prop}$. Therefore, station A requires $2t_{prop}$ seconds to find out whether it has successfully captured the channel.

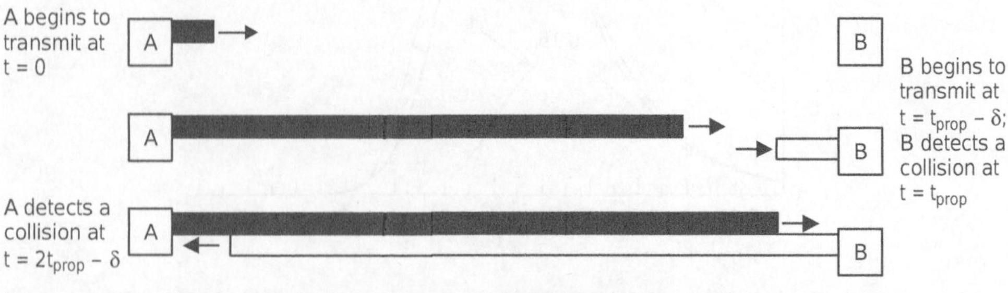

Fig. 6.9 In CSMA-CD, it takes $2t_{prop}$ (the reaction time) to find out whether the channel has been captured

In CSMA-CD a station with a frame first senses the channel and transmits if the channel is idle. If the channel is busy, the station uses one of the possible strategies from CSMA; *i.e.*, the station can persist, back off immediately, or persist and attempt transmission with probability p. If a collision is detected during transmission, then a short jamming signal is transmitted to ensure that other stations know that collision has occurred before aborting the transmission, and the back off algorithm is used to schedule a future resensing time.

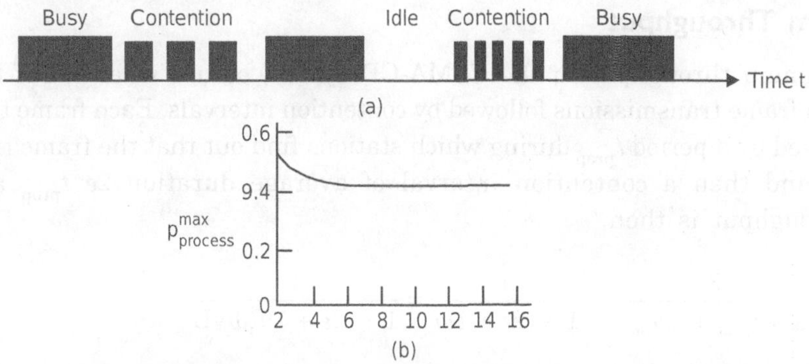

Fig. 6.10 Frame transmission times and contention periods

(iii) Three States of the Channel

As shown in figure 6.10, the channel can be in three states: **busy transmitting frame, idle**, or in a **contention period** where stations attempt of capture the channel. The throughput performance of 1-Persistent CSMA-CD can be analyzed by assuming that time is divided into minislots of length $2t_{prop}$ seconds to ensure that stations can always detect a collision. Each time the channel becomes idle, stations contend for the channel by transmitting and listening to the channel to see if they have successfully captured the channel. Each such contention interval takes $2t_{prop}$ seconds.

Now, let us calculate the mean time required for a station for successfully capture the channel. Let us consider that n stations are contending for the channel and suppose that each station transmits during a contention mini slot with probability p. The probability of a successful transmission is given by the probability that only one station transmits:

$$P_{success} = n\,p\,(1-p)^{n-1} \qquad ...(6.7)$$

Since the probability that a given station transmits and $n - 1$ do not is given by $p\,(1-p)^{n-1}$ and there are n possible ways in which to select the one station the one station that transmits. To find the maximum achievable throughput, assume that stations use the value of p that maximizes $p_{success}$. By taking a derivative of $P_{success}$ with respect to p and setting it to zero, we find that the probability is maximized when $p = 1/n$.

The maximum probability of success is then

$$P^{max}_{success} = n\,\frac{1}{n}\,(1-1/n)^{n-1} \longrightarrow \frac{1}{e} \qquad ...(6.8)$$

Figure 6.10 (*b*) shows the maximum probability of success rapidly approaches 1/*e* as n increases. if the probability of success in one mini slot is $p_{success}^{max}$, then the average number of mini slots that elapse until a station successfully captures the channel is 1/($p_{success}^{max}$) Assuming a large value if *n*, we have that $p_{success}^{max}$ = 1/*e*, and so the average number of mini slots until a station successfully captures the channel is

$$1/p_{success}^{max} = e = 2.718 \text{ minislots} \qquad ...(6.9)$$

(iv) Maximum Throughput

The maximum throughput in the CSMA-CD system occurs when all of the channel time is spent in frame transmissions followed by contention intervals, Each frame transmission time X is followed by a period t_{prop} during which stations find out that the frame transmission is completed and then a contention interval of average duration 2*e* t_{prop} and, so the maximum throughput is then

$$P_{max} = \frac{X}{X + t_{prop} + 2et_{prop}} = \frac{1}{1 + (2e + 1)a} = \frac{1}{1 + (2e + 1)Rd/vL} \qquad ...(6.10)$$

Where $a = t_{prop}/X$ is the propagation delay normalized to the frame transmission time. The rightmost term in the above expression is in terms of the bit rate of the medium R, the diameter of the medium d, the propagation speed over the medium v, and the frame length L. The expression shows that CSMA. CD can achieve throughputs that are close to 1 when a is much smaller than 1. For example, if a = 0.01, then CSMA-CD has a maximum throughput of 94 percent. The CSMA-CD scheme provides the basis for the Ethernet LAN protocol.

(v) Grater Variability

As the load approaches the maximum throughput in equation (6.10), transfer delay increases as collisions occur more frequently. Also, CSMA-CD does not provide an orderly transfer of frames. The random back off mechanism and the random occurrence of collisions imply that frames need not be transmitted in the order that they arrived. Indeed once a frame is involved in a collision; it is quite possible for other later arrivals to be transferred ahead of it. This behaviour implies that in CSMA-CD frame delays exhibit greater variability than in first-in-first out statistical multiplexers.

(vi) Maximum, Achievable Throughputs of Random Access Schemes

Figure 6.11 shows a comparison of the maximum throughput of the main random access MAC techniques discussed in this section. For small values of a, CSMA-CD has the highest maximum throughput followed by CSMA. As an increases, the maximum throughput of CSMA-CD and **CSMA** decrease since the reaction times are approaching the frame transmission ties. As a approaches 1, the throughput of these schemes become less than that of ALOHA and slotted ALOHA. As indicated before, ALOHA and slotted ALOHA are not sensitive to a since their operation does not depend on the reaction time.

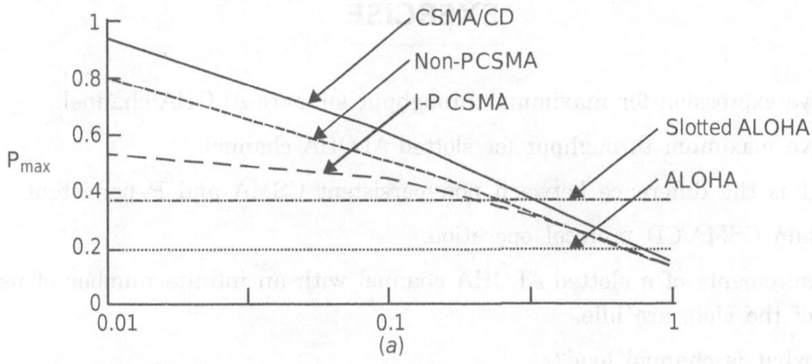

Fig. 6.11 Maximum achievable throughputs of random access schemes

SUMMARY

- The role of Medium Access Control (MAC) sub layer is to resolve the contention for the shared media between adjacent nodes.
- ALOHA are two types, pure ALOHA and slotted ALOHA.
- Pure ALOHA—does not require global time synchronization.
- Slotted ALOHA—requires time synchronization.
- A station can transmit whenever they have data to send. To determine whether a transmission was successful, a sender waits for an acknowledgement from the receiver for a time period. If no acknowledgement is received, the message will be sent again.
- The throughput S is defined as average successful traffic transmitted between stations per unit time. The unit of time is slot-time, which is the time required to transmit a frame.
- The offered traffic is the average number of packets per slot time which are presented to the network for transmissions by users.
- The maximum achievable throughput for a particular type of access scheme is called the **capacity of the channel.**
- In slotted ALOHA, the channel time is divided into time slots and the stations are allowed to transmit at specific instance of time.
- In **1-Persistent CSMA**, stations with a frame to transmit sense the channel.
- **Non-Persistent CSMA** attempts to reduce the incidence of collisions. Stations with a frame to transmit sense the channel.
- The class of **p-Persistent CSMA** schemes combines elements of the**1-Persistent CSMA** and **Non-Persistent CSMA**.
- The CSMA schemes improve over the ALOHA schemes by reducing the vulnerable period from one or two-frame transmission times to a single propagation delay.

EXERCISE

1. Derive expression for maximum throughput for pure ALOHA channel.
2. Derive maximum throughput for slotted ALOHA channel.
3. What is the difference between non–persistent CSMA and P–persistent CSMA?
4. Explain CSMA/CD protocol operation.
5. Measurements of a slotted ALOHA channel with an infinite number of user. Show that 40%of the slots are idle.
   (*i*) what is channel load?
   (*ii*) what is through put?
6. What is CSMA/CD? Explain in brief.
7. Define following terms for a pure ALOHA system
   (*i*) Throughput,
   (*ii*) offered traffic,
   (*iii*) Channel capacity.
8. Consider the delay of pure ALOHA versus slotted ALOHA at low load which one is less? Explain your answer.
9. Compare pure ALOHA and slotted ALOHA.
10. Explain in brief Multiple Access protocol of MAC sub layer.
11. What is the role of MAC?
12. Explain the need of carrier sense multiple access.
13. Write short note on
    (*i*) 1-persistent CSMA
    (*ii*) non-persistent CSMA
    (*iii*) p-persistent CSMA
14. What is the basic operation of CSMA –CD?
15. Explain the three states of the channel. what is the use of back off Algorithm?

Chapter 7

COLLISION FREE PROTOCOLS

7.1 COLLISION FREE PROTOCOL

- Collisions in any system adversely affect the overall system performance. This can be observed especially when the distance between stations is large and the packet length is short. There are some protocols, which can resolve this problem of collision and contention.
- The protocols are

1. A bit-map protocol
2. Binary count down

7.1.1 A Bit-map Protocol

- Let there are N stations each having unique address 0 to N-1 and contention period is equally divided into N slots.
- If station 0 wants to transmit, it will transmit a 1-bit during the zeroth slot. No station is allowed to transmit during this slot. Again if station 3 wants to transmit, a 1-bit during third slot, it has to transmit in contention slot. After passing all N slots, all stations in queue will start transmitting signals.
- Since it is predecided that which station is going to transmit next, there will not be any collision.
- When last station has transmitted its signal another N bit contention period will start. Fig. 7.1 shows the operation of this protocol.

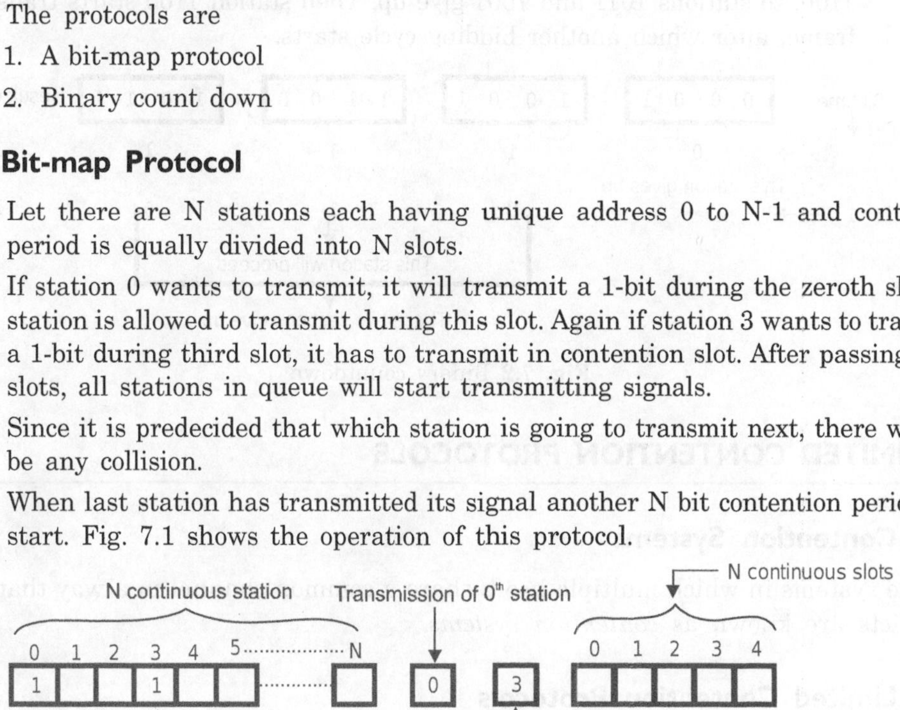

Fig. 7.1 A Bit-map protocol operation

- The station that wants to transmit is broadcast on the channel, before the actual transmission. This protocol is also called as *reservation protocol.*

7.1.2 Binary Countdown

- Binary countdown protocol is used to overcome the overhead 1 bit per station. In binary countdown binary station addresses are used.
- A station wanting to use the channel broadcasts its address as a binary bit string, starting with high-order bit. All addresses are assumed to be of same length.
- Here we will see the example to illustrate the working of binary countdown. In the method different station address are O Red together to decide the priority of transmitting.
- If these stations 0001, 1001, 1100, 1011 all are trying to seize the channel for transmission. The stations at first will broadcast its most significant address bit 0, 1, 1, 1 respectively.
- The most significant bits are O Red together. Station 0001 see the 1 MSB in other station addresses and knows that a higher numbered station is competing for the channel, so it gives for the current round.
- Other three stations 1001, 1100, 1011 will continue. The next bit is 1 at stations 1100, so stations 1011 and 1001 give up. Then station 1100 starts transmitting a frame, after which another bidding cycle starts.

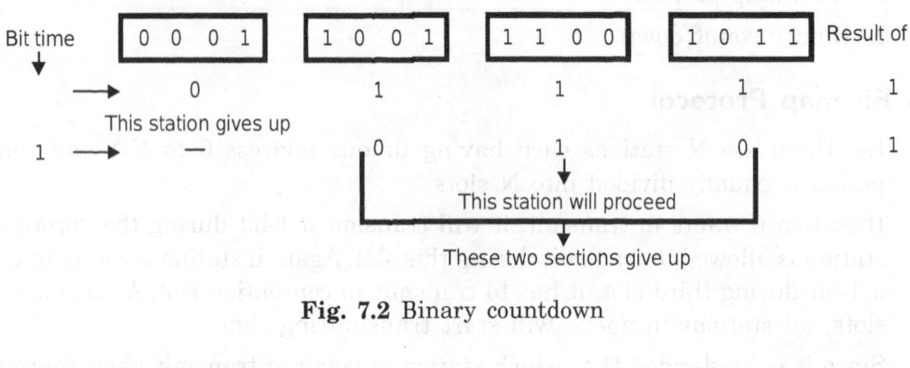

Fig. 7.2 Binary countdown

7.2 LIMITED CONTENTION PROTOCOLS

7.2.1 Contention Systems

The systems in which multiple users share a common channel in a way that can lead to conflicts are known as *contention systems.*

7.2.2 Limited Contention Protocols

The best properties of the contention and collision-free protocols, arriving at a new protocol that used contention at low loads to provide low delay; but used a collision-free technique at high load to provide good channel efficiency. Such protocols are called as *limited contention protocols.*

- Limited contention protocol combines the best properties of the contention and collision free protocol. This protocol uses contention (pure or slotted ALOHA) at low loads to provide low delay and collision free technique (Bit map or binary count down) and at high load to provide good channel efficiency.
- The contention protocols like CSMA/CD are symmetric in nature *i.e.*, each station attempts to acquire the channel with some probability P, with all stations using the same P.
- In case of limited contention protocols the overall performance is improved by assigning different probabilities to different stations.
- Curve for probability for a symmetric contention is shown in Fig. 7.3.

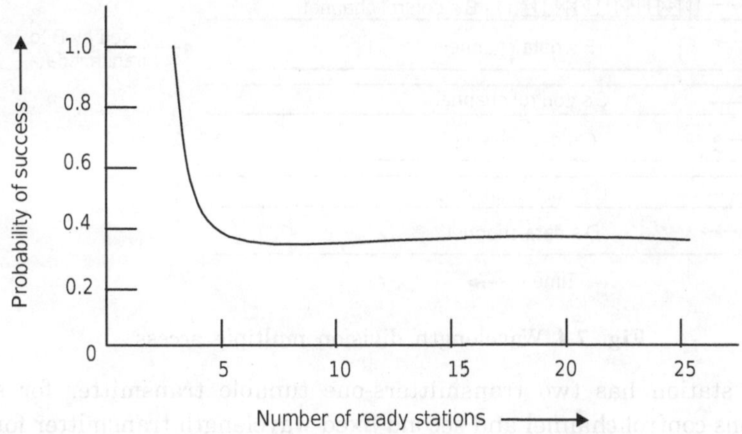

Fig. 7.3 Probability for symmetric contention

- The probability curve shows that for small number of stations, the chances of success are good, but as soon as the number of stations reaches near five the probability drops to asymptotic value of 1/e.
- If amount of competition is decreased probability of acquiring channel is increased. Limited contention protocol works on this principle. The numbers of stations are divided into groups. By making as appropriate divisions into groups, the amount of contention for each slot can be reduced, thus operating each slot near the left hand. The most important thing is assigning stations to slots. This is done by binary count down or bit map protocol technique.

7.3 WDMA (WAVELENGTH DIVISION MULTIPLE ACCESS)

In this protocol, **WDMA (Wavelength Division Multiple Access)**, each station is assigned two channels. A **narrow channel** is provided as a control channel to signal the station, and a **wide channel** is provided so the station can output data frames.

Each channel is divided up into groups of time slots, as depicted in Fig. 7.4. Let us call the number of slots in the control channel m and the number of slots in the data channel n + 1, where n of these are for data and the last one is used by the station to report on its status (mainly, which slots on both channels are free). On both channels, the sequence of slots repeats endlessly, with slot 0 being marked in a special way so latecomers can detect it. All channels are synchronized by a single global clock.

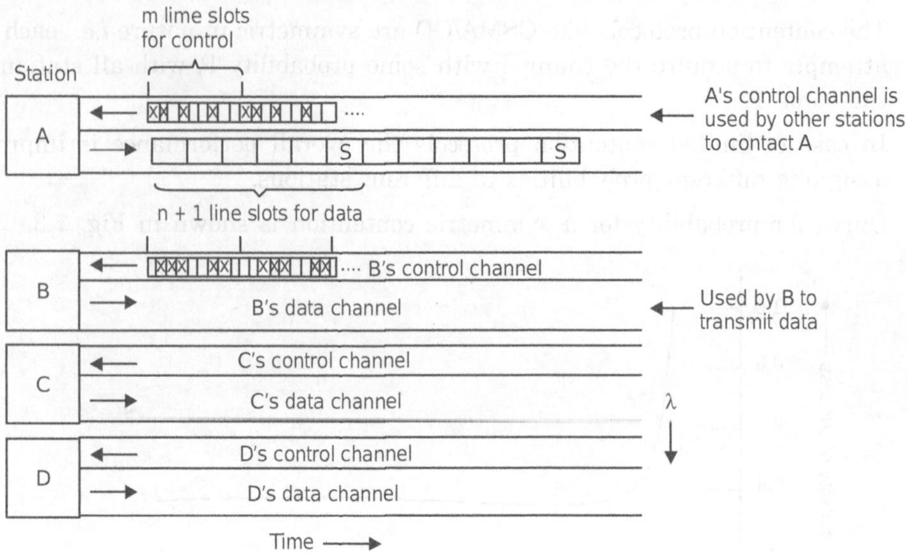

Fig. 7.4 Wavelength division multiple access

- Each station has two transmitters-one tunable transmitter for sending other stations control channel and second fixed-wavelength transmitter for transmitting data, packets or data frames.
- Also each station has two receivers. One tunable receiver for selecting a data transmitter to listen and second fixed wavelength receiver for listening to its own control channel.
- Every station listens to its control channel for incoming request after registering a request that the station has to tune to the remote station (transmitter's) wavelength to receive the data packets. An interferometer is used for wavelength tuning.
- If two different stations try to grab a control slot of the same station, no station will get the channel for data transfer. This will be monitored as failure in the status slot (of control channel) of that common station. Both the stations will have to try again.
- WDMA protocol supports three different classes of traffic.
  1. Constant data rate connection oriented traffic - *e.g.*, uncompressed video signal.
  2. Variable data rate connection oriented traffic - *e.g.*, file transfer
  3. Data gram traffic - *e.g.*, user datagram protocol.
- If station A wants to communicate with station B, station A tunes its data receiver to B's data channel to check for status slot. Status slot tells which control slots are free. Station A picks one of the free slots and a connection request is inserted.

Since station B constantly monitors its control channel, it senses the request and assigns the free slot. This assignment is registered in status slot of control channel. In this way the connection is established.

- WDMA protocols are used in fiber optic LANs, where different conversations at different wavelength takes place simultaneously.

7.4 MACA

It stands for **multiple access with collision avoidance.** MACA protocol is based on IEEE 802.11 wireless standards. The basic idea behind it is, the sender to stimulate the receiver into outputting a short frame. So stations nearby can detect this transmission and avoid transmitting themselves for the duration of upcoming data frames. MACA is illustrated in Fig. 7.5.

Let us consider how A sends a frame to B. A starts by sending an RTS (Request To Send) frame to B, as shown in Fig. 7.5 (*a*). This short frame (30 bytes) contains the length of the data frame that will eventually follow. Then B replies with a CTS (Clear to Send) frame, as shown in Fig.7.5 (*b*). The CTS frame contains the data length (copied from the RTS frame). Upon receipt of the CTS frame, A begins transmission.

Now let us see how stations overhearing either of these frames react. Any station hearing the RTS is clearly close to A and must remain silent long enough for the CTS to be transmitted back to A without conflict. Any station hearing the CTS is clearly close to B and must remain silent during the upcoming data transmission, whose length it can tell by examining the CTS frame.

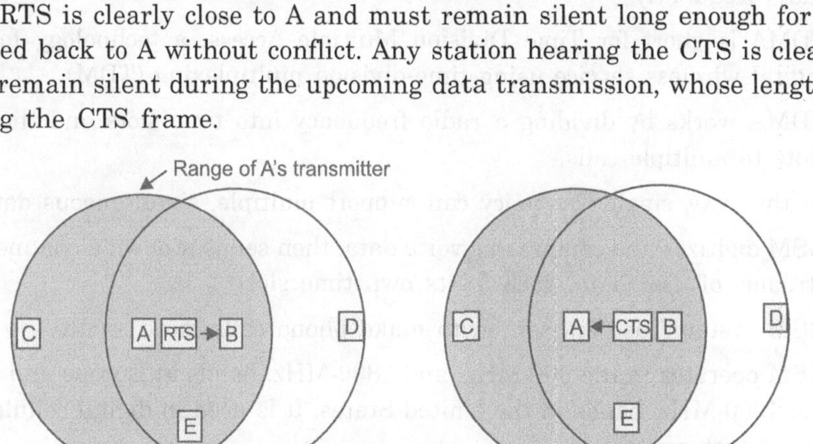

Fig. 7.5 The MACA protocol. (*a*) A sending an RTS to B. (*b*) B responding with a CTS to A

In Fig. 7.5 C is within range of A but not within range of B. Therefore it hears the RTS from A but not the CTS from B. As long as it does not interfere with the CTS, it is free to transmit while the data frame is being sent. In contrast, D is within range of B but not A. It does not hear the RTS but does hear the CTS. Hearing the CTS tips it off that it is close to a station that is about to receive a frame, so it defers from sending anything until that frame is expected to be finished. Station E hears both control messages, and like D, must be silent until the data frame is complete.

7.5 GSM (GLOBAL SYSTEM FOR MOBILE)

- GSM is short for Global System for Mobile communications, which is one of the leading digital cellular systems.
- The GSM standard for digital cell phones was established in Europe in the mid 1980s.
- GSM has now become the international standard in Europe, Australia and much of Asia and Africa.
- In covered areas, cell-phone users can buy one phone that will work anywhere where the standard is supported. To connect to the specific service providers in these different countries, GSM users simply switch subscriber identification module (SIM) cards.
- SIM cards are small removable disks that slip in and out of GSM cell phones. They store all the connection data and identification numbers you need to access a particular wireless service provider.
- Unfortunately, the 1900-MHz GSM phones used in the United States are not compatible with the international system.
- GSM uses narrowband TDMA, which allows eight simultaneous calls on the same radio frequently.
- TDMA is short for Time Division Multiple Access, a technology for delivering digital wireless service using time-division multiplexing (TDM).
- TDMA works by dividing a radio frequency into time slots and then allocating slots to multiple calls.
- In this way, single frequency can support multiple, simultaneous data channels.
- GSM digitizes and compresses voice data, then sends it down a channel with other streams of user data, each in its own time slot.
- GSM systems use encryption to make phone calls more secure.
- GSM operates in the 900-MHz. and 1800-MHz. bands in Europe and Asia, and in the 1900-MHz. bands in the United States. It is used in digital cellular and PCS-based systems.
- GSM is also the basis for Integrated Digital Enhanced Network (IDEN), a popular system introduced by Motorola and used by Nextel.

7.5.1 Uses of GSM

GSM uses narrowband TDMA, which allows eight simultaneous calls on the same radio frequency.

7.5.2 What is a SIM Card?

- The **SIM–Subscriber Identity Module** is a chip card, the size of a first-class postage stamp.

- It is a key element in over 600 million GSM (Global System for Mobile) mobile phones–representing about 70 percent of the mobile handset market.
- A SIM is actually a tiny computer chip that gives a cellular device its unique phone number.
- It has memory (for data and applications), a processor and the ability to interact with the users.
- Current SIMs typically have 16 to 64 Kb of memory, which provides plenty of room for storing hundreds of personal phone numbers, text messages and other data.

7.5.3 Advantages of GSM

GSM (Global System for Mobile) communications is a technique that uses narrowband TDMA, which allows eight simultaneous calls on the same radio frequency. TDMA is short for Time Division Multiple Access.

TDMA technology uses time division multiplexing (TDM) and divides a radio frequency into time slots and then allocates these slots to multiple calls thereby supporting multiple, simultaneous data channels.

A GSM system has up to a maximum of 200 full-duplex channels per cell. Each channel consists of a downlink frequency (from the base station to the mobile stations) and an uplink frequency (from the mobile stations to the base station). Each frequency band is 200 kHz wide as shown in Fig. 7.6.

Each of the 124 frequency channels supports eight separate connections using time division multiplexing. Each currently active station is assigned one time slot on one channel. Theoretically, 992 channels can be supported in each cell, but many of them are not available, to avoid frequency conflicts with neighboring cells. In fig. 7.6, the eight shaded time slots all belong to the same channel, four of them in each direction. If the mobile station assigned to 890.4 /935.4 MHZ and slot 2 wanted to transmit to the base station, it would use the lower four shaded slots (and the ones following them in time), putting some data in each slot until all the data had been sent.

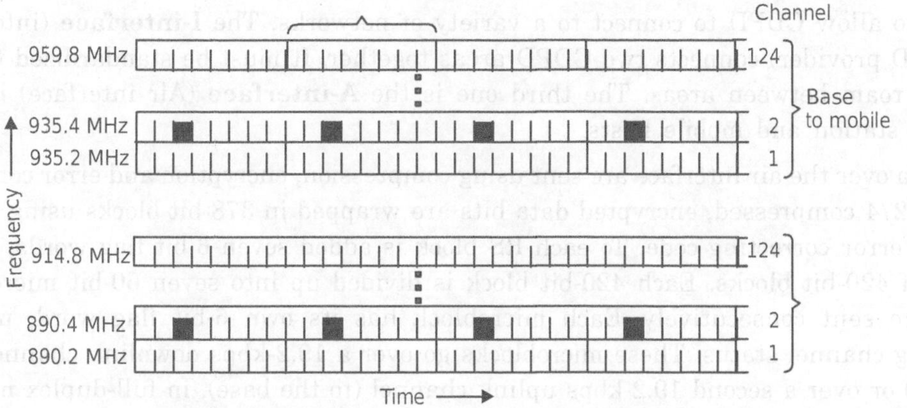

Fig. 7.6 GSM uses 124 frequency channels, each of which use an eight-slot TDM system

The TDM slots shown in Fig. 7.6 are part of a complex framing hierarchy. Each TDM slot has a specific structure, and groups of TDM slots form multiframes, also with a specific structure.

7.6 CDPD (CELLULAR DIGITAL PACKET DATA)

A CDPD system consists of **three kinds of stations: mobile hosts, base stations and base interface station** (in CDPD jargon: mobile end systems, mobile data base systems, and mobile data intermediate systems, respectively). These stations interact with stationary hosts and standard routers, of the kind found in any WAN. The mobile hosts are the users' portable computers. The base stations are the transmitters that talk to the mobile hosts. The base interface stations are special nodes that interface all the base stations in a CDPD provider's area to a standard (fixed) router for further transmission through the Internet or other WAN. This arrangement is shown in Fig. 7.7.

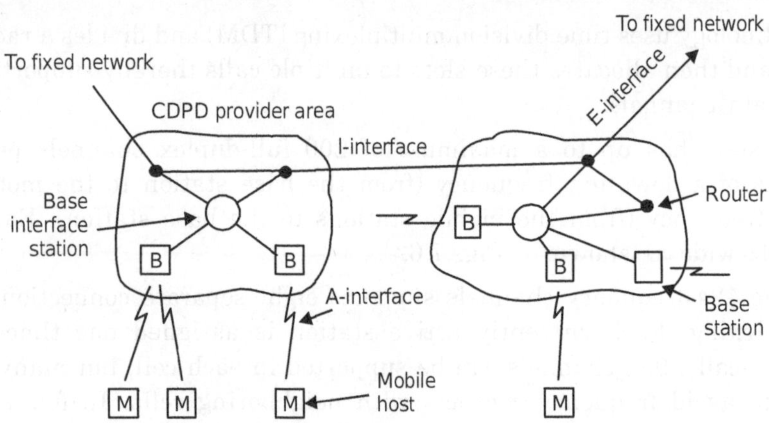

Fig. 7.7 An example CDPD system

Three kinds of interfaces are defined in CDPD. The E-interface (external to the CDPD provider) connects a CDPD area to a fixed network. This interface must be well defined to allow CDPD to connect to a variety of networks. The **I-interface** (internal to the CDPD provider) connects two CDPD areas together. It must be standardized to allow users to roam between areas. The third one is the **A-interface** (Air interface) between the base station and mobile hosts.

Data over the air interface are sent using compression, encryption and error correction. Units of 274 compressed, encrypted data bits are wrapped in 378-bit blocks using a Reed-Solomon error correcting code. To each RS block is added seven 6-bit flag words, to form a total of 420-bit blocks. Each 420-bit block is divided up into seven 60-bit microblocks, which are sent consecutively. Each microblock has its own 6-bit flag word, used for indicating channel status. These microblocks go over a 19.2-kbps downlink channel (from the base) or over a second 19.2-kbps uplink channel (to the base), in full-duplex mode. In effect, both the downlink and uplink channel are slotted in time, as a sequence of 60-bit microblocks. Each microblock lasts for 3.125 msec.

Each CDPD cell has only one downlink/uplink pair available for data. The downlink channel is easy to manage since there is only one sender per cell: the base station. All frames sent on it are broadcast, with each mobile host selecting out those destined for it or for everyone.

The tricky part is the uplink channel, for which all-mobile hosts wishing to send must contend. When a mobile host has a frame to send, it watches the downlink channel for a flag bit telling whether the current uplink slot is busy or idle. If it is busy, instead of just waiting for the next time slot, it skips a random number of slots and tries again. If it again sees that the uplink channel is busy, it waits a longer random time, and repeats the procedure. The statistically average waiting time doubles with each unsuccessful attempt. When it finally finds the channel supposedly idle, it begins transmitting its microblock.

An additional property of CDPD is that data users are second-class citizens. When a new voice call is about to be assigned to a channel currently in use for CDPD, the base station sends a special signal on the downlink, closing down the channel. If the base station already knows the number of the new CDPD channel, it announces it. Otherwise, mobile hosts have to hunt around among a designated set of potential CDPD channels to find it. In this way, CDPD can suck up any idle capacity in a cell, without interfering with the big cash cow, voice.

It should be clear from this description that CDPD was added to the voice system after the latter was already operational, and that its design was subject to the constraint that no changes could be made to the existing voice system. Consequently, when channel selection for voice calls occurs, the algorithm is not aware of the existence of CDPD. This is the reason that the CDPD channel is sometimes suddenly preempted. However, nothing in the design prevents having dedicated CDPD channels. As CDPD grows in popularity, providers are likely to reserve channels exclusively for it.

7.7 CDMA (CODE DIVISION MULTIPLE ACCESS)

Basic Principles

CDMA is a multiplexing technique used with spread spectrum. The scheme works in the following manner. We start with a data signal with rate D, which we call the bit data rate. We break each bit into k chips according to a fixed pattern that is specific to each user, called the user's code. The new channel has a chip data rate of kD chips per second. As an illustration we consider a simple example with k = 6. It is simplest to characterize a code as a sequence of 1s and -1s. Figure 7.8 shows the codes for three users A, B and C, each of which is communicating with the same base station receiver, R. Thus, the code for user A is c_A = {1, -1, -1, 1, -1, 1}. Similarly, user B has code c_B = {1, 1, -1, -1, 1, 1}, and user C has c_C = {1, 1, -1, 1, 1, -1}.

We now consider the case of user A communicating with the base station. The base station is assumed to know A's code. For simplicity, we assume that communication is already synchronized so that the base station knows when to look for codes. If A wants to send a 1 bit, A transmits its code as a chip pattern {1, -1, -1, 1, -1, 1}. If a

0 bit is to be sent, A transmits the complement (1s and -1s reversed} of its code, {-1, 1, 1, -1, 1, -1}. At the base station the receiver decodes the chip patterns. In our simple version, if the receiver R receives chip pattern d = {d1, d2, d3, d4, d5, d6}, and the receiver is seeking to communicate with a user u so that it has at hand u's code, {c1, c2, c3, c4, c5, c6}, the receiver performs electronically the following decoding function:

Su (d) = d1*c1 + d2*c2 + d3*c3 + d4*c4 + d5*c5 + d6*c6

The subscript u on S simply indicates that u is the user that we are interested in. Let's suppose the user u is actually A and see what happens. If A sends a 1 bit, then d is {1, -1, -1, 1, -1, 1} and the preceding computation using S_A becomes

S_A {1, -1, -1, 1, -1, 1} = 1*1 + (-1) *(-1) + (-1) *(-1) + 1 *1 + (-1) *(-1) + 1 *1 = 6

If A sends a 0 bit that corresponds to d = {-1, 1, 1, -1, 1, -1}, we get

S_A{-1, 1, 1, -1, 1, -1} = (-1)*1+1 *(-1) + 1 * (-1) + (-1) * 1 + 1 *(-1) + (-1) *1 = –6

Please note that it is always the case that $-6 < S_A(d) < 6$ no matter what sequence of -1s and 1s that d is, and that the only d's resulting in the extreme values of 6 and -6 are A's code and its complement, respectively. So if S_A produces a + 6, we say that we have received a 1 bit from A; if S_A produces a - 6, we say that we have received a 0 bit from user A; otherwise, we assume that someone else is sending information or there is an error. So why go through all this? The reason becomes clear if we see what happens if user B is sending and we try to receive it with S_A, that is, we are decoding with the wrong code, A's. If B sends a 1 bit, then d = {1, 1, -1, -1, 1, 1,}. Then

S_A{1, 1, -1, -1, 1, 1} = 1 *1 + 1 *(-1) + (-1) *(-1) + (-1) *1 + 1 *(-1) + 1 *1 =0

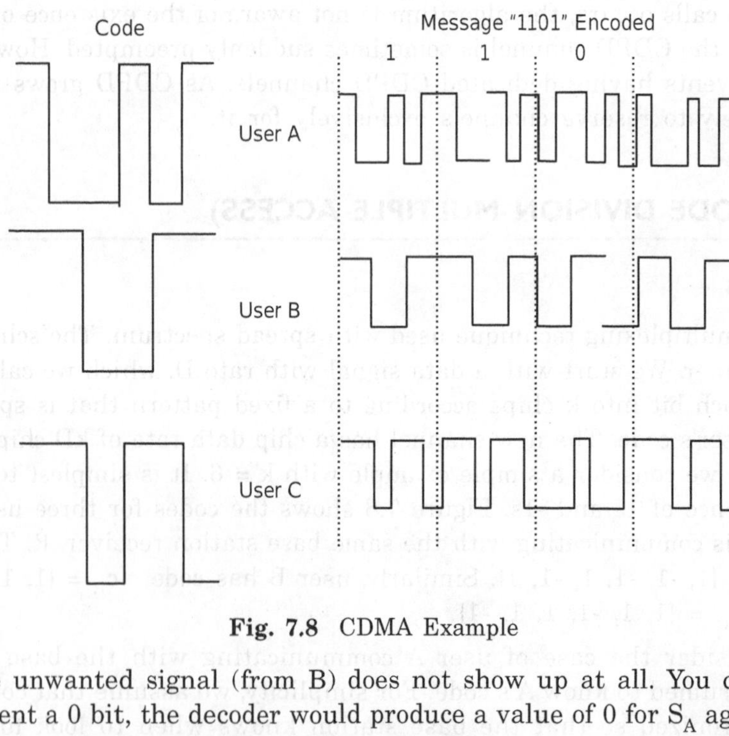

Fig. 7.8 CDMA Example

Thus, the unwanted signal (from B) does not show up at all. You can easily verify that if B had sent a 0 bit, the decoder would produce a value of 0 for S_A again. This means that if the decoder is linear and if A and B transmit signals s_A and s_B, respectively, at the same time, then $S_A(s_A + s_B) = S_A(s_A) + S_A(s_B) = S_A(s_A)$ since the decoder ignores B when it is using A's code. The codes of A and B that have the property that $S_A(c_B) = S_B(c_A) = 0$ are called orthogonal. Such codes are very nice to have but there are not all that many of them. More common is the case when $S_X(c_Y)$ is small in absolute value when $X\ ^1Y$. Then it is easy to distinguish between the two cases when X = Y and $X\ ^1\ Y$. In our examples $S_A(c_C) = S_C(c_A) = 0$, but $S_B(c_C) = S_C(c_B) = 2$. In the latter case the C signal would make a small contribution to the decoded signal instead of 0. Using the decoder, S_u, the receiver can sort out transmission from u even when there may be other users broadcasting in the same cell. Table 7.1 summarizes the example from the preceding discussion.

Table 7.1 CDMA Example

(a) User's codes

User A	1	–1	–1	1	–1	1
User B	1	1	–1	–1	1	1
User C	1	1	–1	1	1	–1

(b) Transmission from A

Transmit (data bit = 1)	1	–1	–1	1	–1	1	
Receiver codeword	1	–1	–1	1	–1	1	
Multiplication	1	1	1	1	1	1	= 6
Transmit (data bit = 0)	–1	1	1	–1	1	–1	
Receiver codeword	1	–1	–1	1	–1	1	
Multiplication	–1	–1	–1	–1	–1	–1	= –6

(c) Transmission from B, receiver attempts to recover A's transmission

Transmit (data bit = 1)	1	1	–1	–1	1	1	
Receiver codeword	1	–1	–1	1	–1	1	
Multiplication	1	–1	1	–1	–1	1	= 0

(d) Transmission from C, receiver attempts to recover B's transmission

Transmit (data bit = 1)	1	1	–1	1	1	–1	
Receiver codeword	1	1	–1	–1	1	1	
Multiplication	1	1	1	–1	1	–1	= 2

(e) Transmission from B and C, receiver attempts to recover B's transmission

B (data bit = 1)	1	1	–1	–1	1	1	
C (data bit = 1)	1	1	–1	1	1	–1	
Combined signal	2	2	–2	0	2	0	
Receiver codeword	1	1	–1	–1	1	1	
Multiplication	2	2	2	0	2	0	= 8

7.7.1 Uses of CDMA

- CDMA (Code Division Multiple Access) uses a spread-spectrum technique where data is sent-in small pieces over a number of discrete frequencies available for use.
- Each user's signal is spread over the entire bandwidth by unique spreading code.
- At the receiver end, the same unique code is used to recover the signal.

7.7.2 Advantages of CDMA

- CDMA (Code Division Multiple Access) on the other hand, unlike GSM, does not assign a specific frequency to each user.
- CDMA uses spread-spectrum technique where every channel uses full available spectrum with CDMA, data is sent in small pieces over a number of discrete frequencies available for use at any time in the specified range.
- All users transmit in the same wide-band chunk of spectrum. Each user's signal is spread over the entire bandwidth by a unique spreading code.

7.8 IEEE LAN STANDARDS

The Institute of Electrical and Electronics Engineers (IEEE) publish several widely accepted LAN-recommended standards. These standards are very important because they encourage the use of common approaches for LAN protocols and interfaces. As a consequence, chip manufacturers are more willing to spend money to develop relatively inexpensive hardware to sell to (they hope) a large market. The IEEE LAN committees are organized as follows:

IEEE 802.1	High-Level Interface (and MAC Bridges)
IEEE 802.2	Logical Link Control (LLC)
IEEE 802.3	Carrier Sense Multiple Access / Collision Detect (CSMA / CD)
IEEE 802.4	Token Bus
IEEE 802.5	Token Ring
IEEE 802.6	Metropolitan Area Networks
IEEE 802.7	Broadband LANs
IEEE 802.8	Fiber Optic LANs
IEEE 802.9	Integrated Data and Voice Networks
IEEE 802.10	Security
IEEE 802.11	Wireless Networks

The IEEE standard are gaining wide acceptance. The European Computer Manufactures Association (ECMA) voted to accept the 802.5 Token Ring as its Standard (ECMA 89). The

NBS, the ISO and ANSI have accepted these standards, and as we shall see, vendors and users groups are also using them.

In addition to the three basic standards of 802.3, 802.4 and 802.5 the IEEE also publishes the metropolitan area network (MAN) standard under the 802.6 number, standard, which deals with interrogated voice / data network is identified with 802.9. The IEEE also sponsors standards concerning broadband LANs under 802.7, optical fiber LANs under 802.8, and security aspects for LANs under 802.10.

The IEEE 802.1 includes a number of standards. Network management is published in this standard, as well as the 802.1 bridges.

The International Organization for Standardization (ISO) is accepting the 802 standards under ISO 8802. As we shall see, vendors and user groups are also using these standards.

7.9 ETHERNET AND IEEE 802.3 LAN STANDARDS

The Ethernet LAN protocol was developed in the early 1970s by Robert Metcalfe and his colleagues working at Xerox as a means of connecting workstations. In the early 1980s DEC, Inlet, and Xerox completed the "DIX" Ethernet standard for a 10 Mbps LAN based on coaxial cable transmission. This standard formed the basis for the IEEE 802.3 LAN standard that was first issued in 1985 for "thick" coaxial cable. The Ethernet and IEEE 802.3 standards differ primarily in the definition of one header field, which we discuss below. The IEEE 802.3 standard has been revised and expanded every few years. Specifications have been issued for operation using "thin" coaxial cable, twisted-pair wires, and single-mode and multimode optical fiber. Higher-speed versions were approved in 1995 (100 Mbps Fast Ethernet) and in 1998 (1000 Mbps Gigabit Ethernet), and in 2002 (10 Gbps Ethernet).

(i) Basic Concept

Table 7.2 shows the various physical layers that have been defined for use with IEEE 802.3. Each of these medium alternatives is designed by three parameters that specify the bit rate, the transmission technique, and the maximum segment length.

Table 7.2 IEEE 802.2 Mbps medium alternatives

	10 Base 5	*10 Base 2*	*10 Base T*	*10 Base F*
Medium	Thick coax	Thin coax	Twisted pair	Optical fiber
Maximum segment length	500 m	185 m	100 m	2 km
Topology	Bus	Bus	Star	Point-to-point link

(ii) 10 Base 5 Standard

The original standard specified 10 Base 5, which made use of thick (10mm) coaxial cable operating at a data rate of 10 Mbps, *using base band* transmission and with a maximum segment length of 500 meters. The transmission uses Manchester coding. This cabling system required the use of a transceiver to attach the NIC card to the coaxial cable. The thick coaxial cable Ethernet was typically deployed along the ceilings in building hallways, and a connection from a workstation is an office would tap onto the cable as shown in Fig. 7.9 (*a*). Thick coaxial cable is awkward to handle and install.

(iii) 10 Base 2 Standard

The 10 Base 2 standard uses this (5 mm) coaxial cable operating at 10 Mbps and with a maximum segment of 185 meters. The cheaper and easier-to-handle thin coaxial cable makes use of T-shaped BNC junctions as shown in Fig. 7.9 (*b*). 10 Base 5 and 10 Base 2 segments can be combined through the use of a repeater that forwards the signals from one segment to the other.

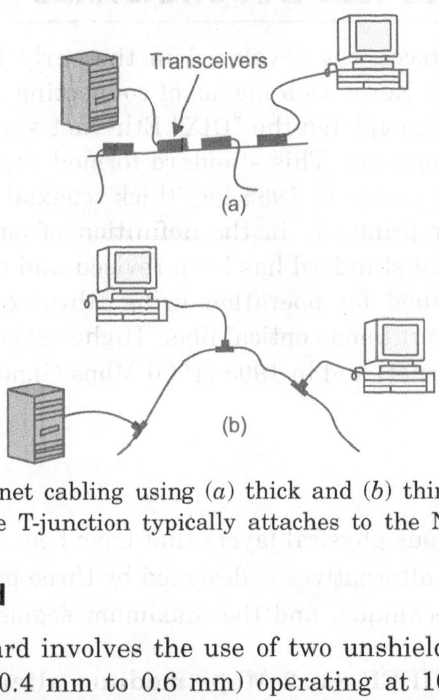

Fig. 7.9 Ethernet cabling using (*a*) thick and (*b*) thin coaxial cable. (The T-junction typically attaches to the NIC)

(iv) 10 Base T Standard

The 10 Base T standard involves the use of two unshielded twisted pairs (UTPs) of copper wires (diameter of 0.4 mm to 0.6 mm) operating at 10 Mbps and connected to a hub as shown in Fig. 7.10(*a*). The T designates the use of twisted pair. The advantage of twisted pair is low cost and its prevalence in existing office wiring where it is used for telephones. Existing wiring arrangements allow the hubs to be placed in telephone wiring closets. The use of 10 Base T standard also involves a move toward a star topology in which the stations connect the twisted pair to a hub where the collisions take place.

(v) 10 Base T Provides Three Approaches

The star topology of 10 Base T provides three approaches to operating the LAN. In all these approaches the stations implement the CDMA-CD protocol.

The difference is the operation of the hub at the center of the star. In the first approach, the hub monitors all transmissions from the stations. When there is only one transmission, the hub repeats the transmission on the other lines. If there is a collision, that is, more than one transmission, then the hub sends a jamming signal to all the stations. This action causes the stations to implement the backoff algorithm. In this approach the stations are said to be into the same **collision domain,** that is, a domain where a collision will occur if two or more stations transmit simultaneously.

A second approach involves operating the hub with an **Ethernet switch,** as shown in Fig. 7.10 (*b*). Ethernet switch is a name commonly used for a product that implements transparent bridging. In a switch, each input port buffers incoming transmissions. The incoming frames are examined and transferred to the appropriate outgoing ports. The incoming frames are examined and transferred to the appropriate outgoing ports. Each output port implements the Ethernet MAC protocol to transmit frames. Collisions will not occur if only a single station is attached to the line. It is example; in this case the group of stations attached to the same line will constitute a collision domain.

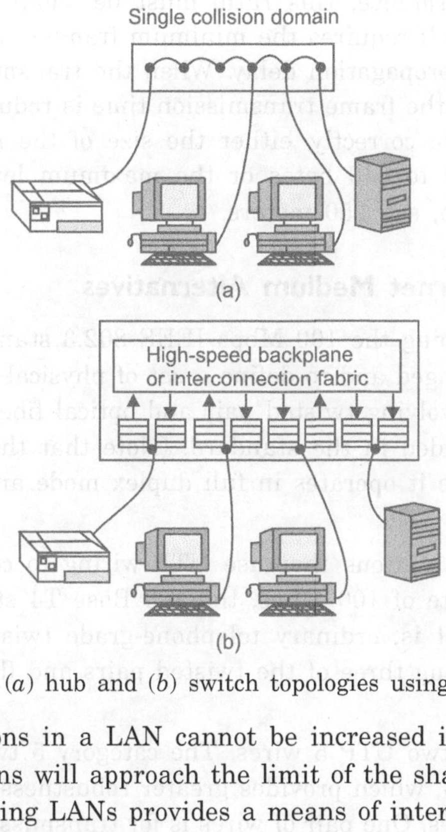

Fig. 7.10 Ethernet (*a*) hub and (*b*) switch topologies using twisted-pair cabling

The number of stations in a LAN cannot be increased indefinitely. Eventually the traffic generated by stations will approach the limit of the shared transmission medium. The introduction of switching LANs provides a means of interconnecting larger numbers of stations without reaching this limit.

A third approach involves having stations transmit in **full-duplex mode.** Normal Ethernet transmission is **half duplex,** because stations transmit data in one direction at a time. In full duplex mode a station can transmit in both directions simultaneously. Consider the case where each port in the switch has only a single station attached to it.

Introducing a dedicated transmission line for each direction enables transmission to take place in both directions simultaneously without collisions. Note that the stations can continue to operate the CSMA-CD protocol, but they will never encounter collisions. All three of these approaches have been implemented in LAN products.

7.10 FAST ETHERNET

(i) Basic Concept

The IEEE 802.3u standard was approved in 1995 to provide Ethernet LANs operating at 100Mbps. The systems that operate under this standard are known as Fast Ethernet. To maintain compatibility with existing standards, the frame format, interfaces, and procedures have been kept the same. Recall that the performance of the CSMA/CD medium access control is sensitive to the radio of the round-trip propagation delay and the frame transmission time. To obtain good performance, this ratio must be small. In addition, the correct operation of the protocol itself requires the minimum frame size transmission time to be larger than the round-trip propagation delay. When the transmission speed is increased from 10 Mbps to 100 Mbps, the frame transmission time is reduced by a factor of 10. For the MAC protocol to operate correctly, either the size of the minimum frame must be increased by a factor of 10 to 640 bytes or the maximum length between stations is reduced by a factor of 10 to, say 250 meters.

(ii) IEEE 802.3 Fast Ethernet Medium Alternatives

The decision in developing the 100 Mbps IEEE 802.3 standards was to keep frame sizes and procedures unchanged and to define a set of physical layers that were entirely based on a hub topology involving twisted pair and optical fiber, as shown in Table 7.3. Coaxial cable was not included in the standard. (Note that the 100 Base F option can extend up to 2000m because it operates in full duplex mode and operates with buffered switched only).

The standard involves stations that use UTP wiring to connect to hubs in a star topology. To obtain a bit rate of 100 Mbps, the 100 Base T4 standards use four UTP 3 wires (UTP category 3, that is, ordinary telephone-grade twisted pair). The 100 Mbps transmission is divided among three of the twisted pairs and flows in one direction at a time.

The 100 Base TX use two UTP 5 wires. The category 5 twisted pair involves more twists per meter than UTP3, which provides greater robustness with respect to interface thus enabling higher bit rates. One pair of wires is for transmission and one for reception, o 100 Base TX can operate in full duplex mode.

A 100 Base FX standard has also been provided that uses two strands of multimode optical to provide full-duplex transmission at 100 Mbps in each direction. The 100 Base FX systems can reach over longer distances than the twisted pair options, and so it is used in interconnecting wiring closets and building in a campus network.

Table 7.3 IEEE 802.3 Fast Ethernet medium alternatives

	100 Base T4	*100 Base T*	*10 Base FX*
Medium	Twisted pair category 3 UTP four pairs	Twisted pair category 5 UTP two pairs	Optical fiber multimode two strands
Maximum segment length	100 m	100 m	2 km
Topology	Star	Star	Star

The 100 Mbps IEEE 802.3 standards provide for two modes of operations and the hubs. In the first mode all incoming lines are logically connected into a single collision domain, and the CSMA/CD MAC procedure is applied. In the second mode the incoming frames are buffered and then switched internally within the hub. In the later approach the CSMA/CD procedure is not used, and instead the IEEE 802.3 standard simply provides a means of accessing the first stage in a LAN that is based or multiplexing and switching.

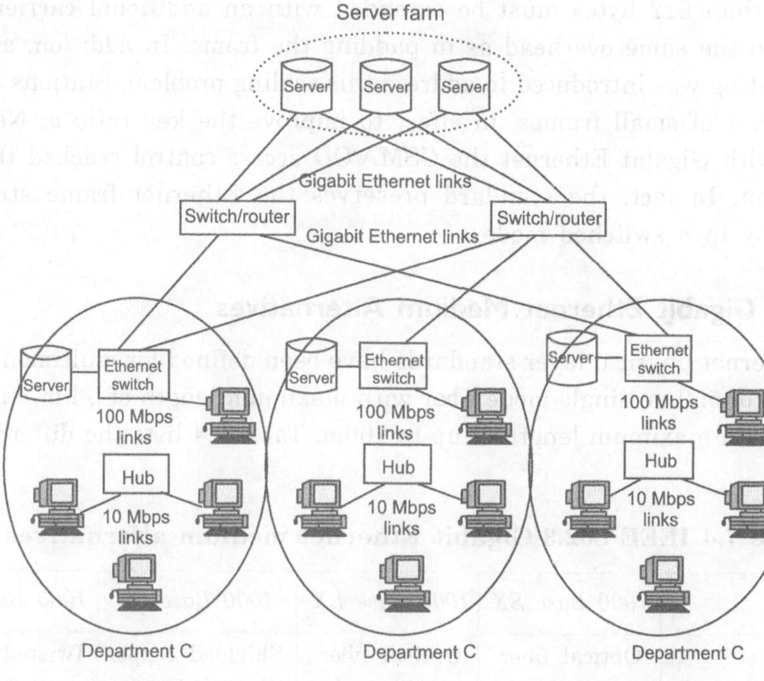

Fig. 7.11 Deployment of Ethernet in a campus network

(iii) Use of Fast Ethernet Switches

Fast Ethernet is deployed in department networks, as shown in Fig. 7.4 where Fast Ethernet switches are used to

1. Aggregate traffic from shared 10 Mbps LANs,
2. Provide greater bandwidth to a server, and
3. Provide greater bandwidth to certain users.

7.11 GIGABIT ETHERNET

(i) Basic Concept

The IEEE 802.3z **Gigabit Ethernet** standard was completed in 1998 and established an Ethernet LAN that increased the transmission speed over that of Fast Ethernet by a factor of 10. The goal was to define new physical layers but to again retain the frame structure and procedures of the 10 Mbps IEEE 802.3 standard.

The increase in speed by another factor of 10 put a focus on the limitations of the CSMA/CD MAC protocol. For example, at a 1 Gbps speed, the transmission of a minimum size frame of 64 bytes can result in the transmission being completed before the sending station senses a collision. For this reason, the slot time was extended to 512 bytes. Frames smaller than 512 bytes must be extended with an additional carrier signal, in effect resulting in the same overhead as in padding the frame. In addition, an approach called frame bursting was introduced to address this scaling problem. Stations are allowed to transmit a burst of small frames, in effect to improve the key ratio a. Nevertheless, it is clear that with Gigabit Ethernet the CSMA/CD access control reached the limits of efficient operation. In fact, the standard preserves the Ethernet frame structure but operates primarily in a switched mode.

(ii) IEEE 802.3 Gigabit Ethernet Medium Alternatives

Gigabit Ethernet physical layer standards have been defined for multimode fiber with maximum length of 550 m, single-mode fiber with maximum length of 5 km, and four-pair category 5 UTP at a maximum length of up to 100m. Table 7.4 lists the different medium alternatives.

Table 7.4 IEEE 802.3-Gigabit Ethernet medium alternatives

	1000 Base SX	*1000 Base LX*	*1000 Base CX*	*1000 Base T*
Medium	Optical fiber multimode two strands	Optical fiber single mode two strands	Shielded copper cable	Twisted pair category 5 UTP
Maxium segment length	500 m	5 km	25 m	100 m
Topology	Star	Star	Star	Star

Gigabit Ethernet is deployed in campus networks as shown in Fig. 7.11. Gigabit Ethernet provides the high bandwidth to connect department switches and server farms to campus backbone switches.

7.12 10 GIGABIT ETHERNET

(i) Basic Concept

The IEEE 802.3ae 10 Gigabit Ethernet draft supplement to the IEEE 802.3 standard was ratified in 2002 to extend the transmission speed to 10 Gbps. Because the ratio of the round-trip propagation delay and the frame transmission time becomes very small, 10 Gigabit Ethernet is defined only for full-duplex mode providing a point-to-point Ethernet connectivity service with the CSMA/CD algorithm disabled. The standard defines two types of physical layer: the LAN PHY and the WAN PHY. Both types differ in framing but support the same capability in terms of distance. The LAN PHY is primarily intended to support existing Ethernet LAN applications while the WAN PHY allows 10 Gigabit Ethernet terminals to be connected through SONET OC-192c equipment.

(ii) IEEE 802.3 10 Gigabit Ethernet Medium Alternatives

The 10 Gigabit specifications uses multiple suffixes to indicate the medium as well as the line coding type. The first set of suffixes indicates the line type. The suffix X denotes the use of 8B10B code. The suffix R denotes the use of 64B66B code, resulting in a more efficient code than the 8B10B code but incurring a higher implementation complexity. The suffix W indicates the encapsulation of 64B66B-encoded data into SONET STS- 192c payload, thus implementing the WAN PHY.

The second set of suffixes indicates the medium type. The suffix S indicates two multimode optical fibers operating at 850 nm wavelengths. The suffixes L and E indicate two single-mode optical fibers operating at 1310 nm and 1550 nm wavelengths, respectively. Finally, the suffix L4 indicates two multimode or single mode optical fibers operating at 1310 nm WDM band. Table 7.5 lists the different medium alternatives.

Table 7.5 IEEE 802.3 10 Gigabit Ethernet medium alternatives

	10G Base SR	*10G Base LR*	*10G Base EW*	*10G Base LX4*
Medium	Two optical fibers multimode at 850 nm 64B66B code	Two optical fibers Single mode at 1310 nm 64B66B	Two optical fibers Single mode at 1550 nm SONET compatibility	Two optical fibers Multimode/ Single mode with four wavelength at 1310 nm band 8B10B code
Maximum Distance	300 m	10 km	40 m	300 m-10 km

7.13 IEEE 802.4 (TOKEN BUS)

- IEEE 802.4 describes a token bus LAN standard.
- The IEEE 802.4 standard for media access control is known as Token bus.
- Token bus is a linear or the tree shaped cable through which different stations are interconnected.
- In token passing method stations, connected on a bus are arranged in a logical ring. When the logical ring is initiated, the highest numbered station may send the first frame. After this it passes permission to its immediate neighbor by sending a special control frame called **a token.** The token propagates around the logical ring, with only the token holder being permitted to transmit frames. Since only one station at a time holds the token, collisions do not occur. There is no relation between the physical location of the station on the bus and its logical sequence number. Fig. 7.12 illustrates the operation of token bus.

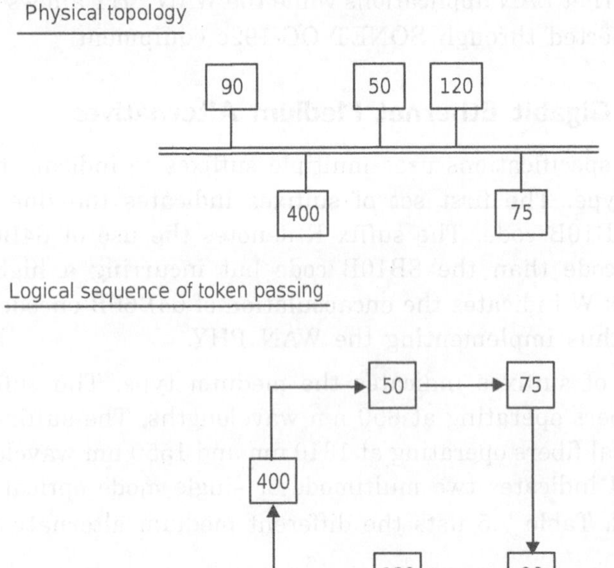

Fig. 7.12 Token passing sequence in a bus

7.13.1 Features of IEEE 802.4

1. It uses highly reliable cable television equipment.
2. It is more deterministic than 802.3.
3. It can handle short minimum frame.
4. It also supports priorities.
5. Token bus has excellent throughput and efficiency at high load.
6. Token bus supports good bandwidth to high priority traffic.

7.13.2 IEEE 802.4 Cable Standards

- The token bus standard specifies three physical layer options in terms of transmission medium, signaling technique, data rate and maximum electrical cable segment length. Table 7.6 summarized these options defined for the IEEE 802.4 medium.

Table 7.6 IEEE 802.4 medium options

Sr. No.	*Medium Options*	*Transmission Medium*	*Signaling Technique*	*Data rate (Mbps)*	*Maximum segment length (m)*
1.	Broad band	Coaxial cable (75 ohm)	Broad band (AM / PSK)	1, 5, 10	Not specified
2.	Carrier band	Coaxial cable (75 ohm)	Broad band (FSK)	1, 5, 10	7600
3.	Optical fiber	Optical fiber	ASK Manchester	5, 10, 20	Not specified

1. *Broad band.* Broadband system supports data channel at 1, 5, 10 Mbps with bandwidths of 1, 5, 6 and 12 MHz, respectively. The standard recommends the use of a single cable split system with a head end frequency translator.
2. *Carrier band.* It is also known as single-channel broadband. Because carrier-band is dedicated to a single data channel, it is not necessary to take care that the modem output be confined to a narrow bandwidth.
3. *Optical fiber.* It is the most recent option at data rates of 5, 10 and 20 Mbps. Either a passive or active star topology can be used.

7.13.3 Frame Format of IEEE 802.4

The frame format as specified by IEEE 802.4 is as shown in Fig. 7.13

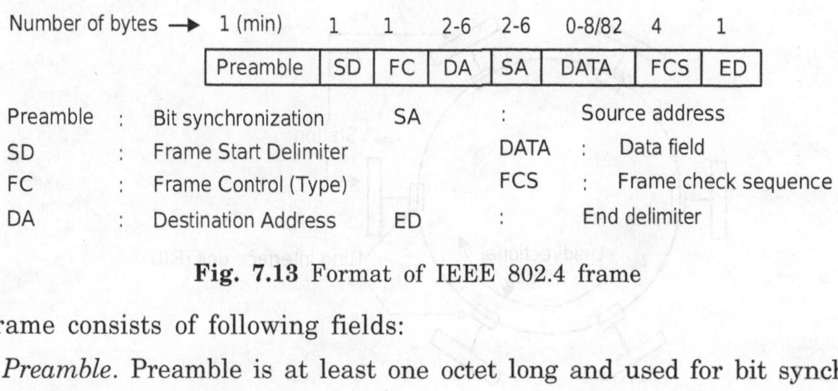

Fig. 7.13 Format of IEEE 802.4 frame

The frame consists of following fields:

(*i*) *Preamble*. Preamble is at least one octet long and used for bit synchronization.

(*ii*) *Start Delimiter (SD)*. It is a unique one-byte pattern, which marks the beginning of a frame.

(iii) *Frame Control (FC).* This field indicates the type of frame. It is one octet long and indicates if the frame is a data frame or control frame. Token is one of the control frames.

(iv) *Source Address (SA).* The source address field is also 2 or 6 octets long.

(v) *Destination Address (DA).* It contains the destination address and it is 2 to 6 bytes long.

(vi) *Frame Check Sequence (FCS).* This field contains a CRC code. It is 4 bytes long and used to check on DA, SA, FC and Data fields.

(vii) *End Delimiter (ED).* This is one byte unique bit pattern, which marks the end of the frame. The total length of the frame from FC to FCS field including the Data field can be at the most 8191 octets.

7.13.4 Performance of IEEE 802.4

- For Token ring, the slightly higher delay compared to CSMA/CD bus occurs. For higher transmission loads the token ring performs well.

7.14 IEEE 802.5 (TOKEN RING)

- In a token ring a special bit pattern, called the token, circulates around the ring whenever all stations are idle. When a station transmits, it breaks the ring and inserts its own frame with destination and source addresses. When the frame eventually returns to the originating station after completing the round, the station removes the frame and closes the ring. Because there is only one token, only one station can transmit at a given instant, thus solving the channel access problem. Fig. 7.14 shows token ring arrangement.
- Each station is connected to the ring through a Ring Interface Unit (RIU). The sequence of token is determined by the physical locations of the stations on the ring.

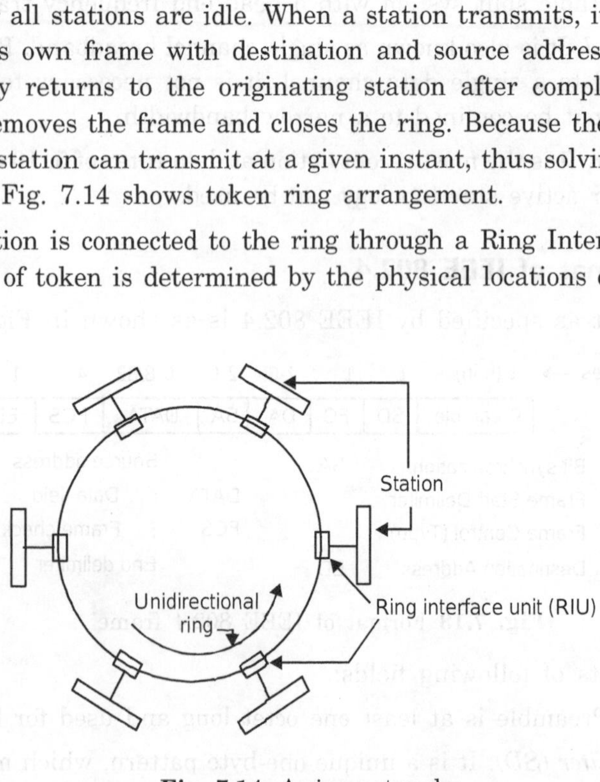

Fig. 7.14 A ring network

7.14.1 Features of IEEE 802.5

1. It uses point-to-point connection.
2. Throughput and efficiency at high load are excellent.
3. Token ring support short frames.

7.14.2 IEEE 802.5 Cable Standards

The token ring standard IEEE 802.5 specifies two types of transmission medium discussed below:

1. *Shielded twisted pair (STP).* It uses differential Manchester signaling technique. Data rate is 4 or 16 Mbps. Maximum number of repeaters allowed is 250.
2. *Unshielded twisted pair (UTP).* It uses differential Manchester signaling technique. Data rate is 4 Mbps; maximum number of repeaters allowed is 250.

7.14.3 Frame Format of IEEE 802.5

The IEEE 802.5 has standardized the formats for the token frame and data frame. They are as shown in Fig. 7.15.

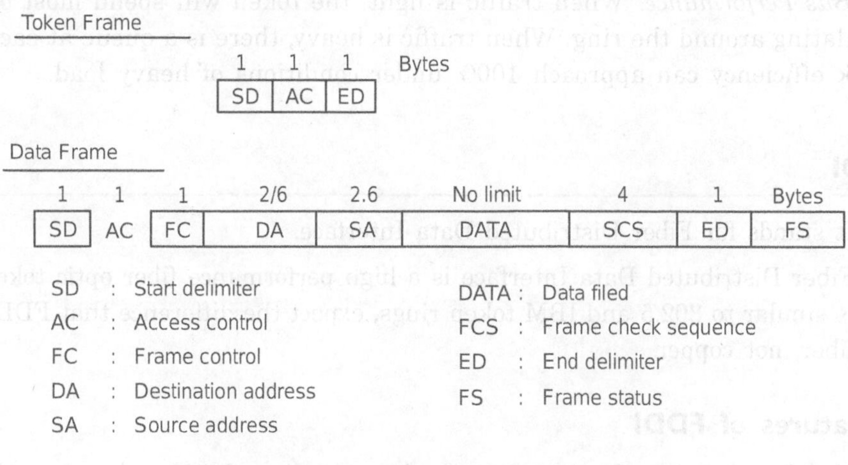

Fig. 7.15 Formats of IEEE 802.5 frames

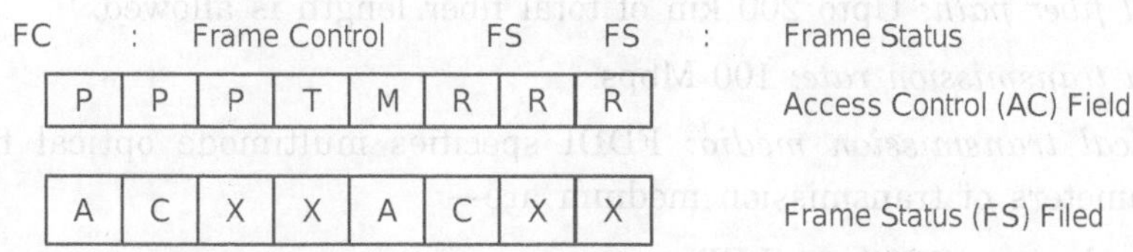

Fig. 7.16 Formats of IEEE 802.5 frames

The token frame and data frame contain the following fields:

Start Delimiter (SD). This is a one byte long field containing a unique pattern which is used to mark the start of the token or data frames.

Access Control (AC). This is also a one octet long field. It consists of the priority bits (P), token bits (T), monitoring bits (M) and reservation bits (R) as shown in Fig. 7.16.

Frame Control (FC). This one byte long field is used to indicate the type of frame, Data frame or control frame. It is also used to distinguish between different types of control frames.

Destination Address (DA). It is 2 to 6 octets long and indicates the destination address.

Source Address (SA). This is also a 2 to 6 octet long field, which indicates the source address.

Data Field (DATA). It can have 0 or more octets. There is no maximum size but the frame transmission time is limited by the token holder timer.

Frame Check Sequence (FCS). The frame check sequence is 4 octets long and contains the CRC code. It checks on DA, SA, FC and data fields.

End Delimiter (ED). It is one octet long and contains a unique bit pattern marking the end of a token or data frame.

Frame Status (FS). This field is one octet long and contains a unique bit pattern marking the end of a token or data frame.

Token Bus Performance. When traffic is light, the token will spend most of its time ideally circulating around the ring. When traffic is heavy, there is a queue at each station. The network efficiency can approach 100% under conditions of heavy load.

7.15 FDDI

- It stands for Fiber Distributed Data Interface.
- Fiber Distributed Data Interface is a high performance fiber optic token ring. It is similar to 802.5 and IBM token rings, expect the difference that FDDI runs on fiber, not copper.

7.15.1 Features of FDDI

- *Number of stations:* Upto 1000 connections are allowed (500 and connected stations).
- *Total fiber path:* Upto 200 km of total fiber length is allowed.
- *Data transmission rate:* 100 Mbps.
- *Optical transmission media:* FDDI specifies multimode optical fiber. Typical parameters of transmission medium are—

  Optical source-1300 nm LED

  Core diameter-62.5 micron

  Cladding diameter-125 micron

  Numerical aperture-0.275

  Band width-500 MHz/km

7.15.2 Data Encoding of FDDI

- 4B5B line code is used for data encoding. Thirty two symbols are possible with 4B5B—
  - 16 symbols for data sets (0 to 15).
  - 3 symbols are used for starting delimiter (J, K, L).
  - 1 symbol is used for encoding delimiter (t).
  - 2 symbols for control indicators (R, S).
  - 3 symbols are used for handshaking (QUIET, IDLE, HALT) between stations.
  - Remaining 7 symbols are invalid.

7.15.3 Frame/Packet Size

- Also frame time should not be less than time taken by token to make a trip around the ring. Therefore frame size can be between 17 and 4500 bytes.

  Frame size ≤ 4500 bytes.

FDDI data frame:

The contents of data frame are–

Data Frame:

8			2/6	21/6	No limit	4	1	1
PA	SD	FC	DA	SA	DATA	FCS	ED	FS

PA–Preamble DA–Destination address

SD–Start delimiter SA–Source address

FC–Frame control DATA–Data field

ED–End delimiter FCS–Frame checks sequence

FS–Frame status

Fig. 7.17 Frame format

(*i*) *Preamble Field (PA).* It consists of IDLE line status symbols. These are used to establish and maintain clock synchronization.

(*ii*) *Start Delimiter Field (SD).* This field is recognized as unique boundary of a frame. It is a sequence of two delimiters (JK).

(*iii*) *Frame Control Field (FC).* It defines the type of frame and its characteristics, such as

- Synchronous or asynchronous frames.
- The length of address field (16 or 48 bits).
- The type of frame (LLC or station management (SMT)).
- Whether the frame is a token.

(*iv*) *Destination Address Field (DA).* A group address that is recognized by more than one station. 16 bit or 48 bit representation of destination.

(*v*) *Source Address Field (SA).* A 16-bit or 48-bit representation of the source, originating the message.

(*vi*) *DATA.* An information field contains data symbols.

(*vii*) *Frame Check Sequence (FCS).* A 32-bit field that contains information from a cyclic redundancy check. This information is used at the destination to check the message for errors.

(*viii*) *End Delimiter (ED).* It marks end of frame. One delimiter symbol "T" is used.

(*ix*) *Frame Status (FS).* It consists of minimum 3 control symbols. These symbols are modified by a receiving station and indicate

- Whether the addressed station has recognized its address.
- Whether the frame has been copied.
- Whether any station has detected an error in the frame.

7.15.4 Network Operation

- FDDI cabling consists of two fiber rings, one transmitting clockwise and the other transmitting counter clockwise as shown in Fig. 7.18 (*a*).
- If either one breaks, the other can be used as a backup. If both break at the same point, due to a fire or other accident in cable duct, the two rings can be joined into a single ring.
- Each station contains relays that can be used to join the two rings or bypass the station in the event of station problems.
- To transmit data, a station must first capture the token. Then it transmits a frame and removes it when it comes a round again, one more difference between FDDI and 802.5 is that in 802.5 a station may not generate a new token until its frame has gone all the way around and come back
- As we know there is dual ring, in FDDI because of the expenses of the dual-ring configuration, FDDI allows nodes to attach to the network by means of a single cable.
- Such nodes are called single attachment stations (SAS) their dual-connected counterparts are called dual attachment stations (DAS) (anticlockwise). A concentrator is used to attach several SAS to the dual ring as shown in Fig. 7.18 (*b*).
- FDDI defines two classes of traffic: synchronous and asynchronous.
- When a node receives a token, it is allowed to send synchronous data, without regard for whether the token is early or late.
- It contrast, a node can send synchronous traffic only when the token is early. Synchronous FDDI means that the traffic is delay sensitive, sending voice or video as synchronous traffic.
- Asynchronous means that the application is more interested in throughput than delay.

- A file transfer application would be asynchronous traffic.
- The FDDI mechanism for ensuring that a valid token is always in circulation is also different from those in 802.5.
- First, all nodes on an FDDI ring monitor the ring to be sure that the token has not been lost. Observe that in a correctly functioning ring, each node should see a valid transmission either in a data frame or in the token.
- The greatest idle time between valid transmissions that a given node should experience is equal to the ring latency plus the time it takes to transmit a full frame.
- The FDDI MAC protocol uses three timers.
- The token holding timer determines how long a station may continue to transmit once it has acquired the token.
- This timer prevents a station from hogging the ring forever. The token rotation timer is restarted everytime the token is seen.

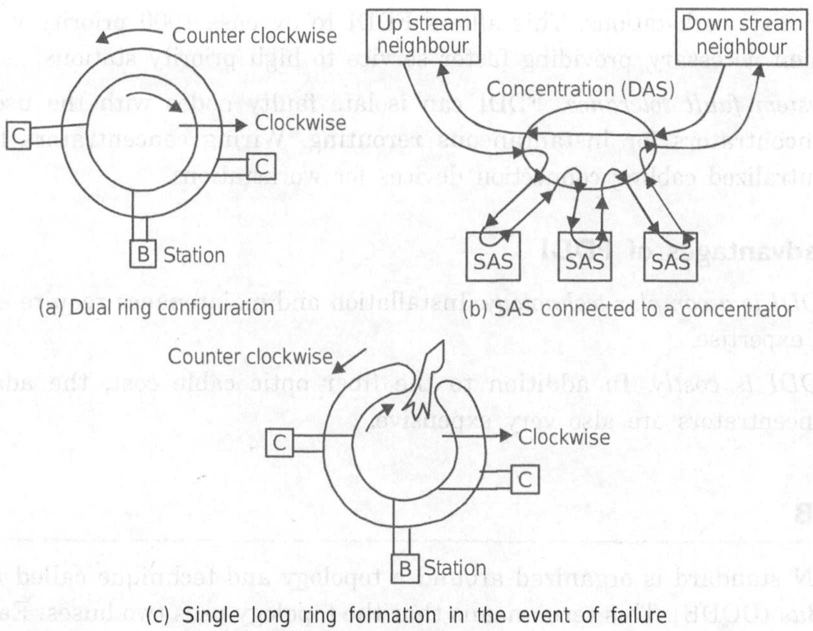

Fig. 7.18

- If this timer expires, it means that the token has not been sighted for too long on interval, it has been lost, so the token recovery procedure is initiated.
- Finally, the valid transmission timer is used to time out and recover from certain transient ring errors.
- FDDI also has priority algorithm. It determines which priority classes may transmit on a given token pass.
- If the token is ahead of schedule, all priorities may transmit, but if it is behind schedule, only the highest ones may send.

7.15.5 Advantages of FDDI

1. *High bandwidth.* It has bandwidth as high as 250 Gbps. High bandwidth allows for tremendous speed. FDDI implementation can handle data rates of 100 Mbps.
2. *Security.* It is difficult to eavesdrop on fiber optic cable transmission.
3. *Physical durability.* Fiber optic cable does not break as easily as do other kind of cables.
4. *Resistance to EMI.* Fiber optic cables are not susceptible to electromagnetic interference.
5. *Cable distance.* Fiber-optic cables transmit signals over 200 kms.
6. *Weight.* Fiber optic cable weighs a lot less than copper wire with similar bandwidth.
7. *Use of multiple tokens.* FDDI uses multiple tokens to improve network speed.
8. *Ability to prioritize workstations.* FDDI can designate some workstations as low priority workstations. This allows FDDI to by pass 1000 priority workstations, when necessary, providing faster service to high priority stations.
9. *System fault tolerance.* FDDI can isolate faulty nodes with the use of wiring concentrators for instantaneous rerouting. Wiring concentrators function as centralized cabling connection devices for workstations.

7.15.6 Disadvantages of FDDI

1. *FDDI is a complex technology.* Installation and maintenance require a great deal of expertise.
2. *FDDI is costly.* In addition to the fiber optic cable cost, the adapters and concentrators are also very expensive.

7.16 DQDB

The MAN standard is organized around a topology and technique called *Distributed Queue Dual Bus* (DQDB). This term means that the topology uses two buses. Each of these buses transmits traffic in one direction only. The implementation for MAN provides for transfer rates from 34 to 150 Mbit/s.

The DQDB provides for two of access. Once access pre-arbitrated services guarantees a certain amount of "bandwidth". This access is useful for isochronous services such as voice and video. The second service *queued arbitrated service* provides access based on demand. It designed to accommodate bursty services such as data transmission.

A MAN is designed with two unidirectional buses. Each bus is independent of the other in the transfer of traffic. The topology can be designed as an open bus or a closed bus configuration. Figure 7.19 shows the two alternatives.

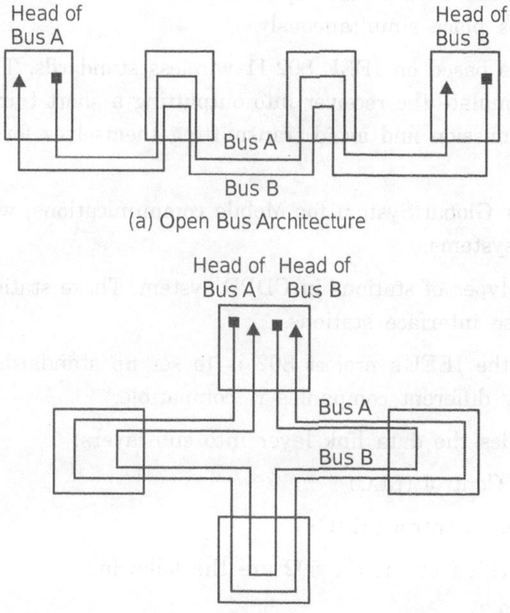

Fig. 7.19 The MAN Bus Architecture

7.16.1 DQDB Operations

The MAN protocol is elegantly simple and is quite attractive because it is distance-independent. Its basic operations may be summarized as follows:

- Node gains access by putting itself in a queue (one for each bus).
- When node is idling, count is made of the requests that pass on bus B (request counter).
- The request counter is decremented by 1 with each empty slot on bus A.
- The node keeps a count of the number of downstream requests and balances that with the number of the empty slot.
- To send, a node put a request on a slot on bus B and remembers the slot count.
- By sending the request counter to a countdown counter node can determine an empty slot.
- When counter = 0, node uses the slot.

SUMMARY

- There are two collision free protocols: a bitmap protocol and binary countdown.
- The systems in which multiple user share a common channel in a way that can lead to conflicts are known as contention systems.
- Limited contention protocol combines the best properties of the contention and collision free protocol.

- WDMA protocols are used in fiber optic LANs, where different conversations at different wavelength takes place simultaneously.
- MACA protocol is based on IEEE 802.11 wireless standards. The basic idea behind it is, the sender to stimulate the receiver into outputting a short frame. So stations nearby can detect this transmission and avoid transmitting themselves for the duration of upcoming data frames.
- GSM is short for Global System for Mobile communications, which is one of the leading digital cellular systems.
- There are three types of stations in CDPD system. These stations are mobile hosts, base stations and base interface stations.
- The purpose of the IEEE's project 802 is to set up standards so that LAN equipment manufactured by different companies is compatible.
- Project 802 divides the data link layer into sub layers:

(*a*) Logical Link Control (LLC)

(*b*) Medium Access Control (MAC)

- Three LANs specified by project 802 are the following:-

(*a*) Ethernet (802.3)

(*b*) Token Bus (802.4)

(*c*) Token Ring (802.5)

- CSMA/CD operates as follows: Any station may listen to the line to determine if the line is clear. If clear, transmission can commence. If a collision occurs, transmission stops and the process is repeated.
- Token Bus (IEEE 802.4), used in factory automation and process control, combines features of Ethernet and Token ring.
- Token Ring (IEEE 802.5), employs token passing as its method of transmission initiation.
- Switches in token ring can be encased in a multistation access unit (MAU).
- In token ring, a frame travels from node-to-node, getting regenerated at each node, until the destination is reached.
- FDDI (Fiber Distributed Data Interface) is a LAN protocol using optical fiber as a medium, with a 100 Mbps data rate.
- FDDI consists of a primary ring for data transmission and a secondary ring that assists failure situations.
- FDDI specifies protocols for the physical and data link layers.
- The FDDI data link layer consists of an LLC sub layer and an MAC sub layer. The former is similar to that specified in IEEE 802.2. The later is similar to that of the token ring protocol (802.5).
- In FDDI protocol, token possession is controlled by three time values and two timers.
- Distributed Queue Dual Bus (DQDB) uses two unidirectional buses. The buses travel in opposite direction.
- Data transmission in DQDB occurs through capture of an empty slot and insertion of data into the slot.

- DQDB operates in the physical layer and the MAC sub layer.
- DQDB can also be implemented as a ring topology.
- DQDB is also used by the SMDs for media access.

EXERCISE

1. What is the difference between collision free protocol and limited contention protocols?
2. Explain the operation of:
   (*a*) A bit map protocol
   (*b*) Binary countdown protocol
   (*c*) Limited contention protocol
3. Define WDMA. Also mention its classes.
4. Explain MACA with neat diagram.
5. What is GSM? Explain in brief with its uses.
6. What do you understand by SIM card?
7. Explain the advantage of GSM.
8. Define CDPD with suitable example.
9. Explain the three interfaces in CDPD.
10. Compare E-interface and I- interface.
11. What is the difference between I- interface and A-interface?
12. CDMA is a multiplexing technique? If yes explain with example.
13. What is orthogonal?
14. What is the use of the CDMA?
15. What are the different benefits of the CDMA?
16. Explain different type of IEEE LAN standards.
17. Show the IEEE LAN committees.
18. Explain the physical properties of Ethernet.
19. Explain the difference between 10 Base 2 standard and 10 Base 5 standards.
20. What are the three approaches, which are provided by 10 Base T standards?
21. What is the basic concept of the fast Ethernet?
22. Explain different fast Ethernet medium alternatives.
23. What is the use of fast Ethernet switches?
24. What is the difference between GigaBit Ethernet and 10 GigaBit Ethernet?
25. What do you understand by token bus?
26. Describe the token bus LAN standard.
27. Explain the features of the token bus.
28. Explain the brief IEEE 802.4 cable standards.

29. What is the difference between token bus and token ring?

30. Explain the features of the token ring.

31. Describe the various IEEE 802.5 cable standards.

32. Explain the working principle of FDDI.

33. Describe the FDDI data frame in brief.

34. Explain the network operation of the FDDI.

35. Explain the formats of IEEE 802.5 frames.

36. What are the advantages and disadvantages of the FDDI?

37. What do you understand by DQDB?

38. Explain the DQDB operation with neat diagram.

39. Explain the frame formats of 802.3 and 802.4

40. Explain the working of FDDI network. Also explain the working when one station in the ring has failed. What will happen when one ring fails at one point?

41. Explain the operation of Distributed Queue Dual Bus with the help of a suitable diagram.

Chapter 8

ROUTING

8.1 INTRODUCTION

Routing achieved commercial popularity as late as the mid–1980s. The topic of routing has been covered in Computer Science literature for more than two decades, but routing achieved commercial popularity as late as the mid–1980s. The primary reason for this time lag is that networks in the 1970s were simple, homogenous environments. Only relatively recently has large–scale internetworking become popular.

8.1.1 Definition

"Routing may be defined as the act of moving–information across an internetwork from a source to destination".

Along the way, at least one intermediate node typically is encountered. Routing is often contracted with bridging that might see to accomplish precisely the same thing to the casual observer. The primary difference between the two is that bridging occurs at layer 2 (link layer) of the OSI reference model whereas routing occurs at layer 3 (the network layer). This distinction provides routing and bridging with different information to use in the process of moving information from source to destination, so the two functions accomplish their tasks in different ways.

8.1.2 Functions of Routing

Routing involves two basic functions: determining optimal routing path and transporting information groups (typically called packets) through an internetwork. In the context of the routing process, the later of there is referred to as packet switching. Although packet switching is relatively straightforward, path determination can be very complex.

8.1.3 Path Determination

Routing protocols use metrics to evaluate what path will be the best for a packet to travel. A metric is a standard of measurement. Such as path bandwidth that is used by routing algorithm to determine the optimal path to a destination. To aid the process of path determination, routing algorithm varies depending on the routing algorithm used.

Routing algorithm fill routing tables with a variety of information: Destination/next hop associations tell a router that a particular destination can be reached optimally by sending the packet to a particular router representing the 'next hop' on the way to the final destination. When a router receives an incoming packet, it checks the destination address and attempts to associate this address with a next hop. Figure 8.1 depicts a sample destination/next hop routing table.

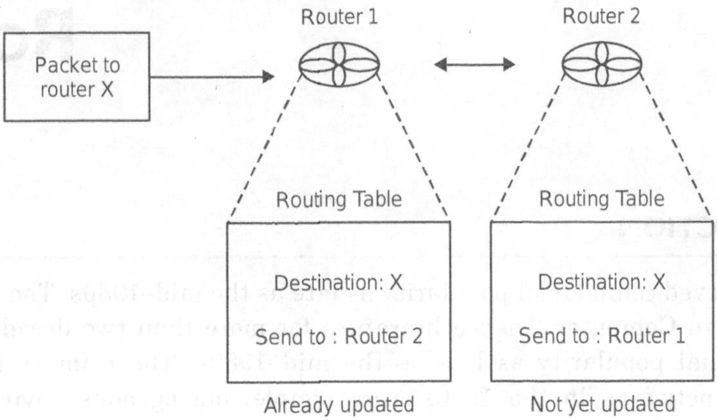

Fig. 8.1 Destination/next hop associations determine the data's optimal path

8.1.4 Types of Routing

Routing is a classified as non adaptive or adaptive routing:

1. Non-adaptive Routing

In some routing protocols, once a pathway to a destination has been selected, the router sends all packets for that destination along that one route. In other words, the routing decisions are not based on the condition or topology of the networks. It is also known as static routing. The disadvantage of static routing is its inability to respond quickly to network failure.

2. Adaptive Routing

Other routing protocols employ a technique called adaptive routing, by which a router may select a new route for each packet (even packet belonging to the same transmission) in response to changes in condition and topology of the networks. Given a transmission from network A to network D, a router may send the first packet by the way of network B, the second packet by way of network C and the third packet by way of network Q, depending on which route is most efficient at the moment.

We can classify adaptive routing into following categories:

1. Isolated adaptive.
2. Distributed adaptive.
3. Centralized adaptive.

In *isolated adaptive* scheme, each node routes the packet on the link with the shortest queues length. This scheme is rarely used since it does not utilize the full information available at node.

In *distributed adaptive* scheme, each node exchanges delay information with other nodes. Based on this information, a node tries to estimate the delay throughout the network and applies suitable routing algorithm.

In *centralized adaptive* scheme, each node reports its information to a central node, which designs the route for the packets.

The disadvantages of adaptive routing are that the system becomes more complex, traffic burden on network increases, too slow, system causes congestion producing oscillation. Adaptive routing is also known as dynamic routing. The other disadvantage of dynamic routing is its complexity in the router.

8.2 FLOODING

This technique requires no network information. A packet is sent by a source node to all its adjacent nodes. At each node, every incoming packet is retransmitted on every outgoing links, except the link that it arrived from. Flooding generates large number of duplicate packets. One way to prevent this is for each node to renumber the identity of those packets it has already sent. When duplicate packets arrive they are discarded. One such measure is to have a hop counter contained in the header of each packet, which is decremented at each hop. When the count reaches zero, the packet is discarded. The counter is set to maximum value *i.e.*, diameter of the subnet.

8.2.1 Examples of Flooding

An example of the latter tactic is shown in Fig. 8.2. A packet is to be sent from node 1 to node 6 and is assigned a hop count of 3. On the first hop, three copies of the packet are created. For the second hop of all these copies, a total of nine copies are created. One of these copies reaches node 6, which recognizes that it is the intended destination and does not retransmit. However, the other nodes generate a total of 22 new copies for their third and final hop. Note that if a node is not keeping track of the packet identifier, it may generate multiple copies at this third stage. All packets received from the third hop is discarded. In all, node 6 has received four additional copies of the packet.

8.2.2 Uses of Flooding

Flooding is not practical in most applications but it does have some uses. For example in military applications, where large numbers of routers may be blown to bits at any instant, the tremendous robustness of flooding is highly desirable. In distributed database applications, it is sometimes necessary to update the entire database concurrently; in which case flooding can be useful. A third possible use of flooding is as a metric against which other routing algorithms can be compared. Flooding always chooses the shortest path because it chooses every possible path in parallel. Consequently, no other algorithm can produce a shorter delay (if we ignore the overhead generated by the flooding process itself).

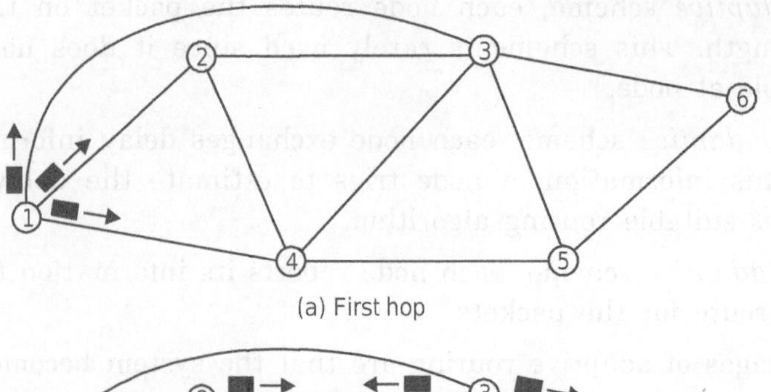

Fig. 8.2 Flooding Example (Hop Count = 3)

8.2.3 Advantage and Disadvantage of Flooding

The main disadvantage of flooding is the total traffic load that it generates, is directly proportional to the connectivity of the network. Also flooding requires much large bandwidth. The advantage of flooding is that it is highly robust. This property finds application in military network that is subjected to extensive damage and in distributed database applications where it is necessary to update database concurrently.

8.2.4 Properties of Flooding

The flooding technique has three remarkable properties:

- All possible routes between source and destination are tried. Thus, no matter what link or node outages have occurred, a packet will always get through if at least one path between source and destination exists.
- Because all routes are tried, at least one copy of the packet to arrive at the destination will have used a minimum hop route.
- All nodes that are directly or indirectly connected to the source node are visited.

8.3 DISTANCE/OPTIMAL VECTOR ROUTING

In distance vector routing, each router periodically shares its knowledge about the entire network with its neighbors. The three keys to understanding how this algorithm works are as follows:

1. *Knowledge about the whole network.* Each router shares its knowledge about the entire network. It sends all of its collected knowledge about the network to its neighbors. At the outset, a router's knowledge of the network may be sparse. How much it knows however, is unimportant: it sends whatever it has.
2. *Routing only to neighbors.* Each router periodically sends its knowledge about the network only to those routers to which it has direct links. It sends whatever knowledge it has about the whole network through all of its ports. This information is received and kept by each neighboring router and used to update that router's own information about the network.
3. *Information sharing at regular intervals.* For example, every 30 seconds, each router sends its information about the whole network to its neighbors. This sharing occurs whether or not the network has changed since the last time information was exchanged.

Sharing Information

To understand how distance vector routing works, examine the internet shown in Fig. 8.3. In this example, the clouds represent local area networks (LANs). The number inside each cloud is that LAN's network ID. These LANs can be of any type (Ethernet, Token Ring, FDDI, etc.). The LANs are connected by routers (or gateways), represented by the boxes labeled A, B, C, D, E, and F.

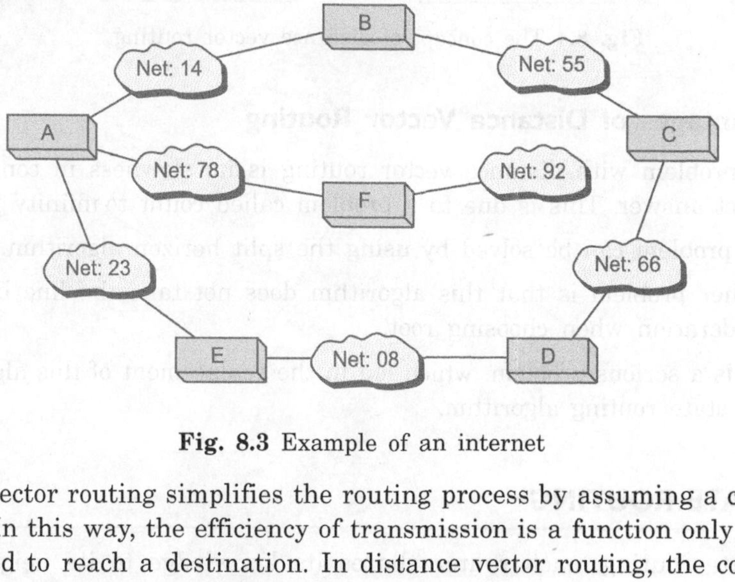

Fig. 8.3 Example of an internet

Distance vector routing simplifies the routing process by assuming a cost of one unit for every link. In this way, the efficiency of transmission is a function only of the number of links required to reach a destination. In distance vector routing, the cost is based on hop count.

Figure 8.4 shows the first step in the algorithm. The text boxes indicate the relationships of the routers in Fig. 8.3 to their neighbors. As you can see, each router sends its information about the internet work only to its immediate neighbors. How, then do non-neighboring routers learn about each other and share knowledge?

A router sends its knowledge to its neighbors. The neighbors add this knowledge to their own knowledge and send the whole table to their own neighbors. In this way the first router gets its own information back plus new information about its neighbor's other neighbors. Each of these neighbors adds its knowledge and sends the updated table on to its own neighbors (to neighbors of the original router), and so on. Eventually, every router knows about every other router in the internetwork.

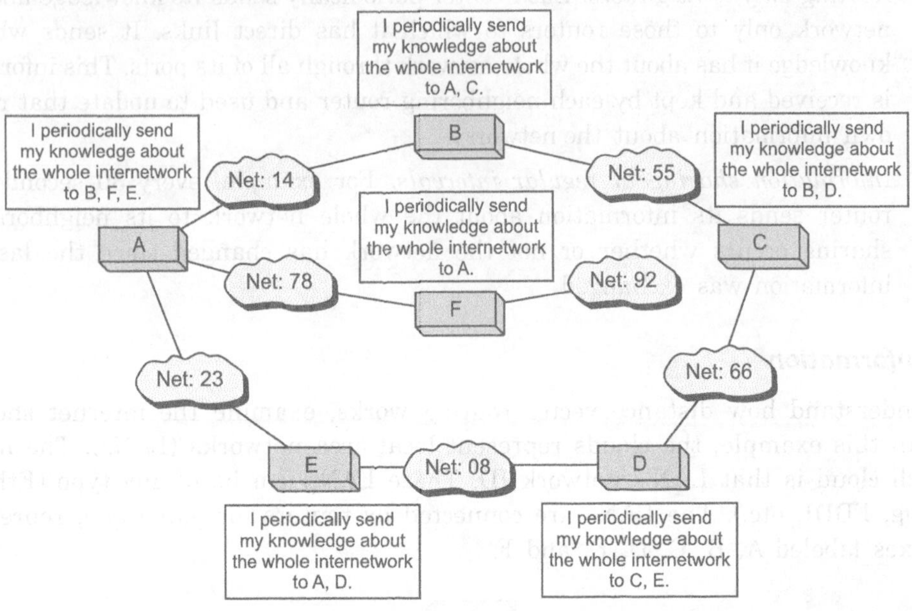

Fig. 8.4 The concept of distance vector routing

8.3.1 Disadvantages of Distance Vector Routing

1. The problem with distance vector routing is its slowness in converging to the correct answer. This is due to a problem called count to infinity problem.
2. This problem can be solved by using the split horizon algorithm.
3. Another problem is that this algorithm does not take the line bandwidth into consideration when choosing root.
4. This is a serious problem, which led in the replacement of this algorithm by the Link state routing algorithm.

8.4 LINK STATE ROUTING

In link state routing, each router shares its knowledge to its neighborhood with every other router in the internetwork. The following are true of link state routing.

1. *Knowledge about the neighborhood.* Instead of sending its entire routing table, a router sends information about its neighborhood only.
2. *To all routers.* Each router sends this information to every other router on the internetwork, not just to its neighbors. It does so by a process called flooding. Flooding means that a router sends its information to all its neighbors (through all of its output ports). Each neighbors sends the packet to all of its neighbors and so on. Every router that receives the packet sends copies to all of its neighbors. Finally, every router (without exception) receives a copy of the same information.

Information sharing when there is a change

Each router sends out information about the neighbors when there is a change.

Information Sharing

Let's examine the link state routing process. The first step in link state routing is information sharing (see Fig. 8.5). Each router sends its knowledge about its neighborhood to every other router in the internetwork.

Packet Cost

Both link state and distance vector are lowest-cost algorithms. In distance vector routing cost refers to hop count. In link state routing, cost is a weighted value based on a variety of factors such as security levels, traffic or the state of a link. The cost from router A to network 14, therefore, might be different from the cost from A to 23.

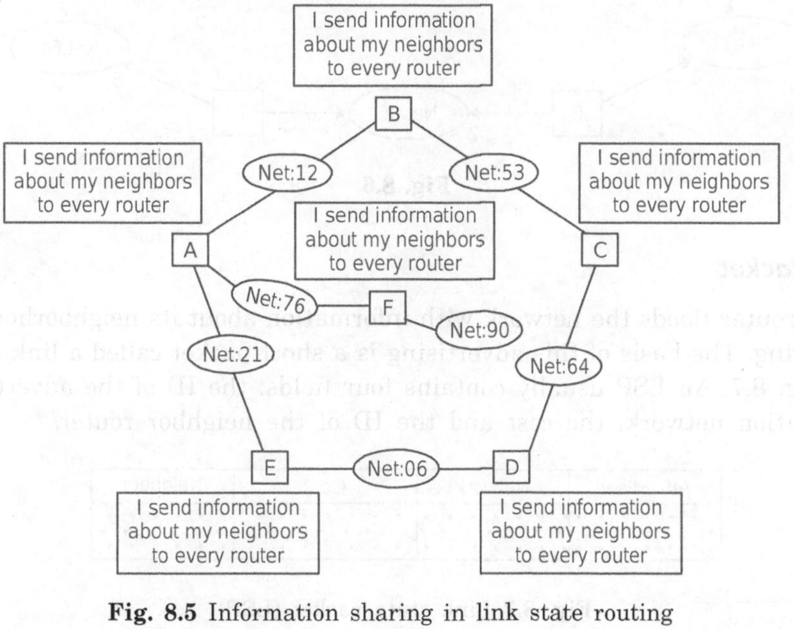

Fig. 8.5 Information sharing in link state routing

In determining a route, the cost of a hop is applied to each packet as it leaves a router and enters a network (Remember, cost is just a weighting and should not be confused with the transmission feeds paid by the sender or receiver). This cost is an outbound cost, meaning that it is applied when a packet leaves the router. Two factors govern how cost is applied to packets in determining a route.

Cost is applied only by routers and not by any other stations on a network. Remember, the link from one router to the next is a network not a point-to-point cable. In many topologies (such as ring and bus), every station on the network examines the header of every packet that passes. If cost was added by every station, instead of by routers alone, it would accumulate unpredictably (the number of stations in a network can change for a variety of reasons, many of them unpredictable.

Cost is applied as a packet leaves the router rather than as it enters. Most networks are broadcast networks. When a packet is in the network, every station, including the router, can pick it up. Therefore, we cannot assign any cost to a packet when it goes from a network to a router.

Figure 8.6 shows our sample interest as it appears to the link state routing algorithm. The cost shown is arbitrary; in actual practice they would reflect attributes of each network.

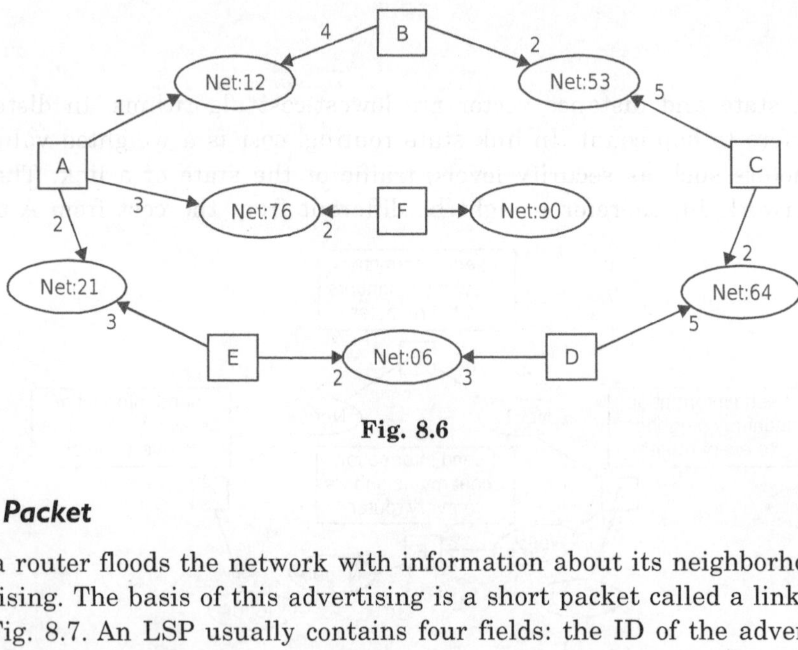

Fig. 8.6

Link State Packet

When a router floods the network with information about its neighborhood, it is said to be advertising. The basis of this advertising is a short packet called a link state packet (LSP); see Fig. 8.7. An LSP usually contains four fields: the ID of the advertiser, the ID of the destination network, the cost and the ID of the neighbor router.

Advertiser	Network	Cost	Neighbor
....	....	....	....
....	....	....	....

Fig. 8.7 Link state packet (LSP)

In the link-state routing, each router shares its knowledge to its neighborhood with all routers in the internetwork.

8.4.1 Difference between Distance Vector and Link State Routing

Table 8.1 Differences between Distance Vector and Link State Routing

Sr. No.	*Distance Vector*	*Link State*
1.	Bellman ford algorithm used to calculate the shortest cost path.	Dijkstras algorithm used to calculate link state cost.
2.	Sends message to their neighbors.	Sends message to every other node in the network.
3.	It is decentralized routing algorithm.	It is centralized global routing algorithm.
4.	Sends larger updates only to neighboring routers.	Send small updates everywhere.
5.	Protocol example—RIP.	Protocol example—OSPF and BGP.
6.	Require less CPU power and less memory space.	Require more CPU power and more memory space.
7.	Simple to implement and support.	Expensive to implement and support.

8.5 HIERARCHICAL ROUTING

- As the size of the network increases, the size of the routing tables of the routers also increases.
- As a result of large routing tables, a large router memory is consumed, more CPU time is needed to scan the tables and more bandwidth is required to send status report about the tables.
- Sometimes the network becomes so large that the size of the router table becomes excessively large and practically it becomes impossible for every router to have an entry for every other router.
- Then the hierarchical routing such as the one used in telephone networks should be adopted.
- In this type of routing the total numbers of routers are divided into different **regions.**
- A router will know everything about the other routers in its own region only. It does not know anything about the internal structure of other regions. This reduces the size of the router table.
- When various networks are connected together, each network is treated as a separate region.
- For very large network the hierarchy is prepared as follows:

  Level 1: Regions

  Level 2: Clusters: It is a group of regions

  Level 3: Zones: zone is a group of clusters

  Level 4: Groups: group contains many zones

Figure 8.8 gives a quantitative example of routing in a two-level hierarchy with five regions. The full routing table for router 1A has 17 entries, as shown in Fig. 8.8(*b*). When routing is done hierarchically, as in Fig. 8.8 (*c*), there are entries for all the local routers as before, but all other regions have been condensed into a single router, so all traffic for region 2 goes via the 1B-2A line, but the rest of the remote traffic goes via the 1C-3B line. Hierarchical routing has reduced the table from 17 to 7 entries. As the ratio of the number of regions to the number of routers per region grows, the savings in table space increase.

Unfortunately, these gains in space are not free. There is a penalty to be paid, and this penalty is in the form of increased path length. For example, the best route from 1A to 5C is via region2, but with hierarchical routing all traffic to region 5 goes via region 3, because that is better for most destinations in region 5.

When a single network becomes very large, an interesting question is: How many levels should the hierarchy have? For example, consider a subnet with 720 routers. If there is no hierarchy, each router needs 720 routing table entries. If the subnet is partitioned into 24 regions of 30 routers each, each router needs 30 local entries plus 23 remote entries for a total 53 entries. If a three-level hierarchy is chosen, with eight clusters, each containing 9 regions of 10 routers, each router needs 10 entries for local routers, 8 entries for routing to other regions within its own cluster, and 7 entries for distant clusters, for a total of 25 entries. Kamoun and Kleinrock (1979) have discovered that the optimal number of levels for an N router subnet is in N, requiring a total of e in N entries per router. They have also shown that the increase in effective mean path length caused by hierarchical routing is sufficiently small that it is usually acceptable.

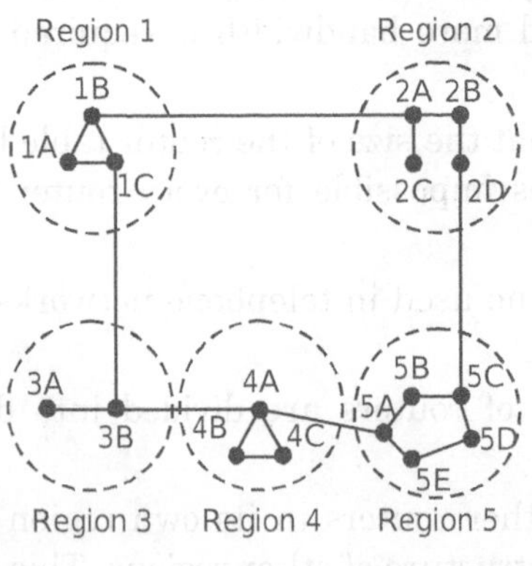

(a) A Network

Dest.	Line	Hops
1A	–	–
1B	1B	1
1C	1C	1
2A	1B	2
2B	1B	3
2C	1B	3
2D	1B	4
3A	1C	3
3B	1C	2
4A	1C	3
4B	1C	4
4C	1C	4
5A	1C	4
5B	1C	5
5C	1B	5
5D	1C	6
5E	1C	5

(b) Full routing table for router 1A

Dest.	Line	Hops
1A	–	–
1B	1B	1
1C	1C	1
2	1B	2
3	1C	2
4	1C	3
5	1C	4

(c) Hierarchical routing table for routing 1A

Fig. 8.8 Hierarchical routing

Disadvantage

The reduced table size has a price tag attached to it. It comes at the expense of increased path length. But it is practically acceptable.

8.6 ROUTING FOR MOBILE HOSTS

- A large number of people have portable computers and they want to work on them whatever they are in the world. Such computers are called as mobile hosts.
- To route a packet to mobile host, the network has to first find it.
- WAN consisting of routers and hosts. Hosts that never move are said to be stationary. They are connected to the network by copper wires or fiber optics.
- Migratory hosts are basically stationary hosts who move from one fixed site to another from time to time but use the network only when they are physically connected to it.
- Roaming hosts actually compute on the run and want to maintain their connections as they move around.
- All hosts are assumed to have a permanent home location that never changes. Hosts also have a permanent home address that can be used to determine their home locations.
- Figure 8.9 shows the model of the world, which is divided into small units. This small unit is called as *area*. Area is typically LAN or wireless cell.

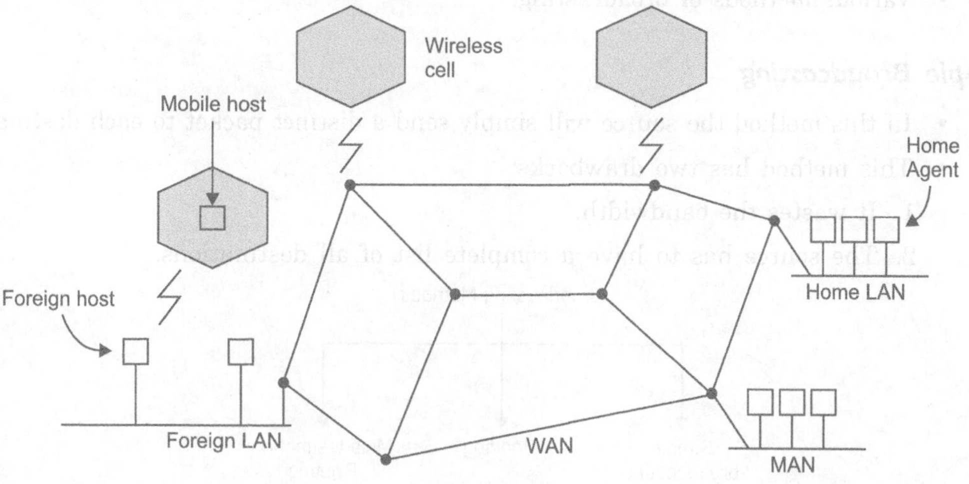

Fig. 8.9

- Each area has one or more *foreign agents,* which are processes that keep tracks of all mobile hosts visiting the area. Each area has also a *home agent*, which keeps tracts of hosts whose home is in the area, but who are currently visiting another area.

- Registration procedure for foreign agent is as follows:
  1. Periodically each foreign agent broadcasts a packet announcing its existence and address. A newly arrived mobile host may wait for one of these messages.
  2. The mobile host registers with the foreign agent, giving its home address, current data link layer address and some security information.
  3. The foreign agent contacts the mobile host's home agent and says: one of your hosts is over here. The message from the foreign agent to the home agent contains the foreign agent's network address.
  4. The home agent examines the security information, which contains a timestamp, to prove that it was generated within the past few seconds. If it is happy, it tells the foreign agent to proceed.
  5. When the foreign agent gets the acknowledgement from the home agent, it makes an entry in its tables and informs the mobile host that it is now registered.
- When a packet is sent to a mobile host, it is routed to the host's home LAN because that is what the address says should be done.

8.7 BROADCAST ROUTING

- In certain applications, the host has to send packets to many or all other hosts.
- Sending a packet to all destinations simultaneously is called as broadcasting.
- Various methods of broadcasting.

1. Simple Broadcasting

- In this method the source will simply send a distinct packet to each destination.
- This method has two drawbacks:
  1. It wastes the bandwidth.
  2. The source has to have a complete list of all destinations.

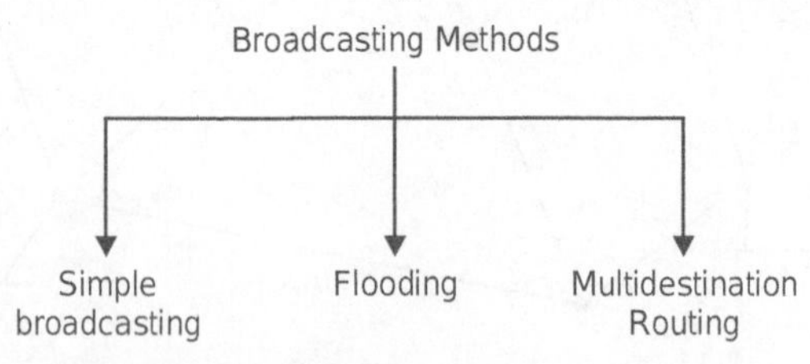

Fig. 8.10 Various methods of broadcasting

2. Flooding

- Flooding is another method used for broadcasting. The problem with flooding is that it has a point-to-point routing algorithm.
- So it consumes a lot of bandwidth and generates too many packets.

3. *Multidestination Routing*

- This is the third algorithm used for broadcasting.
- In this algorithm each packet will contain a list of destinations or a bitmap, which indicates the desired destination.
- When such a packet arrives at a router, the router first checks all the destinations. Then it decides the set of output lines that will be required.
- The router then generates a new copy of the received packet for each output line to be used. It includes a list of only those destinations that are to use the line in each packet going out on that line.

An example of the algorithm, called **reverse path forwarding**, is shown in Fig. 8.11. Part (*a*) shows a subnet, part (*b*) shows a sink tree for router I of that subnet, and part (*c*) shows how the reverse path algorithm works. On the first hop, I send packets to F, H, J and N, as indicated by the second row of the tree. Each of these packets arrives on the preferred path to I (assuring that the preferred path falls along the sink tree) and is so indicated by a circle around the letter. On the second hop, eight packets are generated, two by each of the routers that received a packet on the first-hop. As it turns out, all eight of these arrive at previously unvisited routers, and all but one arrive along the preferred line. Of the nine packets generated on the third hop, only two arrive on the preferred path (at C and L), and so only these generate further packets. After five hops and 24 packets, the broadcasting terminates, compared with four hops and 14 packets had the sink tree been followed exactly.

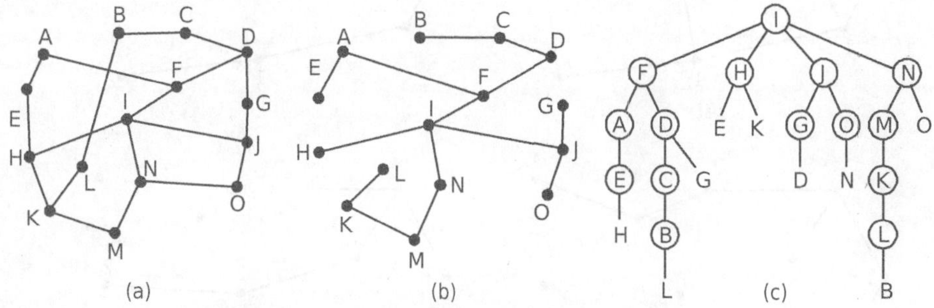

Fig. 8.11 Reserve path forwarding: (*a*) A subnet (*b*) A spanning tree (*c*) The tree built by reverse path forwarding

8.7.1 Advantage of Broadcast Routing

- The advantage of broadcast is that by the use of reverse path forward algorithm it is both reasonably efficient and easy to implement.
- It does not require router to know about spanning tree.
- It is used to transmit the data at multidestination.
- There is no requirement of overhead of destination.

8.7.2 Disadvantages of Broadcast Routing

- The disadvantage of broadcast is that each router must have knowledge of some spanning tree for the method to be applicable.
- Sometimes the information is available (with link state routing) and sometimes is not (with distance vector routing).

8.8 MULTICAST ROUTING

To send messages to well defined groups that are numerically large in size but small compared to the network as a whole. Sending message to such a group is called *multicasting* and its routing algorithm is called *multicast routing*. Multicasting requires group management. Some way is needed to create and destroy groups and to allow processes to join and leave groups.

To do multicasting routing each router computers a spanning tree occurring all others routers. For example in Fig 8.12(*a*) we have a subnet with two groups, 1 and 2. Some routers are attached to hosts that belong to one or both of these groups, as indicated in the figure. A spanning tree for the leftmost router is shown in Fig. 8.12(*b*).

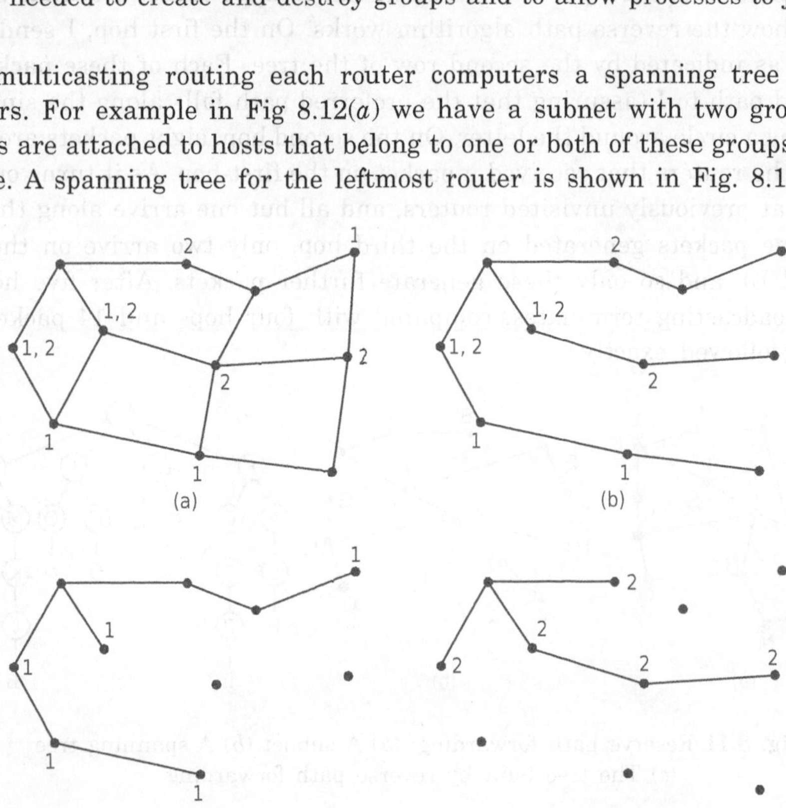

Fig. 8.12 (*a*) A subnet. (*b*) A spanning tree for the leftmost router. (*c*) A multi-cast tree for group 1. (*d*) A multi-cast tree for group 2

When a process sends a multicast packet to a group, the first router examines its spanning tree and prunes it, removing all lines that do not lead to hosts that are members of the group. In our example, Fig. 8.12 (*c*) shows the pruned spanning tree for group1. Similarly, Fig. 8.12 (*d*) shows the pruned spanning tree for group 2. Multicast packets are forwarded only along the appropriate spanning tree. No hosts interested in a particular group and no connections to other routers receives a multicast message for that group, it responds with a PRUNE message, telling the sender not to send it any more multicasts for that group. When a router with no group members among its own hosts has received such messages on all its lines, it, too, can respond with a PRUNE message. In this way, the subnet is recursively pruned.

One potential **disadvantage** of this algorithm is that it scales poorly to large networks. Suppose that a network has n groups, each with an average of m members. For each group m pruned spanning trees must be stored, for a total of mn trees. When many large groups exist, considerable storage is needed to store all the trees.

8.9 FLOW BASED ROUTING

A static algorithm that uses both topology and load or routing, is called *flow-based routing*. In some networks, the mean data flow between each pair of nodes is relatively stable and predictable. For example, in a corporate network for a retail store chain, each store might send orders, sales reports, inventory updates, and other well-defined types of messages to known sites in a predefined pattern, so that the total volume of traffic varies little from day to day. Under conditions in which the average traffic from I to j is known in advance and, to a reasonable approximation, constant in time, it is possible to analyze the flows mathematically to optimize the routing.

The basic idea behind the analysis is that for a given line, if the capacity and average flow are known, it is possible to compute the mean packet delay on that line from queuing theory. From the mean delays on all the lines, it is straightforward to calculate a flow-weighted average to get the mean packet delay for the whole subnet. The routing problem then reduces to finding the routing algorithm that produces the minimum average delay for the subnet. Fig. 8.13.

To use this technique, certain information must be known in advance. First the subnet topology must be known. Second, the traffic matrix, $F_{ij,}$ must be given. Third, the line capacity matrix, C_{ij} specifying the capacity of each line in bps must be available. Finally, a (possibly tentative) routing algorithm must be chosen.

As an example of this method, consider the full-duplex subnet of Fig. 8.13(*a*). The weights on the arcs give the capacities, C_{ij}, in each direction measured in kbps. The matrix of Fig. 8.13(*b*) has an entry for each source-destination pair. The entry for source i to destination j show the route to be used for i-j traffic, and also the number of packets/sec to be sent from source i to destination j. For example, 3 packets/sec go from B to D, and they use route BFD to get there. Notice that some routing algorithm has already been applied to derive the routes shown in the matrix.

Given this information, it is straightforward to calculate the total in line i, 9_i. For example, the B-D traffic contributes 3 packets/sec to the BF line and also 3 packets/sec to the FD line. Similarly, the A-D traffic contributes 1 packet/sec to each of three lines. The total traffic in each eastbound line is shown in the 9_i column of Fig. 8.14. In this example, all the traffic is symmetric, that is, the XY traffic is identical to the YX traffic, for all X and Y. In real networks this condition does not always hold. The figure also shows the mean number of packets/sec on each line, : C_i assuming a mean packet size of 1/: = 800 bits.

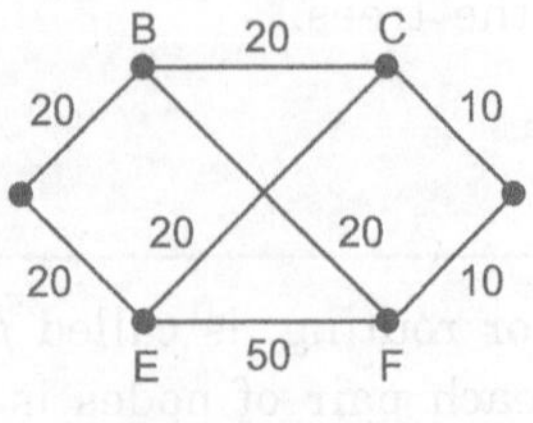

(a)

Destination (columns) / Source (rows):

	A	B	C	D	E	F
A		9 AB	4 ABC	1 ABCD	7 AE	4 AEF
B	9 BA		8 BC	3 BFD	2 BFE	4 BF
C	4 CBA	8 CB		3 CD	3 CE	2 CEF
D	1 DFBA	3 DFB	3 DC		3 DCE	4 DF
E	7 EA	2 EFB	3 EC	3 ECD		5 EF
F	4 FEA	4 FB	2 FEC	4 FD	5 FE	

(b)

Fig. 8.13 (*a*) A subnet with line capacities shown in kbps. (*b*) The traffic in packets/sec and the routing matrix

The next to last column of Fig. 8.14 gives the mean delay for each line derived from the queuing theory formula

$$T = 1/ (:C - 9)$$

Where 1/: is the mean packet size in bits, C is the capacity in bps, and 9 is the mean flow in packets/sec. For example, with a capacity : C = 25 packets/sec and an actual flow 9 = 14 packets/sec, the mean delay is 91 msec. Note that with 9 = 0, the mean delay is still 40 msec, because the capacity is 25 packets/sec. In other words, the "delay" includes both queuing and service time.

i	Line	λ_i (pkts/sec)	C_i (kbps)	μC_i (pkts/sec)	T_i (msec)	Weight
1	AB	14	20	25	91	0.171
2	BC	12	20	25	77	0.146
3	CD	6	10	12.5	154	0.073
4	AE	11	20	25	71	0.134
5	EF	13	50	62.5	20	0.159
6	FD	8	10	12.5	222	0.098
7	BF	10	20	25	67	0.122
8	EC	8	20	25	58	0.098

Fig. 8.14 Analysis of the subnet of figure 8.13 using a mean packet size of 800 bits. The reverse traffic (BA, CB, etc) is the same of the forward traffic

To compute the mean delay time for the entire subnet, we take the weighted sum of each of the eight lines, with the weight being the fraction of the total traffic using that line. In this example the mean turns out to be 86 msec.

To evaluate a different routing algorithm, we can repeat the entire process, only with different flows to get a new average delay. If we restrict ourselves to only single path routing algorithms, as we have done so far, there are only a finite number of ways to route packets from each source to each destination. It is always possible to write a program to simply try them all, one after another, and find out which one has the smallest mean delay. Since this calculation can be done off line in advance the fact that it may be time consuming is not necessarily a serious problem.

8.10 SHORTEST PATH ROUTING

The concept of a **shortest path** deserves some explanation. One-way of measuring path length is the number of hops. Using this metric, the paths ABC and ABE in Fig. 8.15 are equally long. Another metric is the geographic distance in Kilometers. In which case ABC is clearly much longer than ABE (assuming the figure is drawn to scale).

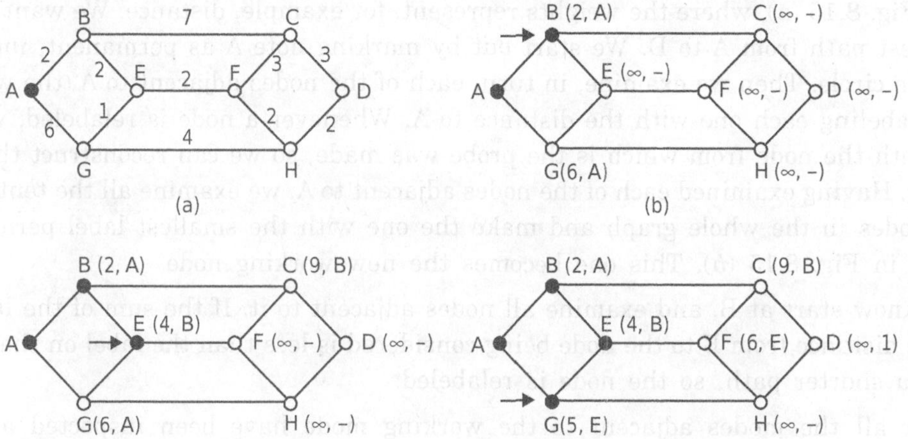

Fig. 8.15 The first five steps used in computing the shortest path from A to D. The arrows indicate the working node

However, many other metrics are also possible besides hops and physical distance. For example, each arc could be labeled with the mean queuing and transmission delay for some standard test packet as determined by hourly test runs. With this graph labeling, the shortest path is the fastest path, rather than the path with the fewest arcs or Kilometers.

In the most general case, the labels on the arcs could be computed as a function of the distance, band with, average traffic, communication cost, mean queue length, measured delay, and other factors. By changing the weighting function, the algorithm would than compute the *"shortest"* path measured according to anyone of a number of criteria, or a combination of criteria.

Several algorithms for computing the shortest path between two nodes of a graph are known. This one is due to dijkstra (1959). Each node is labeled (in parentheses) with its distance from the source node along the best-known path. Initially, no paths are known, so all nodes are labeled with infinity. As the algorithm proceeds and paths are found, the labels may change, reflecting better paths. A label may be either tentative or permanent. Initially, all labels are tentative. When it is discovered at a label represents the shortest possible path from the source to that node, it is made permanent and never changed thereafter.

To illustrate how the labeling algorithm works, look at the weighted, undirected graph of Fig. 8.15 (*a*), where the weights represent, for example, distance. We want to find the shortest path from A to D. We start out by marking note A as permanent, indicated by filled in circle. Then we examine, in turn, each of the nodes adjacent to A (the working node), relabeling each one with the distance to A. Whenever a node is relabeled, we also label it with the node from which is the probe was made, so we can reconstruct the final path later. Having examined each of the nodes adjacent to A, we examine all the tentatively labeled nodes in the whole graph and make the one with the smallest label permanent, as shown in Fig. 8.15 (*b*). This one becomes the new working node.

We know start at B, and examine all nodes adjacent to it. If the sum of the label on B and the distance from B to the node being considered is less than the label on that node, we have a shorter path, so the node is relabeled.

After all the modes adjacent to the working mode have been inspected and the tentative labels changed if possible, the entire graph is searched for the tentatively labeled node with the smallest value. This node is made permanent and become the working node for the next round. Fig. 8.15 shows the first five steps of the algorithm.

To see why the algorithm works, look at Fig. 8.15(*c*). At that point we have just made E permanent. Suppose that there were a shorter path than ABE, say AXYZE. There are two possibilities: either node Z was already been made permanent, or it has not been. If it has, then E has already been probed (on the round following the one when Z was made permanent), so the AXYZE path has not escaped our attention.

Now consider the case where Z is still tentatively labeled. Either label at Z is greater than or equal to that at E, in which case AXYZE can not be a shorter path than ABE, or it is less than that of E, in which case Z and not E will become permanent first, allowing E to be probed from Z.

SUMMARY

- Routing may be defined as the Process of moving information across an internetwork from a source to destination.
- Routing is done in the third layer of an OSI model. So the main function of the network layer is routing packets from the source machine to the destination machine.
- The routing algorithm is that of the network layer software responsible for deciding which output line an incoming packet should be transmitted on.
- Some properties that are desirable in a routing algorithm are: correctness, simplicity, robustness, stability, fairness and optimality.
- Routing algorithm can be grouped into two major classes: non-adaptive and adaptive.
- Non-adaptive algorithms do not base their routing decisions on measurements or estimates of the current traffic and topology. Instead the choice of the route to use to get from I to J (for all I and J) is computed is advance off line, and downloaded to the routers when the network is booted. This is also sometimes known as static routing.
- Adaptive routing, change their routing decisions to reflect changes in the topology and usually the traffic as well.
- Adaptive routing algorithms are again categorized into three categories: isolated adaptive, distributed adaptive and centralized adaptive.
- There are two methods to calculate the shortest path between two routers: distance vector routing and link state routing.
- In distance vector routing each router periodically shares its own knowledge about the network with its immediate neighbor routers.
- In distance vector routing, each router has a table with information about networks (ID, cost, and the router to access the particular network).
- In link state routing, each router creates its own link-state packet (LSP). Every other router receives this LSP through the flooding process. All routers, have the same information, this is compiled into the link state database. From this common database each router finds its own shortest path to the other routers by using the Dijkstra algorithm.
- Sending a packet to all the destinations simultaneously is termed as broadcasting.
- Broadcasting can be divided into three methods: Simple broadcasting, Flooding and Multi destination routing.

EXERCISE

1. What do you mean by the term routing?
2. What is the LSP database, and how is it created?
3. Contrast and compare distance vector routing with link state routing?
4. In routing, what does the term shortest mean?
5. Why is adaptive routing superior to non-adaptive routing?

6. What are the two most popular routing algorithms?
7. What are the three main elements of distance vector routing?
8. Describe an initial routing table for a distance vector router.
9. What are the three main elements of link state routing?
10. What algorithm does link state routing use to calculate the routing tables?
11. Explain the term routing along with its functions?
12. What do you mean by the term "Path Determination" in reference to routing?
13. Write a short note on any two technique used in routing?
14. Explain in detail the flooding routing algorithm? Also state its advantages and disadvantages.
15. Enumerate the hierarchical routing in detail?
16. Illustrate the concept of routing for mobile hosts?
17. Explain in detail the concept of shortest path routing?
18. What is the difference between broadcast routing and multicast routing?
19. Write short note on:
    (*a*) Broadcast Routing
    (*b*) Multicast Routing
    (c) Distance-vector Routing
20. Explain flow-based routing in brief with the help of a suitable example.
21. Explain in detail the concept of shortest path routing with the help of an example.

Chapter 9

Congestion Control

9.1 CONGESTION CONTROL

An important issue in a packet-switched network is **congestion**. Congestion in a network may occur if the **load** on the network & the number of packets sent to the network & is greater than the *capacity* of the network & the number of packets a network can handle. **Congestion control** refers to the mechanisms and techniques to control the congestion and keep the load below the capacity.

We may ask why there is congestion on a network. Congestion happens in any system that involves waiting. For example, congestion happens on a freeway because any abnormality in the flow, such as an accident during rush hour, creates blockage.

Congestion in a network or internetwork occurs because routers and switches have queues & buffers that hold the packets before and after processing. A router, for example, has an input queue and an output queue for each interface. When a packet arrives at the incoming interface, it undergoes three steps before departing, as shown in Fig. 9.1.

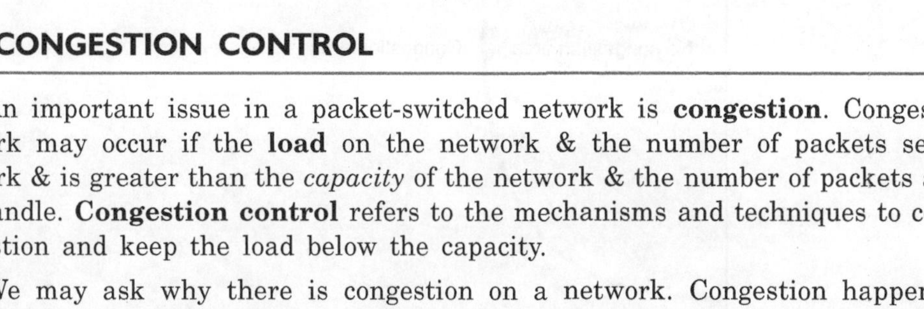

Fig. 9.1 Packet delay and network load

1. The packet is put at the end of the input queue while waiting to be checked.
2. The processing module of the queue and uses its routing table and the destination address to find the route.
3. The packet is put in the appropriate output queue and waits its turn to be sent.

We need to be aware of two issues. First, if the rate of packet arrival is higher than the packet processing rate, the input queues become longer and longer. Second, if the packet departure rate is less than the packet processing rate, the output queues become longer and longer.

Network Performance

Congestion control involves two factors that measure the performance of a network: *delay* and *throughput.*

1. Delay versus Load

Figure 9.2 shows the relationship between packet delay and network load.

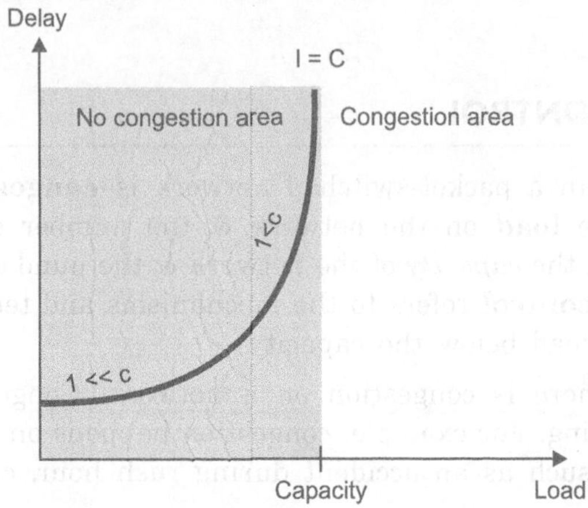

Fig. 9.2 Delay versus network load

Note that when the load is much less than the capacity of network, the delay is at a minimum. This minimum delay is composed of propagation delay and processing delay, both of which are negligible. However, when the load reaches the network capacity, the delay increases sharply because we now need to add the waiting time in the queues (for all routers in the path) to the total delay. Note that the delay becomes infinite when the load is greater than the capacity. If this is not obvious, consider the size of the queues when almost no packet reaches the destination, or reaches the destination with infinite delay: the queues become longer and longer. Delay has a negative effect on the load and consequently the congestion. When a packet is delayed, the source, not receiving the acknowledgement, retransmits the packet, which makes the delay, and the congestion, worse.

2. Throughput versus Load

Throughput in a network as the number of packets passing through the network in a unit of time. We can then plot the throughput versus the network load, as shown in Fig. 9.3.

Notice that when the load is below the capacity of the network, the throughput increases proportionally with the node. We expect the throughput to remain constant after the load reaches the capacity, but instead the throughput declines sharply. The reason is the discarding of packets by the routers. When the load exceeds the capacity, the queues become full and the routers have to discard some packets. Discarding packets does not reduce the number of packets in the network because the sources retransmit the packets, using time-out mechanisms, when the packets do not reach the destinations.

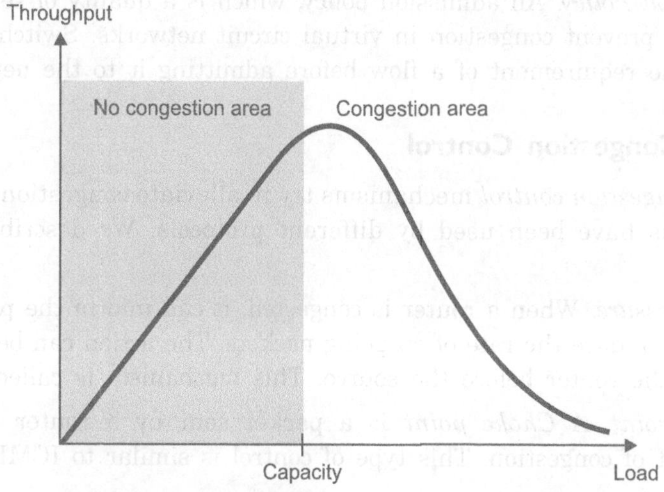

Fig. 9.3 Throughput versus network Load

9.2 PRINCIPLE OF CONGESTION CONTROL

Congestion control refers to techniques and mechanisms that can either prevent congestion, before it happens, or remove congestion, after it has happened. In general, we can divide congestion control mechanisms into two broad categories: open-loop congestion control (prevention) and closed-loop congestion control (removal).

1. Open-Loop Congestion Control

In *open-loop congestion control*, policies are applied to prevent congestion before it happens. In these mechanisms, congestion control is handled by either the source or the destination. We give a brief list of policies that can prevent congestion.

(*a*) *Retransmission Policy.* A good retransmission policy can prevent congestion. The retransmission policy and the retransmission timers must be designed to optimize efficiency and at the same time prevent congestion.

(*b*) *Window Policy.* The type of window at the sender may also affect congestion. The Selective Repeat window is better than the Go-Back-N window for congestion control.

(*c*) *Acknowledgement Policy.* The acknowledgement policy imposed by the receive may also affect congestion. If the receiver does not acknowledge every packet it receives, it may slow down the sender and help prevent congestion.

(*d*) *Discarding Policy.* A good discarding policy by the routers may prevent congestion and at the same time may not harm the integrity of the transmission. For example, in audio transmission, if the policy is to discard less sensitive packets when congestion likely to happen, the quality of sound is still preserved and congestion is prevented.

(*e*) *Admission Policy.* An admission policy, which is a quality of service mechanism, can also prevent congestion in virtual circuit networks. Switches in a flow first check the requirement of a flow before admitting it to the network.

2. Closed-Loop Congestion Control

Closed-loop congestion control mechanisms try to alleviate congestion after it happens. Several mechanisms have been used by different protocols. We describe a few of them here.

(*a*) *Back Pressure.* When a router is congested, it can inform the previous upstream router to reduce the rate of outgoing packets. The action can be recursive all the way to the router before the source. This mechanism is called backpressure.

(*b*) *Choke Point. A Choke point* is a packet sent by a router to the source to inform it of congestion. This type of control is similar to ICMP's source quench packet.

(*c*) *Implicit Signaling.* The source can detect an implicit signal concerning congestion and slow down its sending rate. For example, the mere delay in receiving an acknowledgement can be a signal that the network is congested.

(*d*) *Explicit Signaling.* The routers that experience congestion can send an explicit signal, the settling of a bit in a packet, for example, to inform the sender or the receiver of congestion. Explicit signaling, as we will see in Frame Relay congestion control, can occur in either the forward or the backward direction.

(*i*) *Backward Signaling:* The bit can be set in a packet moving in the direction opposite to the congestion. This bit can warn the source that there is congestion and that it needs to slow down to avoid the discarding of packets.

(*ii*) *Forward Signaling:* The bit can be set in a packet moving in the direction of the congestion. This bit can warn the destination that there is congestion. The receiver in this case can use policies, such as slowing down the acknowledgements, to alleviate the congestion.

9.3 EXAMPLES OF CONGESTION CONTROL

To better understand the concept of congestion control, let us give two examples: one in TCP and the other in Frame Relay.

9.3.1 Congestion Control in TCP

As we have side, an Internet is a combination of networks and connecting devices (*e.g.,* routers). A packet from a sender may pass through several routers before reaching its final destination. A router has a buffer that stores the incoming packets, processes them, and forwards them. If a router receives packets faster than it can process, congestion might occur and some packets could be dropped. When a packet does not reach the destination, no acknowledgement is sent for it. The sender has no choice but to retransmit the lost packet. This may create more congestion and more dropping of packets, which means more retransmission and more congestion. A point may that be reached in which the whole system collapses and no more data can be sent. TCP therefore needs to find some way to avoid this situation.

TCP assumes that the cause of a lost segment is due to congestion in the network.

We know that the sender window size is determined by the available buffer space in the receiver. In other words, we assumed that it is only the receiver that can dictate to the sender the size of the sender's window. We totally ignored another entity here - the network. If the network cannot deliver the data as fast as they are created by the sender, it needs to tell the sender to slow down. In other words, in addition to the receiver, the network is a second entity that determines the size of the sender's window in TCP.

If the cause of the lost segment is congestion, retransmission of the segment does not remove the cause-it aggravates it.

Congestion Window

In TCP, the sender's window size is determined not only by the receiver but also by congestion in the network.

The sender has two pieces of information: the receiver-advertised window size and the congestion window size. The actual size of the window is the minimum of these two.

Actual window size = minimum (receiver window size, congestion window size)

Congestion Avoidance

To avoid congestion, the sender TCP has two strategies; one is called *slow start and additive increase,* and the second is called *multiplicative decrease.*

Slow Start: At the beginning of a connection, TCP sets the congestion window size to the maximum segment size. For each segment that is acknowledged, TCP increases the size of the congestion window by one maximum segment size until it reaches a threshold of one-half of the allowable window size. This is called *slow start,* which is totally misleading because the process is not slow at all. The size of the congestion window increases exponentially. The sender sends one segment, receives one acknowledgement, increases the size to two segments, sends two segments, receives acknowledgements for two segments, increases the size to four segments, sends four segments, receives acknowledgement for four segments, increase the size to eight segments, and so on. In other words, after receipt of the third acknowledgement, the size of the window has been increased to eight segments. The rate is exponential (2^3-8). Slow start is used with additive increase.

Additive Increase

To avoid congestion before it happens, one must slow down this exponential growth. After the size reaches the threshold, the size is increased one segment for each acknowledgement even if an acknowledgement is for several segments. The additive-increase strategy continues as long as the acknowledgements arrive before their corresponding time-outs or the congestion window size reaches the receiver window value.

Multiplicative Decrease

If congestion occurs, the congestion window size must be decreased. The only way the sender can guess that congestion has occurred is through a lost segment. If the sender does not receive an acknowledgement for a segment before its retransmission timer has matured, it assumes that there is congestion. Because networks today are to some extent noise-free, it is more probable that a segment is lost than that it is corrupted. The strategy says if a time-out occurs, the threshold must be set to one-half of the last congestion window size, and the congestion window size should start from 1 again. In other words, the sender returns to the slow start phase. Note that the threshold is reduced to one-half of the current congestion window size each time a time-out occurs. This means that the threshold is reduced exponentially (multiplicative decrease). Figure 9.4 shows the idea.

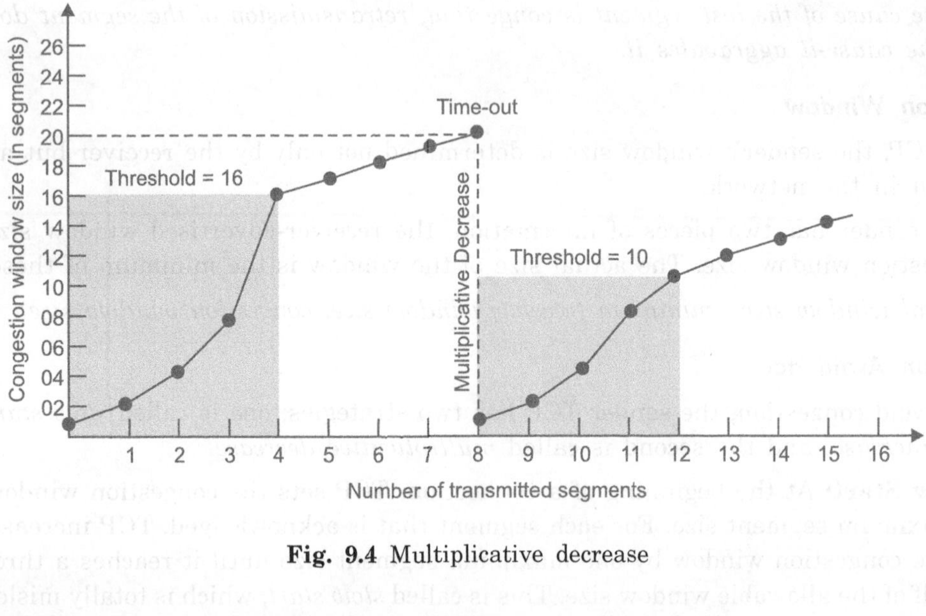

Fig. 9.4 Multiplicative decrease

9.3.2 Congestion Control in Frame Relay

Congestion in a Frame Relay network decreases throughput and increased delay. A high throughput and low delay are the main goals of the Frame Relay protocol. Frame Relay does not have flow control. Frame Relay allows the user to transmit bursty data. This means that a Frame Relay network has the potential to be really congested with traffic, thus requiring congestion control.

Congestion Avoidance

For congestion avoidance, the Frame Relay protocol uses 2 bits in the Frame to explicitly warn the source and the destination of the presence of congestion.

BECN

The **Backward Explicit Congestion Notification (BECN)** bit warns the sender of congestion in the network. One might ask how this accomplished since the frames are traveling away from the sender. In fact, there are two methods: The switch can use a predefined connection (DLCI = 1023) to send special frames for this specific purpose. The sender can respond to this warning by simply reducing the data rate. Figure 9.5 shows the use of BECN.

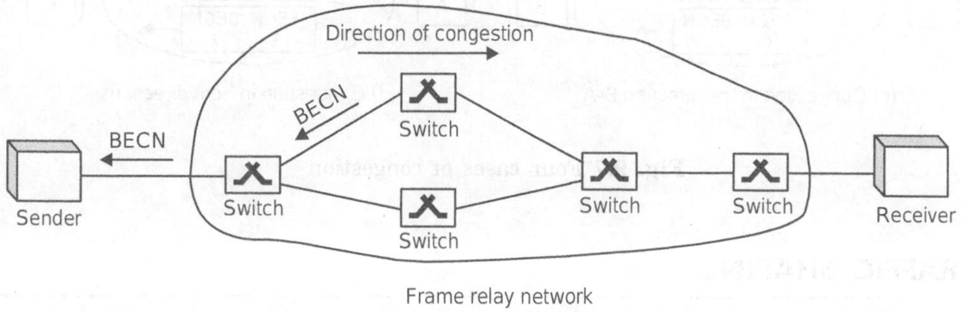

Fig. 9.5 BECN

FECN

The **Forward Explicit Congestion Notification (FECN)** bit is used to warn the receiver of congestion in the network. It might appear that the receiver cannot do anything to relieve the congestion. However, the Frame Relay protocol assumes that the sender and receiver are communicating with each other and are using some type of flow control at a higher level. For example, if there is an acknowledgement mechanism at this higher level, the receiver can delay the acknowledgement, thus forcing the sender to slow down. Figure 9.6 shows the use of FECN.

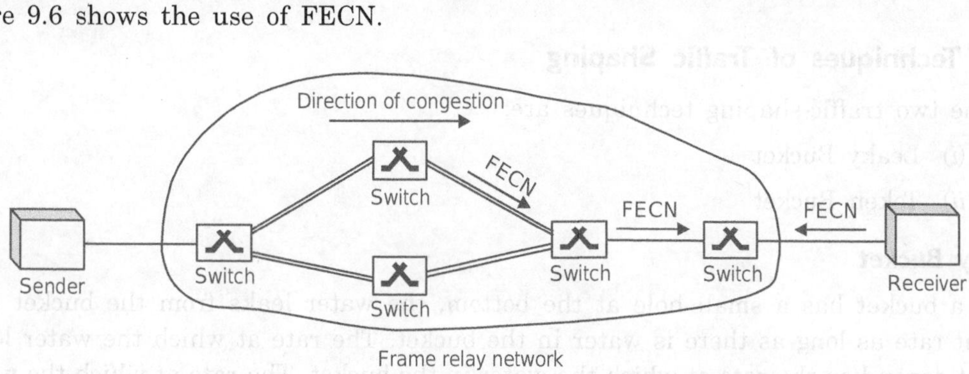

Fig. 9.6 FECN

When two endpoints are communicating using a Frame Relay network, four situations may occur with regard to congestion. Figure 9.7 shows these four situations and the values of FECN and BECN.

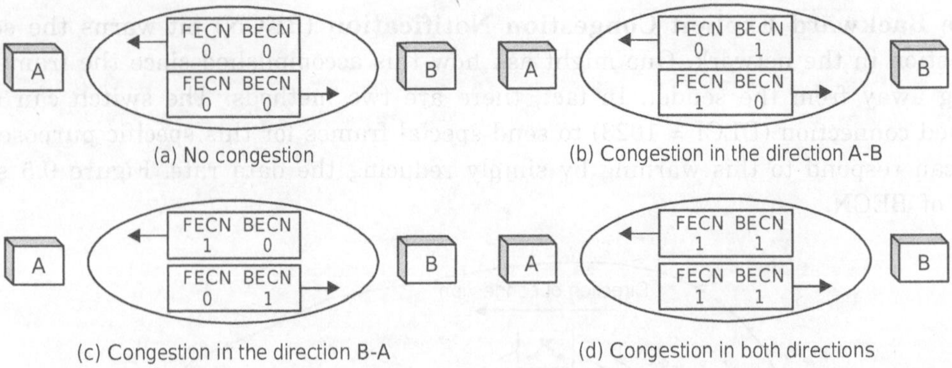

Fig. 9.7 Four cases of congestion

9.4 TRAFFIC SHAPING

Traffic Shaping is a mechanism to control the amount and the rate of the traffic sent to the network. Two techniques can shape traffic: leaky bucket and token bucket.

- Traffic shaping is about regulating the average rate of data transmission.
- Traffic Shaping smooth out the traffic on the server, rather than on the client side.
- Monitoring a traffic flow is called traffic policing. Agreeing to a traffic shape and policing it afterward are easier with virtual circuit subnets than with datagram subnets.
- Traffic shaping is an open loop method of congestion control.

9.4.1 Techniques of Traffic Shaping

The two traffic-shaping techniques are:

(*i*) Leaky Bucket

(*ii*) Token Bucket

I Leaky Bucket

If a bucket has a small hole at the bottom, the water leaks from the bucket at a constant rate as long as there is water in the bucket. The rate at which the water leaks does not depend on the rate at which the water in the bucket. The rate at which the water leaks does not depend on the rate at which the water is input to the bucket unless the bucket is empty. The input rate can vary, but the output rate remains constant. Similarly, in networking, a technique called *leaky bucket* can smooth out bursty traffic. Bursty chunks are stored in the bucket and sent out at an average rate. Figure 9.8 shows a leaky bucket and its effects.

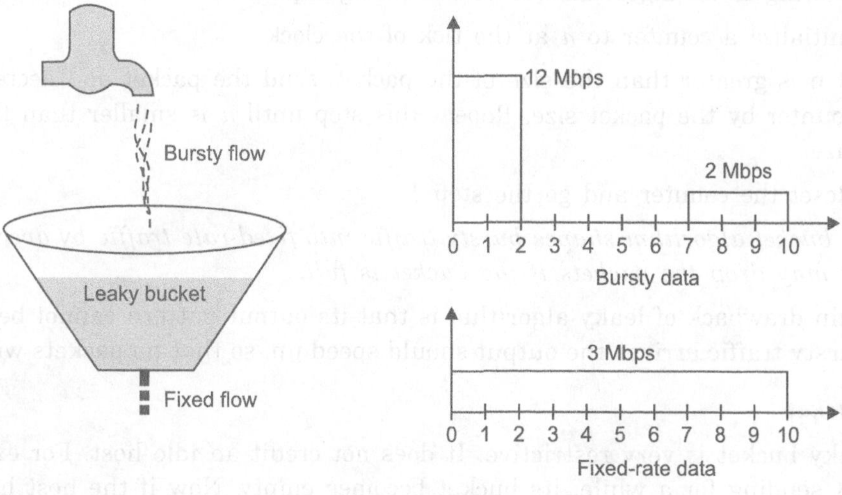

Fig. 9.8 Leaky bucket

In the figure, we assume that the network has committed a bandwidth of 3 Mbps for a host. The use of the leaky bucket shapes the input traffic to make it conform to this commitment. In the figure the host sends a burst of data at a rate of 12 Mbps for 2 s, for a total of 24 megabits of data. The host is silent for 5 s and then sends data at a rate of 2 Mbps for 3 s, for a total of 6 megabits of data. In the entire host has sent 30 megabits of data in 10 s. The leaky bucket smoothes the traffic by sending out data at a rate of 3 Mbps during the same 10 s. Without the leaky bucket, the beginning burst may have hurt the network by consuming more bandwidth than is set aside for this host. We can also see that the leaky bucket may prevent congestion. As an analogy, consider the freeway during rush hour (bursty traffic). If, instead, commuters could stagger their working hours, congestion on our freeways could be avoided.

A simple leaky bucket implementation is shown in Fig. 9.9. A FIFO queue holds the packets. If the traffic consists of fixed-size packets (*e.g.*, cells in ATM networks), the process removes a fixed number of packets from the queue at each tick of the clock. If the traffic consists of variable-length packets, the fixed output rate must be based on the number of bytes or bits.

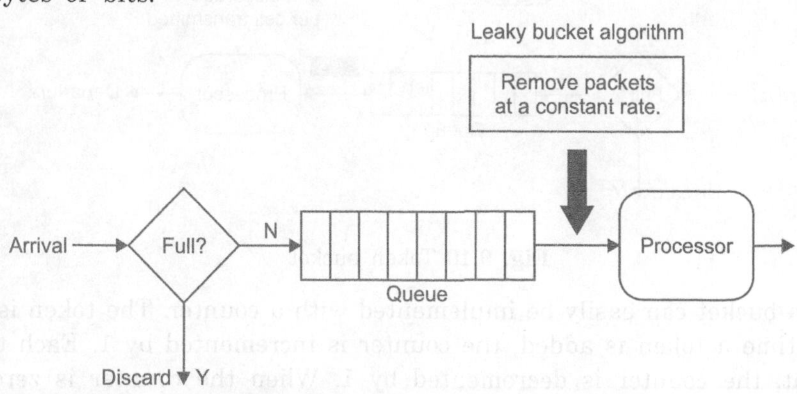

Fig. 9.9 Leaky bucket implementation

The following is an algorithm for variable-length packets:

1. Initialize a counter to *n* at the tick of the clock.
2. If n is greater than the size of the packet, send the packet and decrement the counter by the packet size. Repeat this step until *n* is smaller than the packet size.
3. Reset the counter and go the step 1.

A leaky bucket algorithm shapes bursty traffic into fixed-rate traffic by averaging the data rate. It may drop the packets if the bucket is full.

The main drawback of leaky algorithm is that its output pattern cannot be modified *i.e.*, if the bursty traffic arrives the output should speed up, so that no packets will be lost.

2. Token Bucket

The leaky bucket is very restrictive. It does not credit an idle host. For example, if a host is not sending for a while, its bucket becomes empty. Now if the host has bursty data, the leaky bucket allows only an average rate. The time when the host was idle is not taken into account. On the other hand, the *token bucket* algorithm allows idle hosts to accumulate credit for the future in the form of tokens. For each tick of the clock, the system sends n tokens to the bucket. The system removes one token for every cell (or byte) of data sent. For example, if n is 100 and the host is idle for 100 ticks, the bucket collects 10,000 tokens. Now the host can consume all these tokens in one tick with 10,000 cells, or the host takes 1000 ticks with 10 cells per tick. In other words, the host can send bursty data as long as the bucket is not empty Fig. 9.10 shows the idea.

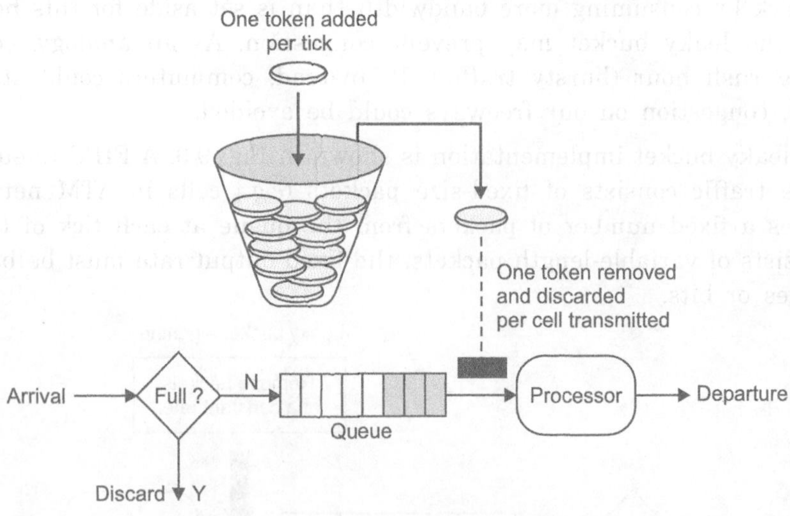

Fig. 9.10 Token bucket

The token bucket can easily be implemented with a counter. The token is initialized to zero. Each time a token is added, the counter is incremented by 1. Each time a unit of data is sent, the counter is decremented by 1. When the counter is zero, the host cannot send data.

The token bucket allows bursty traffic at a regulated maximum rate.

Combining Token Bucket and Leaky Bucket

The two techniques can be combined to credit an idle host and at the same time regulate the traffic. The leaky bucket is applied after the token bucket; the rate of the leaky bucket needs to be higher than the rate of tokens dropped in the bucket.

Resource Reservation

A flow of data needs resources such as a buffer, bandwidth, CPU time, and so on. The quality of service is improved if these resources are reserved beforehand. One QoS model called Integrated Services, which depends heavily on resource reservation to improve the quality of service.

Admission Control

Admission control refers to the mechanism used by a router, or a switch, to accept or reject a flow based on predefined parameters called flow specifications. Before a router accepts a flow for processing, it checks the flow specification to see if its capacity (in terms of bandwidth, butter size, CPU speed, etc.) and its previous commitments to other flows can handle the new flow.

Comparison of Leaky Bucket and Token Bucket Regulator

Sr. No.	*Leaky Bucket*	*Token Bucket*
1.	Output stream has fixed rate of delivery even for bursty input.	Allows some burstiness in the output stream by giving faster response to sudden bursts of input.
2.	Leaky bucket discards packets when the bucket fills up.	When bucket fills up token are discarded not the packets.

9.5 CHOKE PACKETS

- This approach can be used in virtual circuits as well as in the datagram subnets.
- In this technique each router associates a real variable with each of its output lines. This real variable say "u" has a value between 0 and 1 and it indicates the percentage utilization of that line.
- If the value of "u" goes above the threshold then that output line will enter into a "warning" state. The router will check each newly arriving packet to see if its output line is in the "warning state".
- If it is in the warning state then the router will send back a **choke packet** signal to the sending host.
- The sender host will not generate any more choke packets.
- Several variations on the congestion control algorithm have been proposed, depending on the value of thresholds.

- Depending on the threshold value, the choke packets can contain a mild warning, a stern warning or an ultimatum.
- Another variation can be in items of queue lengths or buffer utilization instead of using the line utilization as a deciding factor.

9.5.1 Disadvantage of Choke Packets

The problem with choke packet technique is that the action to be taken by the source host on receiving a choke packet is voluntary and not compulsory.

9.6 LOAD SHEDDING

- Admission controls, choke packets, fair queuing are the techniques suitable for light congestion.
- But if these techniques cannot make the congestion to disappear, then the load shedding technique is to be used.
- When buffers become full routers simply discard packets.
- Which packets to discard may depend on the applications running? For file transfer, an old packet is worth more than a new one. We cannot discard older packets since this will cause a gap in received data.
- For real time voice or video it is probably better to throw away old data and keep new packets.
- Get the application itself to mark packets with discard priority.
- Co-operation from the sender is required while discarding the packets. For many applications, some packets are more important than others.
- For example, certain algorithm for compressing video periodically transmits an entire frame and then sends subsequent frames as differences from the last full frame.
- To implement an intelligent discarding policy, application must mark their packets in priority classes to indicate how important they are. The low priority packets being cheaper to send than the higher priority ones.

SUMMARY

- When too many packets rushing to a node or a part of network, the network performance degrades, and this situation is called as congestion.
- Congestion control is a process of maintaining the number of packets in a network below a certain level at which performance falls off.
- Congestion control makes sure that subnet is able to carry the offered traffic. So congestion control is different process than flow control.
- Congestion control refers to the mechanisms and techniques to control the congestion and keep the load below the capacity.

- Congestion control involves two factors that measure the performance of a network is: delay and throughput.
- Congestion control mechanisms are divided into two broad categories: open-loop congestion control and closed-loop congestion control.
- Flow control is handled through the Backward Explicit Congestion Notification (BECN) bit and/or the Forward Explicit Congestion Notification (FECN) bit of the address field of the frame.
- The two techniques for traffic shaping are leak bucket and token bucket techniques.
- The leaky bucket algorithm is a model for frame transmission at a switch. The queue output bits at a fixed rate while the bits enter the queue at a variable rate.
- The token bucket algorithm provides a different kind of traffic shaping than the leaky bucket algorithm.
- The leaky bucket algorithm does not allow idle hosts to save up permission to send large bursts later while the token bucket algorithm does allow saving, up to the maximum size of the bucket, n.
- The token bucket algorithm throws away tokens when the bucket fills up but never discards packets. In contrast, the leaky bucket algorithm discards packets when the bucket fills up.

EXERCISE

1. What do you mean by the term congestion control?
2. Explain the term traffic shaping.
3. Illustrate some of the principles of congestion control.
4. Enumerate the factors by which we can measure the performance of a network?
5. Explain with the help of a diagram the relationship between the packet delay and the network load?
6. Explain the categories of congestion control mechanism?
7. Write short note on the following:
   (*a*) Open–loop congestion control
   (*b*) Closed–loop congestion control
8. Explain the terms backward signaling and forward signaling.
9. Explain the term congestion control with the help of a suitable example?
10. What do you mean by traffic shaping. Explain only one of the technique by which traffic can be shaped?
11. Write short note on the following:
    (*a*) Leaky bucket technique
    (*b*) Token bucket technique
12. What is the meaning of forward explicit congestion notification.

13. Compare and contrast between the leaky bucket technique and token bucket technique of traffic shaping?

14. Write short note on choke packets?

15. What are the advantages and disadvantages of the Choke packets?

16. What do you mean by the term load shedding?

17. What do you mean by the term backward explicit congestion notification?

18. Give the comparison between the terms BECN and FECN?

19. Explain the concept of congestion control in frame relay?

20. Draw the diagram of leaky bucket technique and also explain its concept in detail?

Chapter 10

TCP/IP

10.1 HISTORY OF TCP/IP

The TCP/IP protocol was deployed to the ARPANET network with some persuasion. Not all sites were preparing to convert over their protocols, so Cerf, Jon Postel, and the TCP/IP team turned off the NCP network channel numbers on the ARPANET IMP's for a full day in mid 1982, so that only sites using TCP/IP could still operate. To emphasize the point, they disabled NCP again for two days later that fall. The full switchover to TCP/IP was performed on January 1, 1983, without too many problems, although a few recalcitrant sites were down as long as three months while they retrofitted their systems.

In 1984, the US Department of Defense made TCP/IP the standard for all military computers networking, which gave it a high profile and stable funding.

In 1985, Dan Lynch and the Internet Architecture Board held a three-day workshop on TCP/IP for the computer industry, which was attended by about 50 researchers and 250 vendor representatives.

In September 1988, Lynch organized an Internet convention that later became the Interop trade show. Fifty companies were invited to the first show to demonstrate interoperation of their TCP/IP packages, and five thousand engineers attended. The interoperability demonstration was successful, validating TCP/IP's open design and showing that the network standard could become a multi-vendor product.

About TCP/IP

The Internet protocols consist of a suite of communication protocols, of which the two best known are the *Transmission Control Protocol (TCP) and the Internet Protocol (IP)*. The Internet protocol suite not only includes lower-layer protocols (such as TCP and IP), but it also specifies common applications such as electronic mail, terminal emulation, and file transfer. This chapter provides a broad introduction to specifications that comprise the Internet protocols. Discussions include IP addressing and key upper-layer protocols used in the Internet. Specific routing protocols are addressed individually later in this document.

Internet protocols were first developed in the mid-1970s, when the Defense Advanced Research Projects Agency (DARPA) became interested in establishing a packet-switched network that would facilitate communication between dissimilar computer systems at research institutions. With the goal of heterogeneous connectivity in mind, DARPA funded research by Stanford University and Bolt, Beranek, and Newman (BBN). The result of this development effort was the Internet protocol suite, completed in the late 1970s.

TCP/IP later was included with Berkeley Software Distribution (BSD) UNIX and has since become the foundation on which the Internet and the World Wide Web (WWW) are based.

10.2 INTRODUCTION TO TCP/IP

Definition

TCP/IP (Transmission Control Protocol/Internet Protocol) is the basic communication language or protocol of the Internet. It can also be used as a communications protocol in a private network (either an intranet or an extranet). When you are set up with direct access to the Internet, your computer is provided with a copy of the TCP/IP program just as every other computer that you may send messages to or get information from also has a copy of **TCP/IP.**

OR

The internet is a decentralized global network of millions of computers & computer networks. These n\w are used to communicate messages or information to each other and they all follow a common set of protocols called **TCP/IP.**

10.2.1 Application Layers for TCP/IP

There are two application layers for TCP/IP:

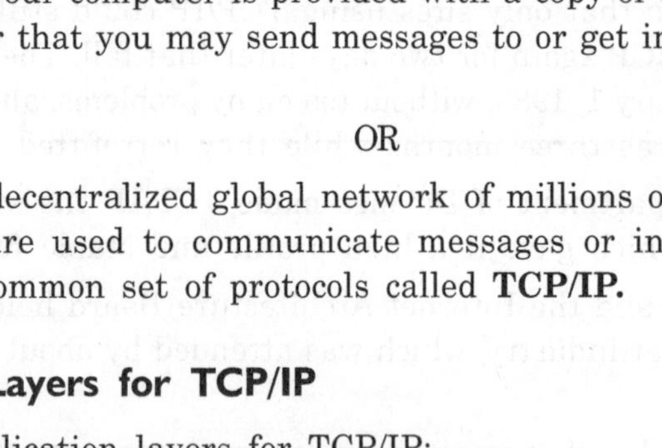

Fig. 10.1 Two application layers for TCP/IP

1. Higher Layer

The higher layer is the TCP *i.e.*, TRANSMISSION CONTROL PROTOCOL manages the assembling of a message or file into smaller packets that are transmitted over the Internet and received by a TCP layer that reassembles the packets into the original message.

The TCP also ensures the safe delivery at the destination & the assembling of all the packets to get the complete lot of data at the destination computers.

2. Lower Layer

The lower layer is the IP *i.e.*, INTERNET PROTOCOL handles the address part of each packet so that it gets to the right destination. Each gateway computer on the network checks this address to see where to forward the message. Even though some packets from the same message are routed differently than others, they'll be reassembled at the destination.

10.3 THE FIVE-LAYER TCP/IP MODEL

There are five types of layers in the TCP/IP model:-

1. Application layer.
2. Transport layer.
3. Network layer.
4. Data link layer.
5. Physical layer.

1. The Application Layer

There are many applications available in the TCP/IP suite of protocols. Some of the most useful ones are for sending mail (SMTP), transferring files (FTP), and displaying web pages (HTTP).

Another important application layer protocol is the *Domain Name System (DNS)*. Domain names are significant because they guide users to where they want to go on the Internet.

A. DNS

The Domain Name System is a distributed database of domain name and IP address bindings. A domain name is simply an alphanumeric character string separated into segments by periods. It represents a specific and unique place in the "domain name space." DNS makes it possible for us to use identifiers such as rabbit.com to refer to an IP address on the Internet. Name servers contain information on some segment of the DNS and make that information available to clients who are called *resolvers*.

- Every TCP/IP implementation has a software routine called the *name resolver (NR)* to request a DNS lookup from a name server (NS)
- Two types of name resolution:
  - o *Recursive resolution*—NR asks NS to resolve names for which it does not have an authoritative answer by querying other name servers (*predominant method*).
  - o *Iterative resolution*—NR asks NS to provide the IP address of a NS that can provide an authoritative solution.

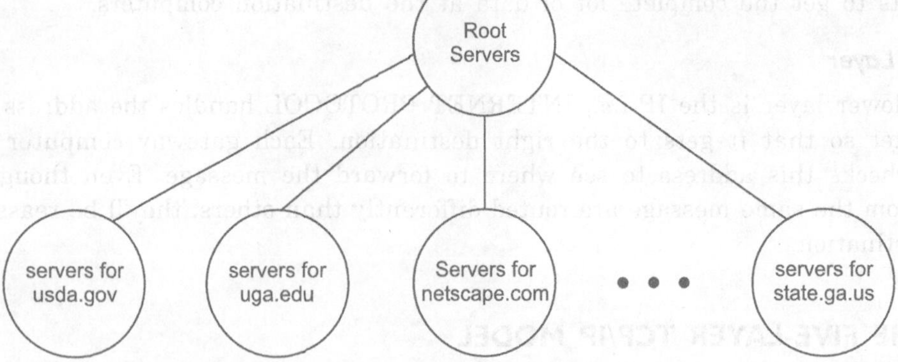

Fig. 10.2 Domain name system

2. The Transport Layer

There are two primary transport layer protocols: Transmission Control Protocol (TCP) and User Datagram Protocol (UDP). They provide end-to-end communication services for applications:

A. UDP

This is a minimal service over IP, adding only optional check summing of data and multiplexing by port number. UDP is often used by applications that need multicast or broadcast delivery, services not offered by TCP. Like IP, UDP is connectionless and works with datagram's.

- UDP provides an unreliable, connectionless delivery.
- Application programs using UDP are responsible for message loss, duplication, delay, out-of-order delivery, and loss of connectivity.
- Examples of applications that use UDP transport include Network Time Protocol (NTP), Sun's Network File System (NFS), and the Simple Network Management Protocol (SNMP).
- Each UDP message is called a *user datagram.*

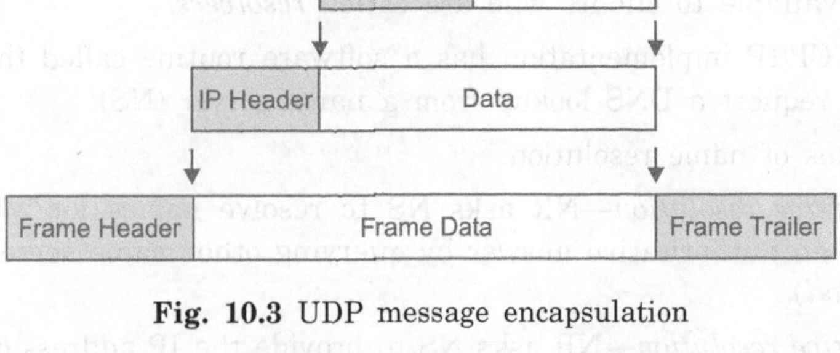

Fig. 10.3 UDP message encapsulation

0	16	31
UDP Source Port	UDP Destination Port	
UDP Message Length	UDP Checksum	
Data		
......		

Fig. 10.4 UDP message format

The various fields of the UDP Message Format are discussed as follows:

- *Source port address:* The source port address is the address of the application program that has created the message.
- *Destination port address:* The destination port address is the address of the application program that will receive the message.
- *Total length:* The total length field defines the total length of the user datagram in bytes.
- *Checksum:* The checksum is a 16-bit field used in error detection.
- UDP messages are stored in queues on destination host, one queue per destination port.

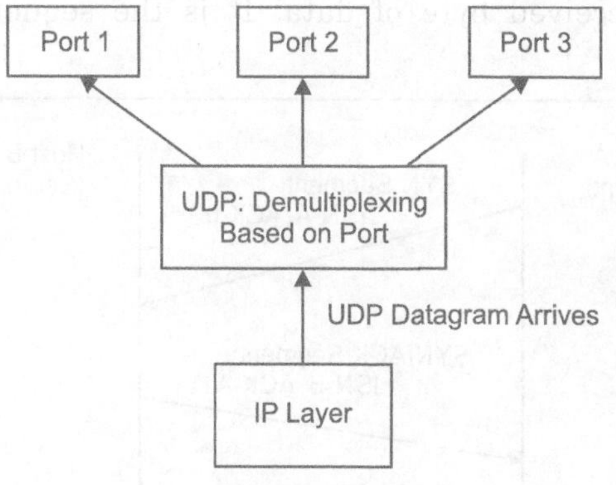

Fig. 10.5

B. TCP

TCP is a connection-oriented transport service; it provides end-to-end reliability, re-sequencing, and flow control. TCP enables two hosts to establish a connection and exchange streams of data, which are treated in bytes. The delivery of data in the proper order is guaranteed. TCP can detect errors or lost data and can trigger retransmission until the data is received, complete and without errors.

TCP Connection Socket

A TCP connection is done with a 3-way handshake between a client and a server. The following is a simplified explanation of this process.

- The client asks for a connection by sending a TCP segment with the SYN control bit set.
- The server responds with its own SYN segment that includes identifying information that was sent by the client in the initial SYN segment.
- The client acknowledges the server's SYN segment.

The connection is then established and is uniquely identified by a 4-tuple called a *socket or socket pair.*

(Destination IP address, Destination port number) and (Source IP address, source port number).

TCP Header

Every TCP segment has a header. The header comprises all necessary information for reliable, complete delivery of data. Among other things, such as IP addresses, the header contains the following fields:

Sequence Number. This 32-bit number contains either the sequence number of the first byte of data in this particular segment or the Initial Sequence Number (ISN) that identifies the first byte of data that will be sent for this particular connection.

The sequence number is used to ensure the data is reassembled in the proper order before being passed to an application protocol.

Acknowledgement Number. This 32-bit number is the other host's sequence number + 1 of the last successfully received byte of data. It is the sequence number of the next expected byte of data.

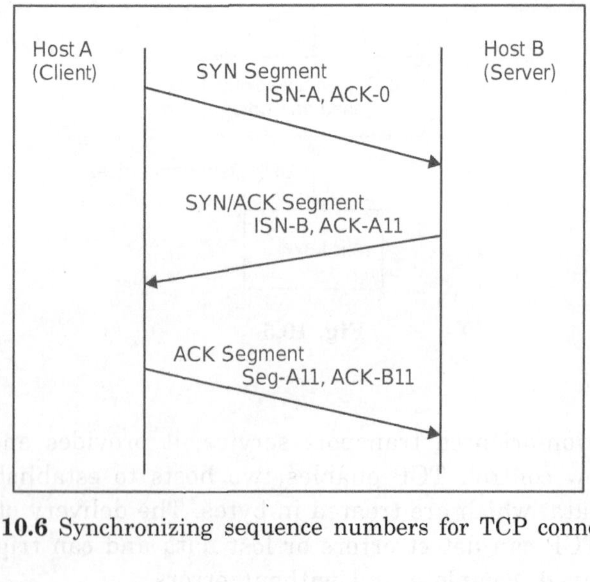

Fig. 10.6 Synchronizing sequence numbers for TCP connection

3. The Network Layer

A. ARP

The Address Resolution Protocol is used to translate virtual addresses to physical ones. The network hardware does not understand the software-maintained IP addresses.

There are three general addressing strategies:

1. Table lookup
2. Translation performed by a mathematical function
3. Message exchange

ARP employs the third strategy, message exchange. ARP defines a request and a response. Only the computer whose IP address matches the request sends a response.

4. The Data Link Layer

The main task of the data link layer is to take a raw transmission facility and transform it into a line that appears free of transmission errors in the network layer.The data link layer should provide error control between adjacent nodes.

Network Frames

- The basic unit of a physical network is a **frame**
- General form of a network frame is shown below:

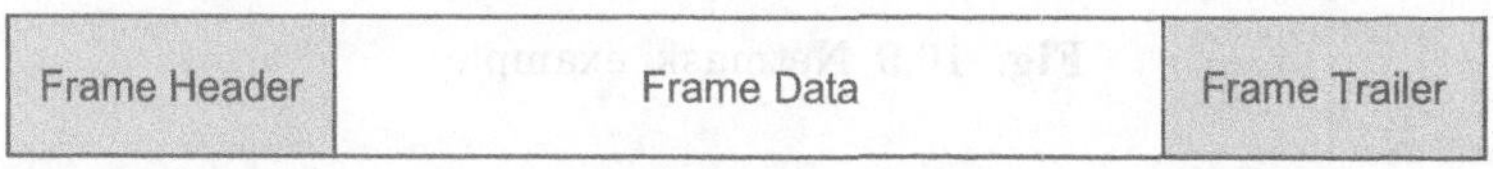

Fig. 10.7 General form of a network frame

- Network frame formats
  - o Ethernet frames
    - – Version 2 format

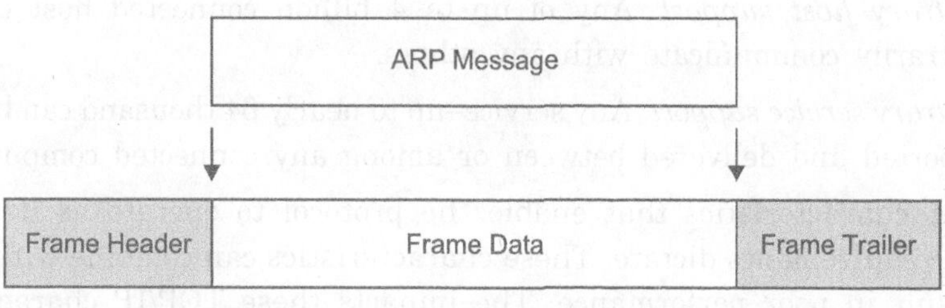

Fig. 10.8 ARP message format

5. The Physical Network

The physical network is a collection of computers, communications devices, wiring, etc. that communicate directly with one another (*e.g.*, Ethernet, Token Ring).

A. IP Addresses

- IP addresses are unique, 32-bit addresses.
- They correspond to connections, not hosts (generally, move connection ⇒ change IP address).

- IP addresses are referenced by humans via dotted decimal (or dotted quad) notation, one number per 8 bits (1 octet or byte), *e.g.*, 128.192.6.7.
- These addresses consist of three primary classes A, B, and C (class D is for multicast) of the form [netid, hostid].
- Netmask determines which portion of an IP address is the network address and which is the host address.
- An IP address bit is a **network** address bit if the corresponding net mask bit is 1.
- An IP address bit is a **host** address bit if the corresponding netmask bit is 0.
- Netmask example is shown below:

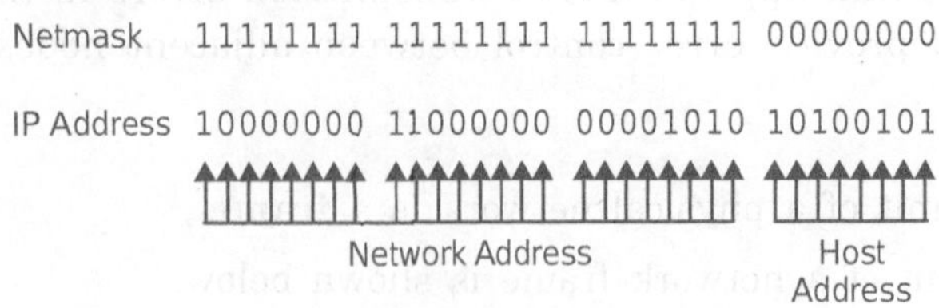

Fig. 10.9 Netmask example

10.4 CHARACTERISTICS OF TCP/IP

1. *Connectionless.* Signal transport paths aren't required to be continuously available.
2. *Adaptive routing diversity.* Transport paths and other network characteristics are not fixed but learned and capable of being altered at any time.
3. *Arbitrary host support.* Any of up to 4 billion connected host computers can arbitrarily communicate with any others.
4. *Arbitrary service support.* Any service–up to nearly 64 thousand can be concurrently supported and delivered between or among any connected computer hosts.

TCP/IP has characteristics that enable the protocol to operate as its standardized implementation requirements dictate. These characteristics can combine with development choices that result in poor performance. The impacts these TCP/IP characteristics have on an application depend on whether the application is transactional or streaming.

Another aspect of TCP/IP is slow-start, which takes place whenever a connection is established. Slow-start is an artificial limit on the number of data segments that can be sent before acknowledgment of those segments is received. Slow-start is designed to limit network congestion. When a connection over Ethernet is established, regardless of the receiver's window size, a 4KB transmission can take up to 3-4 RTT due to slow-start.

A TCP/IP optimization called the Nagle Algorithm can also limit data transfer speed on a connection. The Nagle Algorithm is designed to reduce protocol overhead for applications that send small amounts of data, such as Telnet, which sends a single character at a time. Rather than immediately send a packet with lots of header and little data, the stack waits for more data from the application, or an acknowledgment, before proceeding.

When a TCP connection is closed, connection resources at the node that initiated the close are put into a wait state, called TIME-WAIT, to guard against data corruption if duplicate packets linger in the network. This ensures both ends are finished with the connection. This can cause depletion of resources required per-connection, such as RAM and ports, when applications open and close connections frequently.

10.5 INTERNET PROTOCOL (IP)

- The Internet Protocol (IP) is an:
  - o **Unreliable** (delivery not guaranteed)
  - o **Connectionless** (packets independent of one another)
  - o **Best-effort** (attempt to deliver packets)

  packet delivery mechanism.
- Basic unit is the **datagram** (up to 65,535 bytes).
- This is the host network layer delivery protocol designed for the internet.
- IP is a connectionless datagram protocol with no guarantee of reliability.
- Encapsulation of IP datagram in a physical frame.

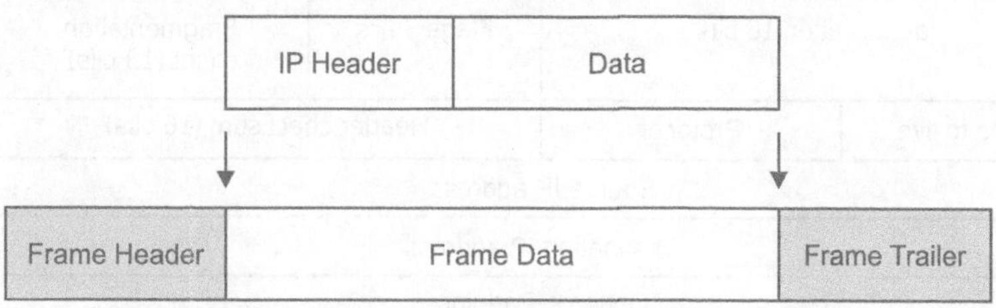

Fig. 10.10 Encapsulation of IP datagram

- It is an unreliable protocol because it does not provide any error control or flow control.
- IP can only detect the error and discards the packet if it is corrupted.
- If IP is to be made more reliable, then it must be paired with a reliable protocol such as TCP at the transport layer.
- Each IP datagram is handled independently and each one can follow a different route to the destination.
- So there is a possibility of receiving out of order packets at the destination. Some packets may even be lost or corrupted.
- IP relies on a higher-level protocol to take care of all these problems.

10.5.1 Datagram

- Packets in IP layer are called datagram. Fig. 10.11 shows the IP datagram format.
- A datagram is a variable length packet with two parts namely the header and data.

- The header is 20 to 60 bytes in length. It contains the information essential for routing and delivery.
- The other part of the datagram is the data field, which is of variable length.

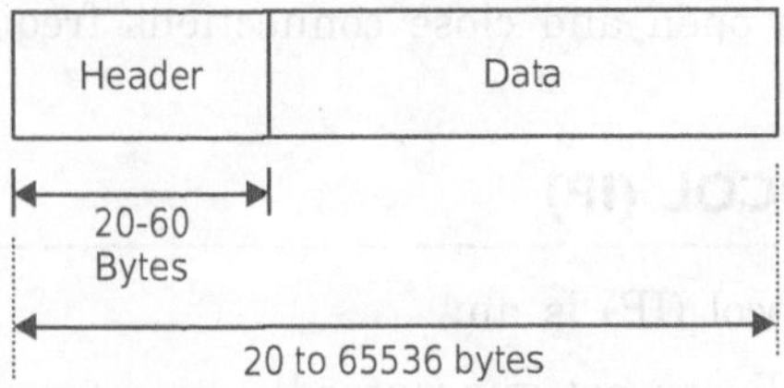

Fig. 10.11 IP datagram format

10.5.2 Structure of IP Frame Header

The IP frame header contains routing information and control information associated with datagram delivery. The IP header structure is as shown in Fig. 10.12.

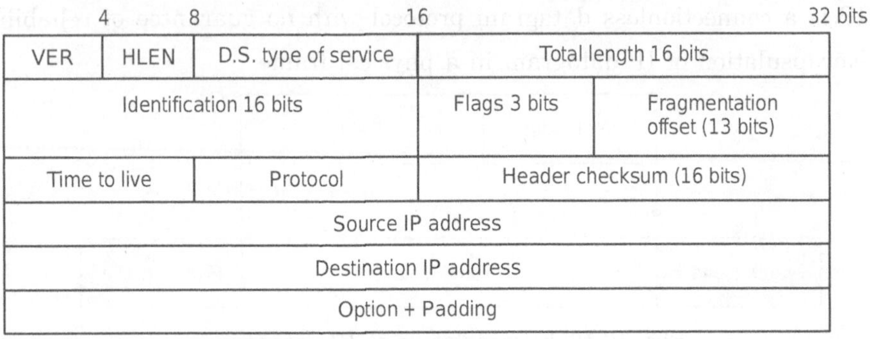

Fig. 10.12 IP header structure

Various fields in the IP header are as follows:

1. *VER (version):* This field defines the version of IP. Current version of IP is IPv4 and the latest version of IP is IPv6. It is a four bit long field.
2. *HLEN (Header length):* This field defines the length of the datagram header in 4-byte word. Its value must be multiplied by 4 to give the length in bytes.
3. *Differential Services (DS):* This field defines the class of the datagram for quality of service purpose.

   Networks may offer service precedence, meaning that they accept traffic only above certain precedence at times of high load. There is a three way trade off between low delay, high reliability and throughput.
4. *Total Length:* This field defines the total length of the IP datagram. The total length includes the length of header as well as the data field.
   - The field length of this fields is 16 bits so the total length of the IP datagram is restricted to (2^{16}-1) = 65535 bytes of which 20 to 60 bytes are the header and the remaining are data.

- This field allows the length of a datagram to be up to 65,535 bytes, although such long datagrams are impractical for most hosts and networks.
- All hosts must be prepared to accept datagram of up to 576 bytes, regardless of whether they arrive whole or in fragments.
- It is recommended that hosts send datagram larger than 576 bytes only if the destination is prepared to accept larger datagram.

5. *Identification, flag and offset:*

- *Identification:* This field identifies the datagram originating from the source host. When a datagram is fragmented, the value in the identification field is copied into all fragments. The identification number helps the destination in reassembling the fragments of the datagram.
- *Flags:* This is a three-bit field. The 3 bits are shown in Fig 10.13.
- First bit is reserved, and it should be 0.
- The second bit is called "Do Not Fragment" bit. If this bit "1" then machine should not fragment the datagram.

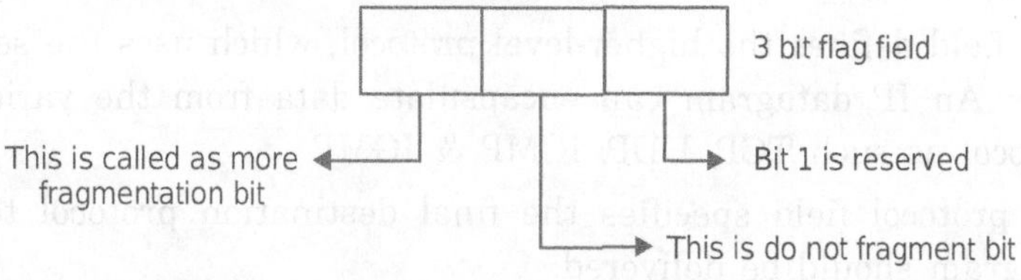

Fig. 10.13 Flag bits

- But if the value of this bit is 0 then the machine should fragment the datagram if only if necessary.
- The third bit is called as "More Fragment Bit". If it is 1 it means that datagram is not the last fragment but if its value is 0 it shows that this is the last or the only fragment.
- *Fragmentation Offset:*
- This is a 13 field, which shows the relative position of this fragment with respect to the whole datagram.
- It is the offset of the data in the original datagram measured in units of 8 bytes.
- To understand this refers Fig. 10.14.
- The original IP packet (datagram) contains 4000 bytes numbered from 0 to 3999. It is fragmented into three fragments.
- The first fragment contains 1400 bytes numbered from 0 to 1399. The offset for this fragment is 0/8 = 0. Similarly the offsets for the other two fragments are 1400/8 = 175 and 2800/8 = 350 respectively as shown in Fig 10.14.
- The offset is measured in units of 8 bytes. Because the length of the offsets field is 13 bits.
- So the fragments should be of size such that the first byte number is divisible by 8.

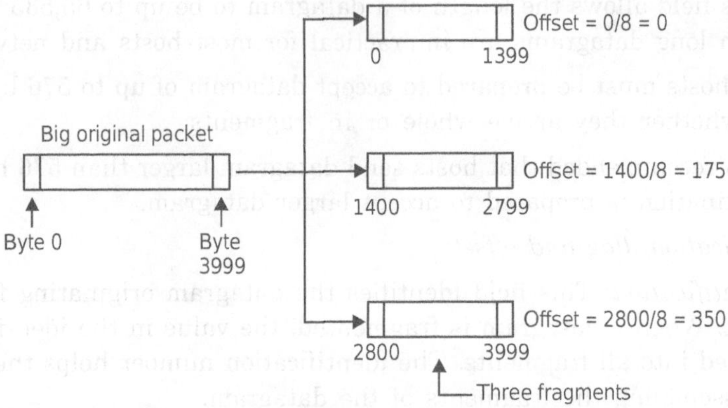

Fig. 10.14 Example of fragmentation

6. *Time to live:* This is an 8 bit long field which controls the maximum numbers of routers visited by the datagram.
7. *Protocol:*
   - This field defines the higher-level protocol, which uses the services of the IP layer. An IP datagram can encapsulate data from the various higher-level protocol as such TCP, UDP, ICMP & IGMP.
   - The protocol field specifies the final destination protocol to which the IP datagram should be delivered.
   - Since IP multiplexes and demultiplexes data from different higher-level protocols, the value of protocol field helps in demultiplexing at a final destination.
8. *Header Checksum:* A checksum in IP packet covers on the header only. Since some header fields change, this recomputed and verified at each point that the internet header is processed.
9. *Source Address:* This field is used for defining the IP address of the source.
10. *Destination Address:* This field is used for defining the IP address of the destination.
11. *Options:*
    - Options are not required for every datagram. They are used for network testing and debugging.
    - IP provides several optional features, allowing the packet's sender to set requirements on the path it takes through the network (source routing), trace the route a packet takes (record route), and label packets with security features.

10.5.3 Services Provided

IP provides following services:

- *Addressing:* IP headers contain 32 bit addresses, which identify the sending and receiving hosts. These addresses are used by intermediate routers to select a path through the network for the packet.

- *Fragmentation:* IP packets may be split, or fragmented, into smaller packets. This permits a large packet to travel across a network which can only handle smaller packets. IP fragments and reassembles packets transparently.
- *Packet time out:* Each IP packet contains a time to live (TTL) field, which is decremented every time a router handles a packet. If TTL reaches zero, the packet is discarded, preventing packets from running in circles forever and flooding a network.
- *Type of Service:* IP supports traffic prioritization by allowing packets to be labeled with an abstract type of service.

10.5.4 Comparison between TCP and UDP

S. No.	*TCP*	*UDP*
1.	TCP connection oriented.	UDP is connectionless.
2.	TCP connection is byte stream.	UDP connection is message stream.
3.	TCP does not support multicasting and broadcasting.	UDP support broadcasting.
4.	It provides error control and flow control.	It does not provide flow control and error control.
5.	TCP supports full duplex transmission.	UDP does not support full duplex transmission.
6.	TCP is reliable.	UDP is unreliable.
7.	TCP packet is called segment.	UDP packet is called user datagram.
8.	Overhead low, but higher than UDP.	Overhead very low.
9.	Transmission speed high, but not as high as UDP.	Transmission speed very high.
10.	Well known applications and protocols—FTP, Telnet, SMTP, DNS HTTP, POP, NNTP, IMAP, BGP, IRC, NFS, (later versions).	Multimedia application DNS, BOOTP, DHCP, TFTP, SNMP, RIP, NFS early versions.

SUMMARY

- The Internet protocols consist of a suite of communication protocols, of which the two best known are the *Transmission Control Protocol (TCP) and the Internet Protocol (IP).*
- TCP/IP (Transmission Control Protocol/Internet Protocol) is the basic communication language or protocol of the Internet. It can also be used as a communications protocol in a private network.
- The internet is a decentralized global network of millions of computers & computer networks.
- The higher layer is the TCP, manages the assembling of a message or file into smaller packets.
- The lower layer is the IP, handles the address part of each packet.

- There are five types of layers in the TCP/IP model:
  1. Application layer.
  2. Transport layer.
  3. Network layer.
  4. Data link layer.
  5. Physical layer.
- The DNS is a distributed database of domain name and IP address bindings.
- UDP, adding only optional check summing of data and multiplexing by port number.
- TCP, provides end-to-end reliability, re-sequencing, and flow control.
- The ARP is used to translate virtual addresses to physical ones.
- Data link layer is to take a raw transmission facility and transform it into a line that appears free of transmission errors in the network layer.
- The Internet Protocol (IP) is an:

  Unreliable (delivery not guaranteed).

  Connectionless (packets independent of one another).

  Best-effort (attempt to deliver packets).
- A datagram is a variable length packet with two parts namely the header and data.
- IP provides following services: **Addressing, Fragmentation, Packet time out and Type of Service**

EXERCISE

1. What do you understand by TCP/IP?

2. Explain application layers for TCP/IP.

3. Explain the TCP/IP model with its layer.

4. What is DNS explain with neat diagram?

5. What is the difference between recursive resolution and iterative resolution?

6. Describe the characteristics of TCP/IP.

7. What do mean by the term internet protocol?

8. Explain the structure of IP frame header.

9. Explain the comparison between TCP and UDP.

10. Describe the different services, which are provided by IP.

11. What is the process of the TCP connection socket?

12. What is the use of the TCP and UDP in transport layer?

Chapter 11

APPLICATION LAYER

11.1 NETWORK SECURITY

Security is a broad topic and covers a multitude of sins. In its simplest form, it is concerned with making sure that nosy people cannot read, or worse yet modify messages intended for other recipients. It is concerned with people trying to access remote services that they are not authorized to use. It also deals with how to tell whether that message purportedly from the IRS saying: "Pay by Friday or else" is really from the IRS or from the Mafia. Security also deals with the problems of legitimate messages being captured and replayed and with people trying to deny that they sent certain messages.

Most security problems are intentionally caused by malicious people trying to gain some benefit or harm someone. A few of the most common perpetrators are listed in Fig. 11.1. It should be clear from this list that making a network secure involves a lot more than just keeping it free of programming errors. It involves outsmarting often intelligent, dedicated and sometimes well-funded adversaries. It should also be clear that measures that will stop casual adversaries will have little impact on the serious ones.

Adversary	*Goal*
Student	To have fun snooping on people's email
Hacker	To test out someone's security system; steal data
Sales rep	To claim to represent all of Europe, not just Andorra
Businessman	To discover a competitor's strategic marketing plan
Ex-employee	To get revenge for being fired
Accountant	To embezzle money from a company
Stockbroker	To deny a promise made to a customer by e-mail
Conman	To steal credit card numbers for sale
Spy	To learn an enemy's military strength
Terrorist	To steal germ warfare secrets.

Fig. 11.1 Some people who cause security problems and why

Network security problems can be divided roughly into four intertwined areas: secrecy, authentication, non repudiation, and integrity control. **Secrecy** has to do with keeping information out of the hands of unauthorized users. This is what usually comes to mind when people think about network security. **Authentication** deals with determining whom you are talking to before revealing sensitive information or entering into a business deal. **Non repudiation** deals with signatures: How do you prove that your customer really placed an electronic order for ten million left-handed doohickeys at 89 cents each when he later claims the price was 69 cents? Finally, how can you be sure that message you received was really the one sent and not something that malicious adversary modified in transit or concocted?

All these issues (secrecy, authentication, non repudiation, and integrity control) occur in traditional systems, too, but with some significant differences. Secrecy and integrity are achieved by using registered mail and locking documents up. Robbing the mail train is harder than it was Jesse James' day.

Also, people can usually tell the difference between an original paper document and a photocopy, and if often matters to them. As a test, make a photocopy of a valid check. Try cashing the original check at your bank on Monday. Now try cashing the photocopy of the check on Tuesday. Observe the difference in the bank's behavior. With electronic checks, the original and the copy are indistinguishable. It may take a while for banks to get used to this.

People authenticate other people by recognizing their faces, voices, and handwriting. Proof of signing is handled by signatures on letterhead paper, raised seals, and so on. Tampering can usually be detected by handwriting, paper, and ink experts. None of these options are available electronically. Clearly, other solutions are needed.

Before getting into the solutions themselves, it is worth spending a few moments considering where in the protocol stack network security belongs. There is probably no one single place. Every layer has something to contribute. In the physical layer, wiretapping can be foiled by enclosing transmission lines in sealed tubes containing argon gas at high pressure. Any attempt to drill into a tube will release some gas, reducing the pressure and triggering an alarm. Some military systems use this technique.

In the **data link layer**, packets on a point-to-point line can be encoded as they leave one machine and decoded as they enter another. All details can be handled in the data link layer, with higher layers oblivious to what is going on. This solution breaks down when packets have to transverse multiple routers, however, because packets have to be decrypted at each router, leaving them vulnerable to attacks from within the router. Also, it does not allow some sessions to be protected (e.g., those involving on-line purchases by credit card) and others not. Nevertheless, **link encryption**, as this method is called, can be added to any network easily and is often useful.

In the **network layer**, firewalls can be installed to keep packets in or keep packets out. In the **transport layer**, entire connections can be encrypted, end to end, that is, process to process. Although these solutions help with secrecy issues and many people are working hard to improve them, none of them solve the authentication or non repudiation problem in a sufficiently general way. To tackle these problems, the solutions must be in the application layer.

11.1.1 Security Attacks

"Security attack is any action that compromises the security of "information" owned by an organization."

ATTACK: An attempted cryptanalysis is termed as an attack.

Classification of Security Attacks

The security attacks are classified into two categories:

1. Active attacks
2. Passive attacks

1. Active Attacks

An active attack attempts to alter the system resources or affect their operation.

OR

Active attack involves some modification of the data stream or the creation of a false stream.

Active attacks are subdivided into four categories:

1. *Masquerade.* A masquerade attack takes place when one entity pretends to be a different entity. It usually includes one of the other forms of active attacks.
2. *Replay.* It involves the passive capture of the data unit and its subsequent retransmission to produce an unauthorized effect.
3. *Modification of messages.* It simply means that some portion of the original message is altered, or that messages are delayed or reordered to produce an unauthorized effect.
4. *Denial of Services.* This prevents or inhibits the normal use or management of communication facilities. This attack may have a specific target: an entity may suppress all messages directed to a particular destination.

2. Passive Attacks

"A passive attack attempts to learn or make use of information from the system but does not affect system resources."

Passive attacks are subdivided into two categories.

1. *Release of message contents.* The release of message contents is easily understood. A telephone conversation, an e-mail message and a transferred file may contain sensitive or confidential information.
2. *Traffic analysis.* Suppose we had a way of masking the contents of a message or other information traffic so that opponents, even if they captured the message, could not extract the information from the message. The common technique for masking contents is encryption.

Note: Passive attacks are very difficult to detect because they do not involve any alteration of the data, these can be prevented by means of encryption. Active attacks are quite difficult to prevent absolutely because to do so requires physical protection of all communication facilities and paths at all times.

11.1.2 Security Services

"Security services are the services that enhance the security of the data processing system and the information transfers of an organization".

The services are intended to counter the security attacks and they make use of one or more security mechanisms to provide the service.

Classification of Security Services

1. *Authentication.* If the message sent by the sender is accurately received by the receiver then it is termed as authentication. Authentication is managed on the network by differ ways:

   (*a*) By sending their PIN number,

   (*b*) By using their ATM card, electronic key etc.

   (*c*) By sending finger prints, DNA patterns etc.

   Two specific authentication services are defined in the standard:

   (*a*) *Peer entity authentication.* Used in association with a logical connection to provide confidence in the identity of the entities connected.

   (*b*) *Data-origin authentication.* In a connectionless transfer, provides assurance that the source of received data is as claimed.

2. *Data Integrity.* If a received communication is exactly what the sender party has send (*i.e.*, Contain no modification, insertion, deletion or replay etc.) then it is said to have integrity. Therefore, the parties must be able to assure themselves that the message they received is exactly what the other party has sent.

   (*a*) *Connection Integrity with recovery.* Provides for the integrity of all user data on a connection and detects any modification, insertion, deletion or replay etc., of any data within an entire data sequence, with recovery attempted.

   (*b*) *Connection Integrity without recovery.* As connection integrity with recovery but provides only detection without recovery.

3. *Non-Repudiation.* It prevents either sender or receiver from denying a transmitted message. Thus when a message is sent, the receiver can prove that the message was in fact sent by the alleged sender. Similarly when a message is received, the sender can prove that the message was in fact received by the alleged receiver.

   (*a*) *Non-repudiation, origin.* Proof that the message was sent by the specified party.

   (*b*) *Non-repudiation, destination.* Proof that the message was received by the specified party.

Example

Suppose customer places the purchase order be a company for buying shares. If the price of a shares goes down on the same day, the sender makes a dispute that he has never placed such a purchase order. Similarly, if the price of a share goes up during the same day, the company may rise a dispute that it has never received such a purchase order.

4. *Access Control.* The prevention of unauthorized use of a resource *i.e.*, this service controls who can have access to a resource, under what conditions access can occur and what those accessing the resource are allowed to do.

   OR

   Access control is the ability to limit and control the access to host systems and applications via communication links.

5. *Data Confidentiality.* Data confidentiality is a service which provides protection of data from unauthorized disclosure. Confidentiality is the protection of transmitted data from passive attacks.

   Four categories of data confidentiality are:

   (*a*) *Connection confidentiality.* The protection of all user data on a connection.

   (*b*) *Connection confidentiality.* The protection of all user data in a single data block.

   (*c*) *Selective-Field confidentiality.* The confidentiality of selected fields within the user data on a connection or in a single data block.

   (*d*) *Traffic Flow confidentiality.* The protection of the information that might be derived from observation of traffic flows, *i.e.*, the attacker should not be able to observe the source and destination frequency, length or other characteristics of the traffic.

11.1.3 Security Mechanisms

Security mechanisms are that which are designed to detect, prevent or recover from a security attack.

Mechanisms are divided into those that are implemented in a specific protocol layer and to those that are not specific to any particular protocol layer or security service.

(a) Specific Security Mechanisms

May be incorporated into the appropriate protocol layer in order to provide some of the OSI security services.

(*i*) *Encipherment.* The use of mathematical algorithms to transform data into a form that is not readily intelligible. The transformation and subsequent recovery of the data depend on an algorithm and zero or more encryption keys.

(*ii*) *Digital Signature.* Data appended to, or a cryptography transformation of, a data unit that allows a recipient of the data unit to prove the source and integrity of the data unit and protect against forgery (for example, by the recipient).

(*iii*) *Access Control.* A variety of mechanisms that enforce access rights to resources.

(*iv*) *Data Integrity.* A variety of mechanisms used to assure the integrity of a data unit or stream of data units.

(*v*) *Authentication Exchange.* A mechanism intended to ensure the identity of an entity by means of information exchange.

(*vi*) *Traffic Padding.* The insertion of bits into gaps in a data stream to frustrate traffic analysis attempts.

(vii) *Routing Control.* Enables selection of particular physically secure routes for certain data and allows routing changes, especially when a breach of security is suspected.

(viii) *Notarization.* The use of a trusted third party to assure certain properties of a data exchange.

(b) Pervasive Security Mechanisms

Mechanisms that are not specific to any particular OSI security service or protocol layer.

(i) *Trusted Functionality.* That which is perceived to be correct with respect to some criteria (for example, as established by a security policy).

(ii) *Security Label.* The marking bound to a resource (which may be a data unit) that names of designates the security attributes of that resource.

(iii) *Event Detection.* Detection of security-relevant events.

(iv) *Security Audit Trail.* Data collected and potentially used to facilitate a security audit, which is an independent review and examination of system records and activities.

(v) *Security Recovery.* Deal with requests from mechanisms, such as event handling and management functions, and takes recovery actions.

11.2 AUTHENTICATION

Authentication plays a very important role in PPP because PPP is designed for use over dial-up links where verification of user identity is necessary. *Authentication* means validating the identity of a user who needs to access a set of resources. PPP has created two protocols for authentication: Password Authentication Protocol (PAP) and Challenge Handshake Authentication Protocol (CHAP).

11.2.1 PAP

The *Password Authentication Protocol (PAP)* is a simple authentication with a two step process:

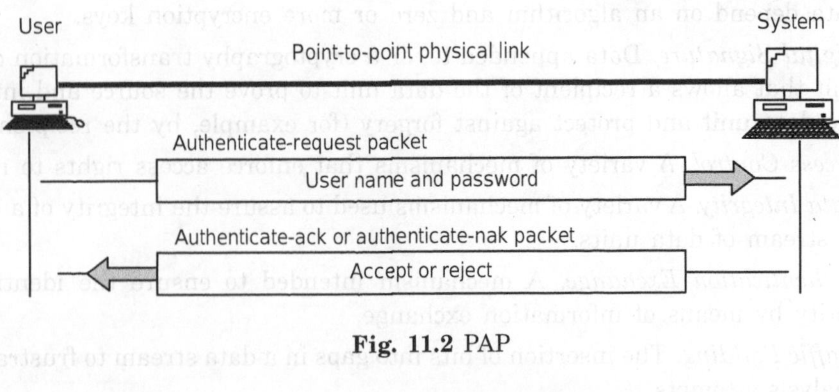

Fig. 11.2 PAP

- The user who wants to access a system sends authentication identification (usually the user name) and a password.
- The system checks the validity of the identification and password and either accepts or denies connection.

For those systems that require more security, PAP is not enough; a third party with access to the link can easily pick up the password and access the system resources. Fig. 11.2 shows the idea of PAP.

PAP Packets

PAP packets are encapsulated in a PPP frame. What distinguishes a PAP packet from other packets is the value of the protocol field, $C023_{16}$. There are three PAP packets: authenticate-request, authenticate-ack, and authenticate-nak. The first packet is used by the user to send the user name and password. The second is used by the system to allow access. The third is used by the system to deny access. Fig. 11.3 shows the format of the three packets.

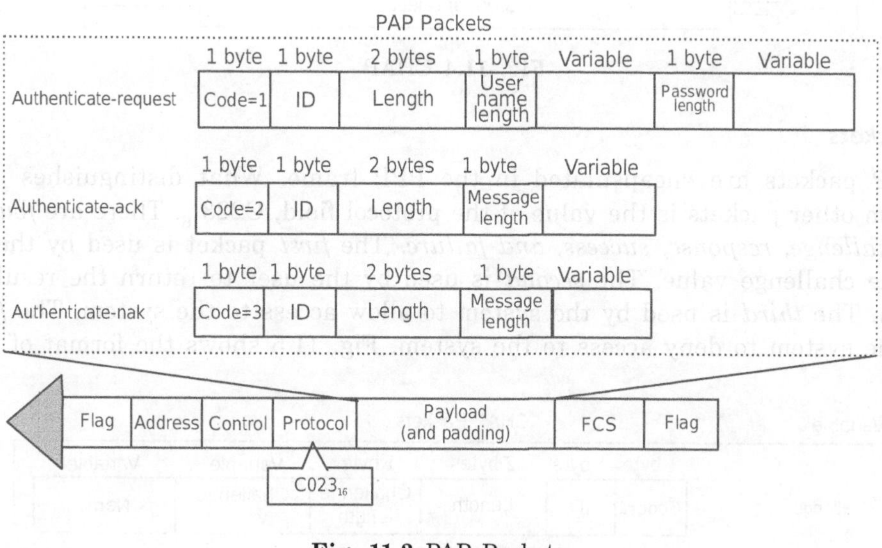

Fig. 11.3 PAP Packets

11.2.2 CHAP

The *Challenge Handshake Authentication Protocol (CHAP)* is a three way handshaking authentication protocol that provides more security than PAP. In this method, the password is kept secret; it is never sent on line.

- The system sends to the user a challenge packet containing a challenge value, usually a few bytes.
- The user applies a predefined function that takes the challenge value and the user's own password and creates a result. The user sends the result in the response packet to the system.
- The system does the same. It applies the same function to the password of the user (known to the system) and the challenge value to create a result. If the

result created is the same as the result sent in the response packet, access is granted; otherwise, it is denied.

CHAP is more secure than PAP, especially if the system continuously changes the challenge value. Even if the intruder learns the challenge value and the result, the password is still secret. Fig. 11.4 shows the idea.

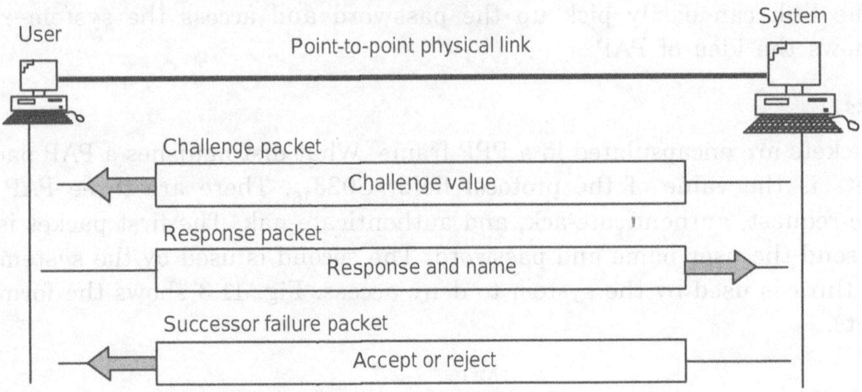

Fig. 11.4 CHAP

CHAP Packets

CHAP packets are encapsulated in the PPP frame. What distinguishes a CHAP packet from other packets is the value of the protocol field, $C223_{16}$. There are *four CHAP packets: challenge, response, success, and failure.* The *first* packet is used by the system to send the challenge value. The *second* is used by the user to return the result of the calculation. The *third* is used by the system to allow access to the system. The *fourth* is used by the system to deny access to the system. Fig. 11.5 shows the format of the four packets.

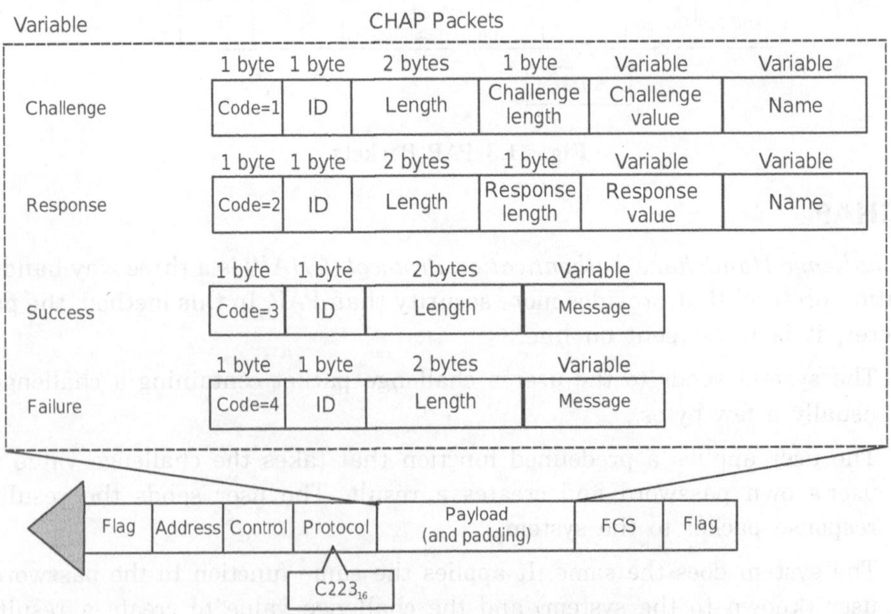

Fig. 11.5 Format of CHAP packets

11.3 SIMPLE NETWORK MANAGEMENT PROTOCOL (SNMP)

The Simple Network Management Protocol (SNMP) is a framework for managing devices in an internet using the TCP/IP protocol suite. It provides a set of fundamental operations for monitoring and maintaining an internet.

11.3.1 Concept of SNMP

SNMP uses the concept of manager and agent. That is, a manager, usually a host, controls and monitors a set of agents, usually routers (see Fig. 11.6).

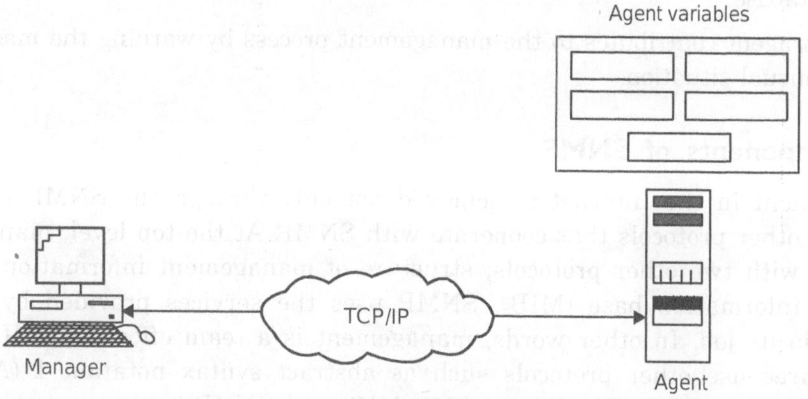

Fig. 11.6 SNMP concept

SNMP is an application-level protocol in which a few manager stations control a set of agents. The protocol is designed at the application level so that it can monitor devices made by different manufacturers and installed on different physical networks. In other words, SNMP frees management tasks from both the physical characteristics of the managed devices and the underlying networking technology. It can be used in a heterogeneous internet made of different LANs and WANs connected by routers or gateways made by different manufacturers.

Managers and Agents

A management station, called a *manager*, is a host that runs the SNMP client program. A managed station, called an *agent*, is a router (or a host) that runs the SNMP server program. Management is achieved through simple interaction between a manager and an agent.

The agent keeps performance information in a database. The manager has access to the values in the database. For example, a router can store in appropriate variables the number of packets received and forwarded. The manager can fetch and compare the values of these two variables to see if the router is congested or not.

The manager can also make the router perform certain actions. For example, a router periodically checks the value of a reboot counter to see when it should reboot itself. It reboots itself, for example, if the value of the counter is 0. The manager can use this feature to reboot the agent remotely at any time. It simply sends a packet to force a 0 value in the counter.

Agents can also contribute to the management process. The server program running on the agent can check the environment and, if it notices something unusual, it can send a warning message (called a *trap*) to the manager.

In other words, management with SNMP is based on three basic ideas:

1. A manager checks an agent by requesting information that reflects behavior of the agent.
2. A manager forces an agent to perform a task by resetting values in the agent database.
3. An agent contributes to the management process by warning the manager of an unusual situation.

11.3.2 Components of SNMP

Management in the Internet is achieved not only through the SNMP protocol but also by using other protocols that cooperate with SNMP. At the top level, management is accomplished with two other protocols; structure of management information (SMI) and management information base (MIB). SNMP uses the services provided by these two protocols to do its job. In other words, management is a team effort by SMI, MIB, and SNMP. All three use other protocols such as abstract syntax notation 1 (ASN.1) and basic encoding rules (BER). We discuss SMI, MIB, and SNMP in the next three sections (see Fig. 11.7).

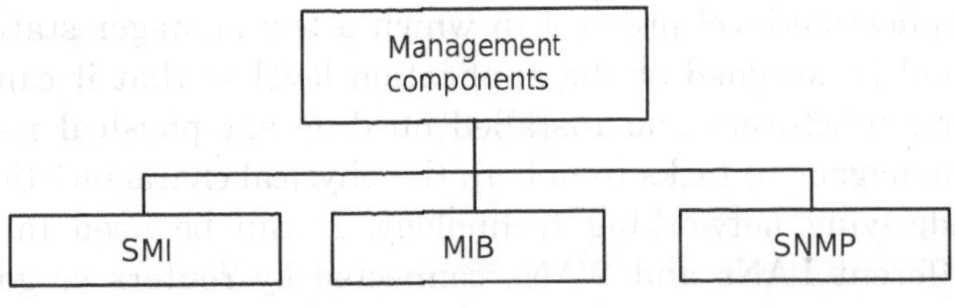

Fig. 11.7 Internet Management Components

SMI

The **Structure of Management Information (SMI)** is a component used in network management. Its functions are to name objects; to define the type of data that can be stored in an object, and to show how to encode data for transmission over the network.

MIB

The **Management Information Base (MIB)** is the second component used in network management. Each agent has its own MIB, which is a collection of all the objects that the manager can manage. The objects in the MIB are categorized under eight different groups: system, interface, address translation, IP, ICMP, TCP, UDP, and EGP. These groups are under the MIB object in the object identifier tree (see Fig. 11.8). Each group has defined variables and/or tables.

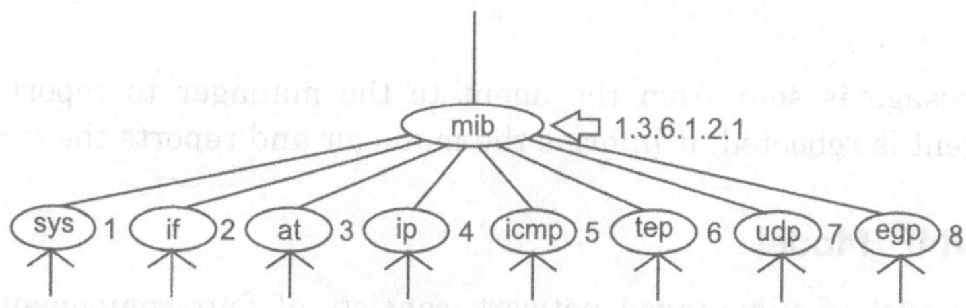

Fig. 11.8 MIB

SNMP

Simple Network Management Protocol (SNMP) defines five messages: Get Request, GetNextRequest, SetRequest, GetResponse, and Trap (see Fig. 11.9).

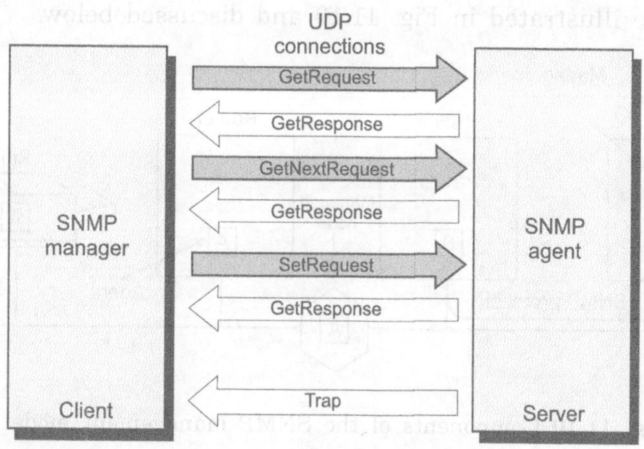

Fig. 11.9 SNMP manager

GetRequest

The GetRequest message is sent from the manager (client) to the agent (server) to retrieve the value of a variable.

GetNextRequest

The GetNextRequest message is sent from the manager to the agent to retrieve the value of a variable. The retrieved value is the value of the object following the defined object in the message. It is mostly used to retrieve the values of the entries in a table. If the manager does not know the indexes of the entries, it cannot retrieve the values. However, it can use GetNextRequest and define the object.

GetResponse

The GetResponse message is sent from an agent to a manager in response to GetRequest and GetNextRequest. It contains the value of the variable(s) requested by the manager.

SetRequest

The SetRequest message is sent from the manager to the agent to set (store) a value in a variable.

Trap

The trap message is sent from the agent to the manager to report an event. For example, if the agent is rebooted, it informs the manager and reports the time of rebooting.

11.3.3 The SNMP Model

The SNMP model of a managed network consists of four components:

1. Managed nodes
2. Management stations
3. Management information
4. A management protocol

These pieces are illustrated in Fig. 11.10 and discussed below.

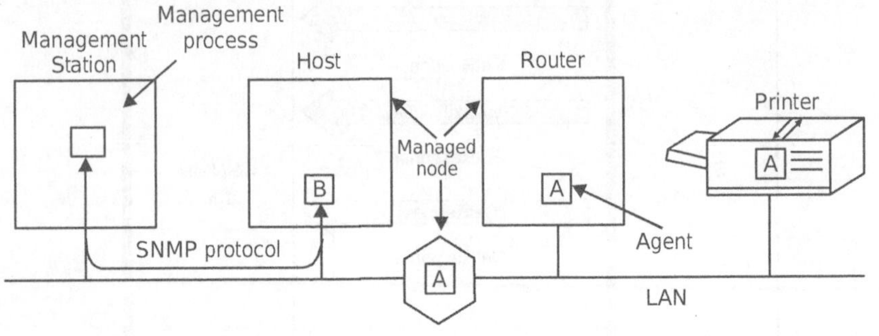

Fig. 11.10 Components of the SNMP management model

1. Managed Nodes

The *managed nodes* can be hosts, routers, bridges, printers, or any other devices capable of communicating status information to the outside world. To be managed directly by SNMP, a node must be capable of running an SNMP management process, called an *SNMP agent.* All computers meet this requirement, as do increasingly many bridges, routers, and peripheral devices designed for network use. Each agent maintains a local database of variables that describe its state and history and affect its operation.

2. Management Stations

Network management is done from *management stations,* which are, in fact, general purpose computers running special management software. The management stations contain one or more processes that communicate with the agents over the network, issuing commands and getting responses. In this design, all the intelligence is in the management stations, in order to keep the agents as simple as possible and minimize their impact on the devices they are running on. Many management stations have a graphical user interface to allow the network manager to inspect the status of the network and take action when required.

Most real networks are multivendor, with hosts from one or more manufacturers, bridges and routers from other companies, and printers from still other ones.

In order to allow a management station (potentially from yet another supplier) to talk to all these diverse components, the nature of the information maintained by all the devices must be rigidly specified. Having the management station ask a router what its packet loss rate is of no use if the router does not keep track of its loss rate. Therefore, SNMP describes (in excruciating detail) the extract information each kind of agent has to maintain and the format it has to supply it in. The largest portion of the SNMP model is the definition of who has to keep track of what and how this information is communicated.

3. Management Information

Very briefly, each device maintains one or more variables that describe its state. In the SNMP literature, these variables are called *objects*, but the term is misleading because they are not objects in the sense of an object-oriented system because they just have state and no methods (other than reading and writing their values). Nevertheless, the term is so ingrained (e.g., used in various reserved words in the specification language used) that we will use it here. The collection of all possible objects in a network is given in a data structure called the *MIB (Management Information Base).*

4. A Management Protocol

The management station interacts with the agents using the SNMP protocol. This protocol allows the management station to query the state of an agent's local objects, and change them if necessary. Most of SNMP consists of this query response type communication.

However, sometimes events happen that are not planned. Managed nodes can crash and reboot, lines can go down and come back up, congestion can occur, and so on. Each significant event is defined in a **MIB module.** When an agent notices that a significant event has occurred, it immediately reports the event to all management stations in its configuration list. This report is called an SNMP **trap**. The report usually just states that some event has occurred. The model of polling at long intervals with acceleration on receipt of a trap is called **trap directed polling.**

This model assumes that each managed node is capable of running an SNMP agent internally. Older devices or devices not originally intended for use on a network may not have this capability. To handle them, SNMP defines what is called a **proxy agent**, namely an agent that watches over one or more non SNMP devices and communicates with the management station on their behalf, possibly communicating with the devices themselves using some nonstandard protocol.

Finally, security and authentication play a major role in SNMP. A management station has the capability of learning a great deal about every node under its control and also has the capability of shutting them all down. Hence it is of great importance that agents be convinced that queries allegedly coming from the management station, in fact, come from the management station.

11.4 CRYPTOGRAPHY

The word cryptography comes from the two Greek Words

Kpu^{TM} 7–means hidden or secret β Kripto

3>Kå 5–means writing β Graph

So,

"Cryptography is the art of secret writing"

OR

"Cryptography is the art and science of keeping messages secure"

OR

"Cryptography is a technique of encoding and decoding the message so they are not understood by any body except sender and receiver."

Cryptography plays a very important role in Internet that is payment details, money transfer contract documents and Business plans etc.

The method consisted of replacing the letters of alphabet in the original text by letters that are of a fixed number of places away.

Plain- A B C D E F G H I J K L M N O P Q R S T U V

Code- C D E F G H I J K L M N O P Q R S T U V W X

Examples. THANK YOU

Using this system a plain message THANKYOU is coded as VJCPMAQW

11.4.1 Dimensions of Cryptography

Cryptographic systems are characterized along three independent dimensions:

1. **The type of operations used for transforming plain text to cipher text.**

   Encryption algorithms are based on two general principles:

   (*a*) Substitution

   (*b*) Transposition

2. **The number of keys used**

   If both sender and receiver use the same keys the system is referred to as symmetric, single-key secret key or conventional encryption. If the sender and receiver use the different keys, the system is referred to as asymmetric, two-key or public key encryption.

3. **The way in which the plain text is processed.**

   There are two ways in which the plain text is processed:

   (*a*) Block cipher

   This processes the input one block of elements at a time, producing output block for each input element.

   (*b*) Stream cipher

   This processes the input elements continuously producing output one element at a time, as it goes along.

11.4.2 Some Terminologies

1. *Cryptographers:* who invent clever secret codes *i.e.*, who practiced cryptography.
2. *Cryptanalysts:* Practitioners of cryptanalysis *i.e.*, who attempt to break the codes.
3. *Cryptology:* The branch of mathematics encompassing both cryptography and cryptanalysis.
4. *Cryptologists:* Practitioners of cryptology

Success of the cryptographers rests on the **Fundamental Tenet of Cryptography** *"If lots of smart people have failed to solve a problem, them it probably won't be solved (soon)."*

11.4.3 Conventional Encryption Model/Symmetric Cipher Model

A simplified model of conventional encryption is shown in the Fig. 11.11.

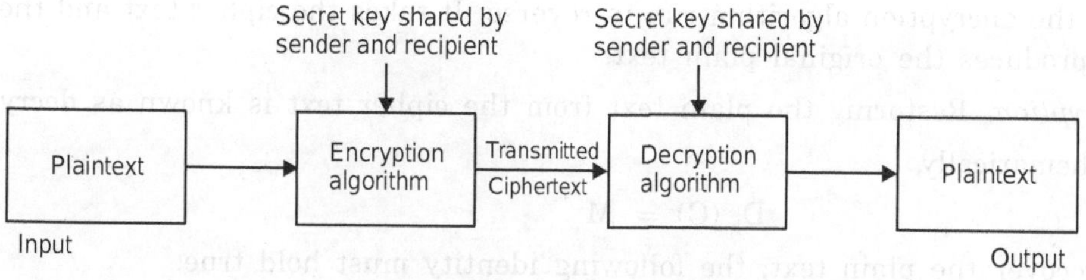

Fig. 11.11 Symmetric cipher model

A conventional encryption scheme has five ingredients

1. Plaintext

Plaintext is the original intelligible message or data that is fed into the algorithm as input. It is denoted by M, for message or P, for plaintext. It can be a stream of bits, a text file, a bitmap, a digital video image etc.

2. Encryption Algorithm

The encryption algorithm performs various substitutions and transformations on the plaintext Encryption/Enciphering. The process of converting from plaintext to cipher text is known as encryption.

Mathematically,

E_k (M) = C

3. Secret Key

The secret key is also input to the encryption algorithm. The key is a value independent of the plain text. The algorithm will produce a different output depending on the specific key being used at a time. It is denoted by K. The range of possible values of the key is termed as *key space.*

4. Cipher Text

It is the scrambled message produced as output. It depends on the plain text and the secret key. For a given message two different keys will produce two different cipher texts. It is denoted by C. It is also a binary data: sometimes the same size as M, sometimes larger.

"Plain text is encrypted; it is called as Cipher text."

Types of Cipher Text

(a) *Transposition System.* A transposition involves rearrangement or change in the sequence of letters of plain text message without any change in their identity.

(b) *Substitution System.* In access entire words, long phrases, long paragraph or even sentences of the plain text are replaced by other words, group of letters, group of figures, etc.

5. Decryption Algorithm

It is the encryption algorithm run in reverse. It takes the cipher text and the secret key and produces the original plain text.

Decryption. Restoring the plain text from the cipher text is known as decryption

Mathematically,

$$D_k(C) = M$$

To recover the plain text, the following identity must hold true:

$$D(E(M)) = M$$

11.4.4 Modes of Operation

A cryptographic mode usually combines the basic cipher, some sort of feedback and some simple operations. The operations are simple because the security is the function of the cipher and not the mode. There are five modes of operation which are discussed one by one:

1. Electronic Code Book Mode (ECB)

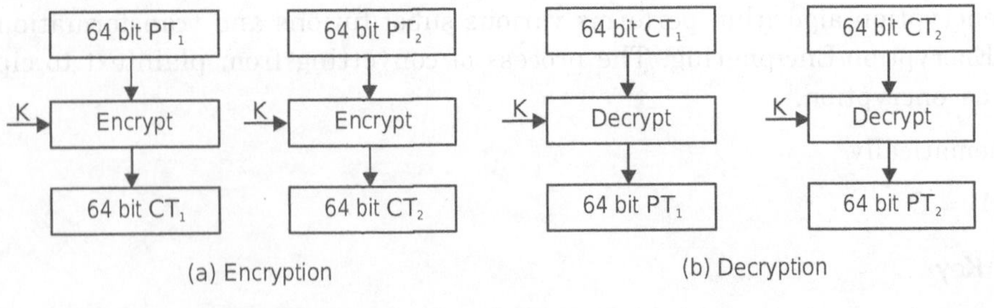

Fig. 11.12 Electronic Code Book Mode (ECB)

- It is the simplest mode of operation.
- The incoming plain text message is divided into blocks of 64 bits each.

- The same key is used in each step of encryption.
- At the receiving end the incoming data is divided into 64 bits block and by using the same key each block is decrypted to produce the corresponding plain text.

Application. Secure transmission of secure values (*e.g.*, an encryption),

2. Cipher Block Chaining Mode (CBC)

In the case of ECB, plain text block always produces the same cipher text block. If a block of plain text occurs more than once in the input, overcome this problem the CBC made ensures that even if a block of plain text repeats in the input it will produce totally different cipher text block.

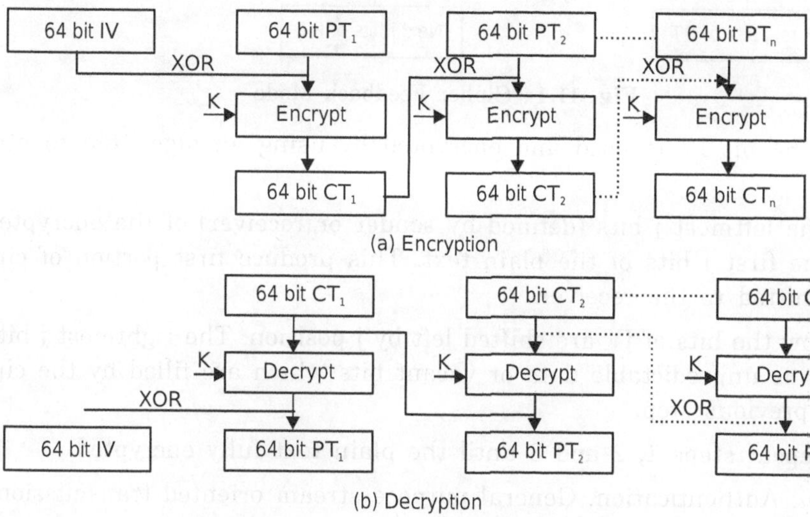

Fig. 11.13 Cipher Block Chaining Mode

- Chaining adds the feedback mechanism to the block cipher.
- In a CBC the results of the encryption of the previous block are feed-back into the encrypts of the current block. Each block is used to modify the encryption of the next block.
- First step receives two inputs, the first block of plain text and a random block of text called initialization vector (IV). IV has no special meaning, it is simply used to make the message unique and is created by the user.

Decryption Process

The cipher text block is passed through the decryption alga using the same key which was used during the encryption process for all plain text block. The output of this step is XOR'ed with the IV to produce the plain text.

Application. Authentication General Purpose block oriented transmission.

3. Cipher Feedback Mode (CFB)

This mode is concerned with the stream cipher.

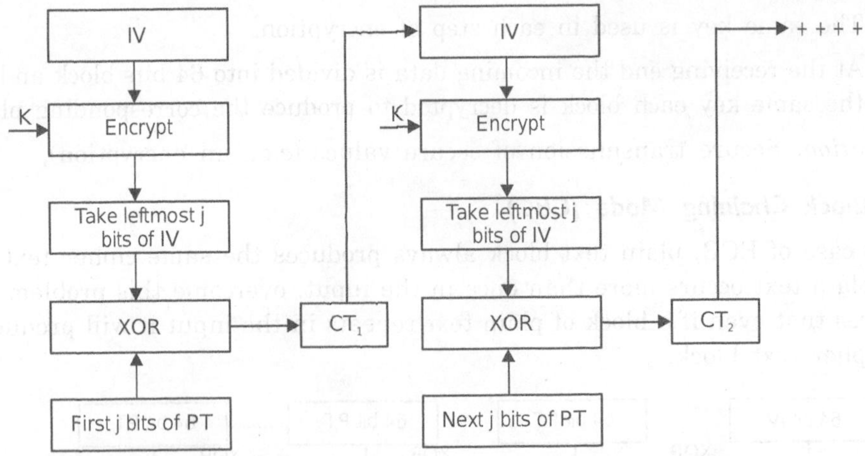

Fig. 11.14 Cipher Feedback Mode

Step 1. A 64 bit IV is used and encrypted by using an algorithm to produce an encrypted IV.

Step 2. The leftmost j bits (defined by sender or receiver) of the encrypted IV are XOR'ed with the first j bits of the plain text. This produce first portion of cipher text which is transmitted to the receiver.

Step 3. Now the bits of IV are shifted left by j position. The rightmost j bit position of the IV contains unpredictable data or vacant bits which are filled by the cipher text created in the previous step.

Step 4. Repeat steps 1, 2 and 3 until the plain text fully encrypted.

Application: Authentication, General purpose stream oriented transmission.

4. Output Feedback Mode (OFB)

OFB is extremely similar to the CFB, the only difference is that in the case of CFB, the cipher text is fed into the next stage of encryption process but in case of OFB the output of the encrypted IV is fed into the next stage of produce the new IV.

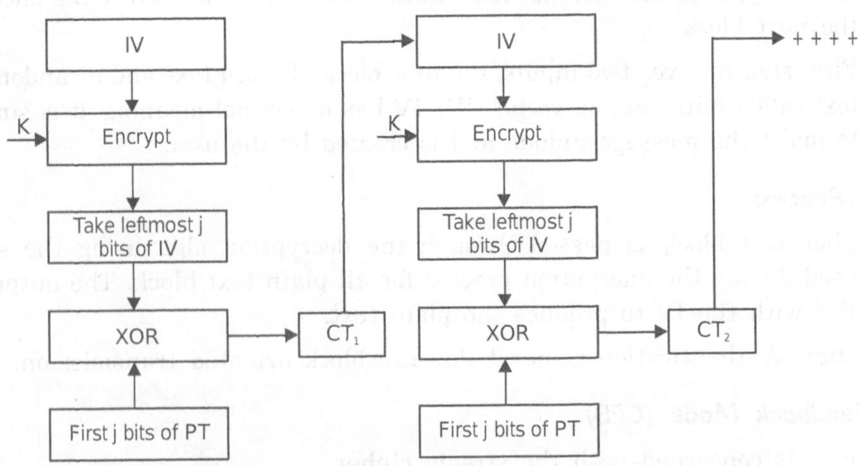

Fig. 11.15 Output Feedback Mode (OFB)

Disadvantage. More vulnerable to a message stream modification attack than in CFB.

Application. Stream oriented transmission over noisy channel (*e.g.*, Satellite communication).

Advantage. Bit errors in transmission do not propagate, For example if bit error occurs in C_1 only the recovered value of P_1 is affected, subsequent plain text units are not corrupted.

5. Counter Mode (CTR)

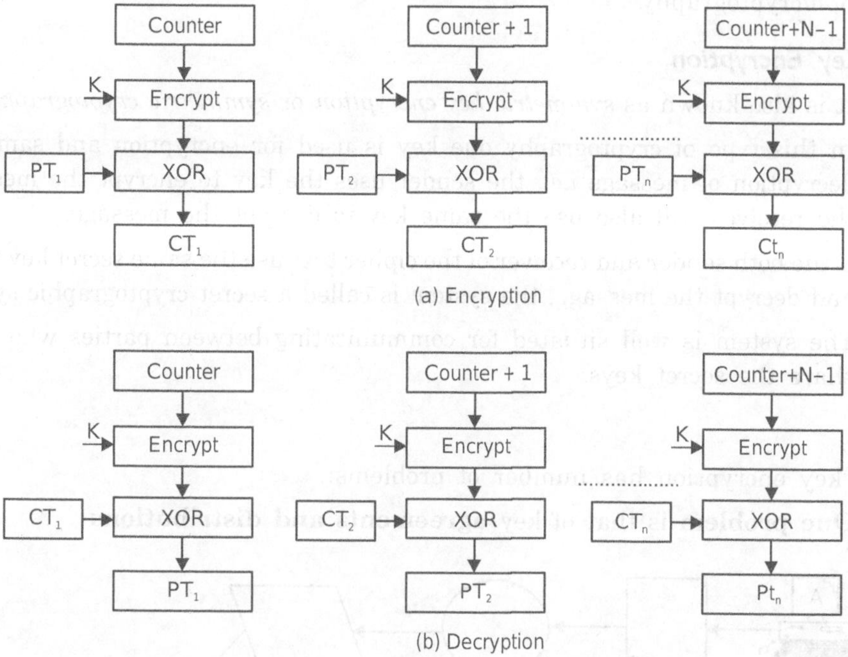

Fig. 11.16 Counter Mode (CTR)

- The counter mode has applications to ATM (Asynchronous Transfer Mode) network, Network security and IPSec (IP security).
- In this mode, a counter is equal to the PT block size is used. The counter value must be different for each. The counter value must be block that is encrypted. In this the counter is initialized to some value and than incremented by 1 for each subsequent block for encryption.

  The counter is encrypted and then XORed with the plain text block to produce cipher text block, there is no chaining.
- *For decryption.* The same sequence of counter values is used, with each encrypted counter XOR'ed with the cipher text block to option the corresponding *plain text* block.
- *Applications.* General purpose block oriented transmission, useful for high requirements.

- *Advantages:*

1. Hardware efficiency
2. Software efficiency
3. Preprocessing
4. Random access
5. Provable security
6. Simplicity

11.4.5 Types of Cryptography

There are two types of cryptography: Secret key encryption/cryptography and Public key encryption/cryptography.

I. Secret Key Encryption

- It is also known as *symmetric key encryption* or *symmetric cryptographic system.*
- In this type of cryptography one key is used for encryption and same key for decryption of message *i.e.*, the sender uses the key to encrypt the message and the receives will also use the same key to decrypt the message.
- If the both sender and receiver of the cipher text use the same secret key to encrypt and decrypt the message, the system is called a secret cryptographic system.
- The system is well situated for communicating between parties who agreed to share the secret keys.

Problems

Secret key encryption has number of problems:

1. **One problem** is that of key **agreements and distributions**

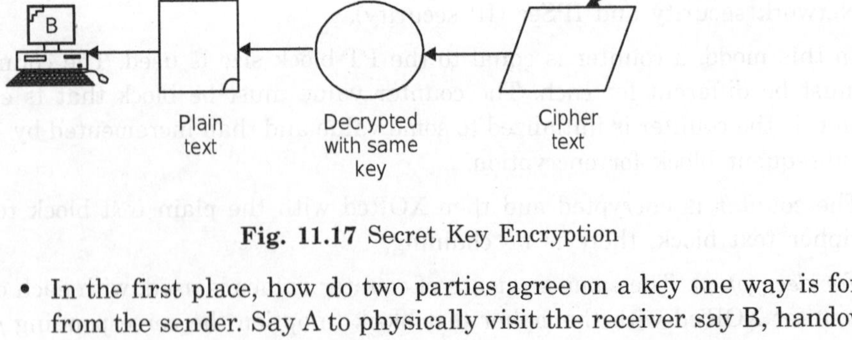

Fig. 11.17 Secret Key Encryption

- In the first place, how do two parties agree on a key one way is for somebody from the sender. Say A to physically visit the receiver say B, handover the key.
- Another way is to courier a paper on which the key is written.
- A third way is to send the key over the network to be and ask for the confirmation but then if an intruder gets the message he can interpret the subsequent message.

2. **Second Problem** is that the **same key is used for encryption and decryption,** one key per communicating parties is required.

   Solution:

   - DES (Data Encryption Standard) specifies a method for encrypting. A way is simple to use DES -3, where key 1 is used to encrypt first, key 2 is used to re encrypt the encrypted lock and key is used once again to re encrypt doubly encrypted block.
   - DES -3 is quite popular and is in wide use.
   - Other popular algorithms are IDEA to RC 5, RC 2, and AES etc.

Advantages of Secret Key Encryption

1. The major advantages of symmetric key algorithm is that it is more efficient than the public key algorithms. It takes less to encrypt a message using the symmetric key algorithm. This is because this key is of smaller size (lengths).
2. Hence symmetric key algorithms are used for encryption and decryption of long message.

Disadvantages of Secret Key Encryption

1. The first disadvantages are that the sender and receiver both should have assume symmetric key. So a large number of keys are required when the numbers of users increases.
2. The distribution of keys between two users can be difficult.

2. Public Key Encryption

It is also called **asymmetric key encryption.** In this type of cryptography, two different keys are used namely public key and private key. One key is used for encryption and the other key must be used for decryption.

Working:

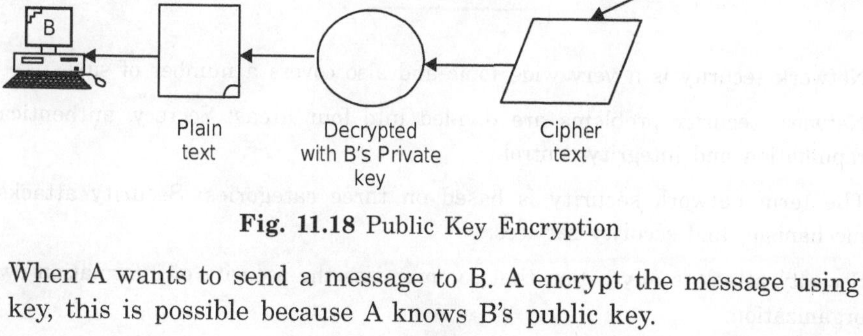

Fig. 11.18 Public Key Encryption

- When A wants to send a message to B. A encrypt the message using B's public key, this is possible because A knows B's public key.

- A sends this message to B.
- B decrypt A's message by using his private key. Note that only B knows about his private key.
- When B wants to send a message to A, exactly reverse steps take place. (B encrypt the message using A's public key).
- Therefore only A can decrypt the message back to its original form using his private key. This is shown in figure11.18.

Advantages Public Key Encryption

1. There is no compulsion of using (sharing) the symmetric key by the sender and receiver.
2. The number of keys required reduces tremendously.

Disadvantages Publie Key Encryption

1. The algorithms used are highly complex.
2. It takes a long time to calculate cipher text from plaintext.
3. It is necessary to verify the association between a sender and this public key.

Comparison of Secret Key and Public Key Cryptosystems

Sr. No.	*Secret key system*	*Public key system*
1.	It is also called as symmetrical key system.	It is also called as asymmetrical key system.
2.	Each sender and receiver pair has to used a unique key.	The sender uses the public key while receiver uses its own private key.
3.	It is more efficient.	It is less efficient.
4.	It is useful for encryption and decryption of long message.	It is used for encryption and decryption of short messages.
5.	A large number of keys are required.	The number of keys is less.

SUMMARY

- Network security is a very wide topic and also covers a number of sins.
- Network security problems are divided into four areas: Secrecy, authentication, non-repudiation and integrity control.
- The term network security is based on three categories: Security attacks, security mechanism, and security services.
- Security attack is any action that compromises the security of information owned by an organization.

- Security services are the service that enhances the security of the data processing system and the information that transfers of an organization.
- Security service can be done or classified in many ways: Authentication, Data Integrity, Non-Repudiation, Access control and Data-confidentiality.
- Security attacks are divided into two categories: active attacks and passive attacks.
- An active attack can be a masquerade, replay, and modification of messages and denial of services.
- A passive attack can be a release of message contents and traffic analysis.
- Security mechanisms are those, which are designed to detect, prevent or recover from a security attack.
- Security mechanisms can be divided into two broad categories: Specific Security Mechanisms and Pervasive Security Mechanisms.
- The word authentication means if a message sent by the sender is accurately received by the receiver.
- Two protocols for authentication created by PPP are Password Authentication Protocol (PAP) and Challenge Handshake Authentication Protocol (CHAP).
- Simple Network Management Protocol (SNMP) is a framework for managing devices in an internet using the TCP/IP protocol suite.
- The three management components of SNMP are SMI, MIB and SNMP.
- The SNMP model of a managed network consists of four components: managed nodes, management stations, management information, and a management protocol.
- Cryptography is the art and science of keeping the messages source.
- The various modes of operation of cryptography are: Electronic code book mode (ECB), Cipher Block Chaining Mode (CBC), Cipher Feed- back Mode (CFB), Output Feedback Mode (OFB), and Counter Mode (CTR).
- The two types of cryptography are: secret key cryptography and public-key cryptography.
- With secret key cryptography (symmetric encryption) a single key is used for both encryption and decryption. The sender uses the key to encrypt the plaintext and sends the cipher text to the receiver. The receiver applies the same key to decrypt the message and recover the plaintext.
- The example of secret key cryptography is Data Encryption Standard (DES).
- With public key cryptography (asymmetric encryption) two different keys are used for both encryption and decryption. The sender uses the one key to encrypt the plaintext and sends the cipher text to the receiver. The receiver applies the other key to decrypt the message and recover the plaintext.
- The example of public key cryptography is RSA (Rivest Shamir Adleman) Cryptosystem.

EXERCISE

1. Write a short note on network security?
2. Give the names of the people who cause the security problems and also state the reason?
3. Explain the various security mechanisms, which are applied in network security?
4. Explain the term authentication?
5. Give the details of two protocols for authentication that are created by PPP.
6. Draw the schematic diagram of the format of the three packets of PAP?
7. Explain the procedure of the password authentication protocol?
8. What do you mean by the term "Security attacks"? Also give the classification of security attacks?
9. Give the various security services, which are given for network security?
10. Write short notes on:
    (*a*) Security attack
    (*b*) Security services
    (*c*) Security mechanisms.
11. What is the difference between data integrity and data confidentiality?
12. What do you mean by the terms authentication and non-repudiation?
13. Explain in detail the concept of Simple Network Management Protocol (SNMP)?
14. What is the role of manager and agents in the SNMP protocol?
15. Write a short note on the messages that are defined by SNMP?
16. Illustrate the SNMP Model in detail?
17. Write a short note on the components of SNMP?
18. What do you mean by cryptography?
19. Give the various dimensions of the term cryptography?
20. Draw the schematic diagram of conventional encryption model. Explain it in detail?
21. What do you mean by the terms encryption and decryption?
22. Explain the various modes of operation?
23. Explain the encryption and decryption of the ECB and CBC modes of operation?
24. Explain the two categories of cryptography?
25. What is the difference between the public key and secret-key cryptosystems?
26. Explain various modes of operations with reference to cryptography with the help of suitable diagrams.